ARKANA

A FURTHER RECORD

P. D. Ouspensky (1878–1947) was born in Moscow. His books *Tertium Organum* (written 1912) and *A New Model of the Universe* (written 1914) revealed his stature as a thinker and his deep preoccupation with the problems of man's existence. After his work with Gurdjieff between 1915 and 1918 his interest centred on the practical study of methods for development of consciousness in man, as expounded in *In Search of the Miraculous* and *The Psychology of Man's Possible Evolution* (both published after his death in 1947) and *The Fourth Way* (1957). It is these methods that are further elucidated in *A Further Record*.

P.D.OUSPENSKY

A FURTHER RECORD

EXTRACTS FROM MEETINGS
1928-1945

ARKANA

LONDON AND NEW YORK

6/11

First published in 1986
Reprinted in 1987
by Arkana Paperbacks
Arkana Paperbacks is an imprint of
Routledge & Kegan Paul Ltd
11 New Fetter Lane, London EC4P 4EE

Published in the USA by
Routledge & Kegan Paul Inc.
in association with Methuen Inc.
29 West 35th Street, New York, NY 10001

Phototypeset by Input Typesetting, Ltd, London
Printed and bound in Great Britain
by The Guernsey Press Co. Ltd,
Guernsey, Channel Islands
© Tatiana M. Nagro 1986

Library of Congress Cataloguing in Publication Data

Uspenskii, P. D. (Petr Demíanovich), 1878-1947.

A further record.

Includes index.
1. Philosophy—Miscellanea.   I. Title.
B4279.U73F87   1986   197'.2   86-3484

British Library CIP Data also available
ISBN 1-85063-056-9

Table of Contents

These extracts were not made or revised by P. D. Ouspensky. As they are printed, for the most part, exactly in the form in which they reached the printer, there are some repetitions. Only the printer is to be blamed for the arrangement and order of the material in sections and for the titles of the sections.

1

Recurrence

MR. O.   Recurrence is in eternity. It is not the same life. This life ends and time ends. There is a theory—and this system admits this theory—that time can be prolonged. I have no evidence. If you think about time, how many attempts were made by spiritualists and others—but there is no evidence.

The study of recurrence must begin with the study of children's minds, and particularly before they begin to speak. If they could remember this time they could remember very interesting things. But unfortunately, when they begin to speak they become real children and they forget after six months or a year. It is very seldom that people remember what they thought before that, at a very early age. They would remember themselves such as they were grown-up. They are not children at all. Then later they become children. If they remember their mentality it is the same mentality as grown-up people have. That is what is interesting.

Q.   Do you know why a child should remember its grown-up mind and not its previous child's mind?

MR. O.   We have so little material to judge about it. I speak only about the way it can be studied. Suppose we try to remember our own—suppose we find it was one or another—trying not to let imagination come in—if we find something, that would be material. In literature you find very little, because people don't understand how to study it. But with my own experience, I met with some very interesting things. Some people I knew had very interesting recollections of first years of life, and they all had the same impression, which was that the mentality was not a child's mentality—how they took people, how they recognized people—it was not a child's psychology. But most people don't remember that at all. You see what I mean. They had a ready mind, such that you cannot imagine this ready mind with quite grown-up reactions could be formed in six months of unconscious life. It had to be before if it is really so, but as I say, it is very difficult to find material.

Q. Why should it disappear when the child learns to talk?

MR. O. It begins to imitate children and do exactly what grown-up people expect from him. They expect him to be a stupid child and he becomes a stupid child.

Q. How could recurrence be of advantage to man?

MR. O. If one begins to remember and if one begins to change and not go by the same circle each time, but do what one wants and what one thinks better; and if one doesn't know about it or even if one knows and doesn't do anything, then there is no advantage in it at all. It is generally the same things repeated and repeated.

Q. Having met the system in one recurrence, will one meet it again in the next?

MR. O. It depends what one did with the system. One could meet the system and say: 'What nonsense these people talk!' It depends how much effort one makes. If one made efforts one could acquire something, and that may remain, if it was not only in surface personality—if it wasn't only formatory.

Q. Does one necessarily follow some line of action in each recurrence?

MR. O. The law about it is that all acquired tendencies repeat themselves. One person acquires a tendency to study or be interested in certain things. He will be interested again. Another acquires a tendency to run away from certain things. Then he will run away again.

Q. Do these tendencies grow stronger?

MR. O. They may, or they may grow in a different direction. There is no guarantee—until one reaches some kind of conscious action, when one has a certain possibility to trust oneself.

Q. Does the parallel time mean that all moments continually exist?

MR. O. Yes. It is very difficult to think about it. Certainly it means eternity of the moment, but our minds cannot think in that way. Our mind is a very limited machine. We must think in the easiest way and make allowances for it. It is easier to think of repetition than of the eternal existence of the moment. You must understand that our mind cannot formulate rightly things as they are. We must have only approximate formulations which are nearer to truth than our ordinary thinking. That is all that is possible. Our mind and our language are very rough instruments and we have to deal with very fine matters and fine problems.

Studying children—this is the easiest way to study it. If we had enough material we could answer many questions. Why, for instance, strange tendencies appear in children, quite opposite to their surrounding circumstances, quite new to the people who surround them. It happens sometimes in many different ways, and they may be very strong tendencies that may change the life and go quite unexpected ways, when there is nothing in heredity to produce that. As I said, heredity in man does not work—it is a fantastic idea. It works in dogs and horses, but not in men.

Q. Does not the question of types come into that?

Mr. O. Yes, but we know nothing about types—not enough to speak about them. And this is why, in most cases it happens that parents don't understand children and children don't understand parents. They never could really understand one another sufficiently or rightly. They are quite different people —strangers to one another—they just happened to meet accidentally at a certain station, and then go in different directions again.

Q. When you said, 'Observe children,' what do you mean?

Mr. O. That is what is so difficult. If you observe tendencies on a big scale, you can find quite unexpected tendencies. You can say it is the result of a certain reason or surroundings, but quite unexpected tendencies can appear in quite young children, and not accidental tendencies that appear and disappear. They will continue throughout life afterwards. In this case, according to this theory, it may be a tendency acquired in a previous life in much later years, and then it appears very early.

Q. From the point of view of recurrence then, may it not be that some important actions that we make between now and the time that we die are really responsible for our tendencies now?

Mr. O. You mean in previous lives? Quite possibly. Only, one thing: this work did not exist before. It may be that other work did—there are many different kinds—but not this. It didn't exist before—that I am perfectly sure of.

Q. What I mean is that it seems such a huge idea to think that between now and the time we die we make the fatal actions which will give us tendencies for next time.

Mr. O. Certainly. Every moment of our lives we may create tendencies that we may not be able to get rid of for ten lives.

That is why in Indian literature they always emphasize this point. It may be in fairy-tale form, but the principle is the same.

APRIL 4TH 1938

Q. MR. O. said that this work has not occurred before. Does this mean also that it will not occur again?

MR. O. There is no guarantee. That will depend on you for yourself. Certainly one thing could be certain—it will not happen in the same way. Maybe there will be groups and schools, only not in the same way and not at the same time. Work is the only thing which is not under the law of recurrence, otherwise it is not work. If it is a little conscious it cannot be under recurrence. Then again in this particular work many things will happen quite differently. What was now at a certain time will begin perhaps twenty years earlier.

Q. In my childhood I was greatly attached to a cousin three years older than myself who died when she was ten. If her brief life has repeated itself four or five times since then, my life as related to hers must also have repeated itself. How is this explained?

MR. O. It is very difficult to explain it, and at the same time mathematically it is very simple. Our calculation of length of this time is based on certain ideas of duration. We say that ten years are less than a longer life of say fifty years. Really there is no guarantee that it is shorter or longer. I said in one page of the 'New Model', suppose for a moment that what looks to us like different duration is the same duration, but the speed is different. There are many things which we take as the foundation of our world which are really illusions. In any case it is not difficult to adjust one life to another life, but our power of visualization is too small and weak for that. We have to leave it as a problem and understand that it may be adjusted somehow.

Q. How is it possible to know what a baby remembers? I thought that one was born with one's centres completely blank and that one remembered with centres.

MR. O. This is a strange thing. Some people, who don't differ much from other people, have strange and quite definite recollections of their first months even. They think they saw people as grown-up people do, not as children. They don't make compound pictures from elements, but they have quite definite impressions of houses, people and so on. They have a quite grown-up mentality.

Q. I can remember things when I was two years old which did not happen at all. How can one verify what a baby remembers before it can speak?

MR. O. How did you know they didn't happen? It could be a dream. I had an experience of that kind. I remember when I was quite a child I was in some place near Moscow and the picture of the place remained in my memory. I wasn't there for about four years after that. Then when I went there I saw it wasn't the same thing as in my memory and I saw my memory was a dream.

Q. If one dies as man No. 4, does one recur as man No. 4 or could one lose it by imitating negative emotions, etc.?

MR. O. No, only man No. 5 can recur as man No. 5. He may not know it, but things will be easier for him. No. 4 has to make again, only it will be easier and earlier.

Q. Could a tendency in one recurrence become habit in the next?

MR. O. It depends which tendency. If it is mechanical it will become a habit. If it is a conscious tendency it cannot become a habit, because they are two different things.

Q. Thinking back over one's life one sees certain crossways where some decision was taken which one thinks was bad. Is there any particular thing one can do in this recurrence so that there is less likelihood that we shall do it in the next?

MR. O. Yes, certainly. One can think, one can change now in these particular points and then if it is sufficiently deep one will remember; if it is not so deep one may remember. In any case there is a chance that in time one will not do something which one did. Many ideas and things like that can pass from one life to another. For instance, someone asked what one could get from the idea of recurrence. If one became intellectually aware of this idea and if the idea became part of one's essence—part of one's general attitude towards life—then one cannot forget it and it will be an advantage to know it early in the next life.

Q. Doesn't the question of sacrifice come in, if there is to be any change in essence or in recurrence?

MR. O. Yes, certainly, one has to pay for everything. If one wants to get one thing one has to give some other thing for it. One cannot have new things and keep the old things. One would have so much luggage one wouldn't be able to move.

MARCH 7TH 1940

Q. As schools are not mechanical they will never recur. Then if we recur there is no assurance that we should ever find the system again.

Mr. O. No assurance, quite right. It is quite true, but there are many different sides to it. It is quite true that things do not recur in exactly the same form, but at the same time one cannot lose anything that one acquired. That means that if one loses one possibility one can find another. But one can lose only by one's own fault, not by the fault of things, although it is necessary to understand that possibilities are not unlimited. Very often I refuse to speak about recurrence because there are many things about it you don't know. You take things too simply. 'Eternal recurrence' means to you that it is eternal, it means always. But there are many different manifestations—eternal may not be eternal at all. If people live an ordinary life and don't accumulate right influences, don't form a magnetic centre, then after some time they lose even the possibility of accumulating magnetic centre: they may die out, because there is a big competition—there are many things we don't know. The first thing that must be understood about eternal recurrence is that it is not eternal at all. When one comes to the possibility, which is a very rare thing because there are many people who never come to the possibility of development, but when one comes to a possibility, at the same time chances become very small, smaller and smaller. The nearer one comes, the easier it is to lose everything. One has less time. When one comes nearer to the possibility it actually affects time as time—the time of this person becomes smaller. This is the answer, but not the answer.

Q. Less time in what sense? We recur less often?

Mr. O. Everybody has his own time; time must be taken like that. Time is an individual possession. There is no general time, one person has more time, another has less time: all people cannot have the same time.

Q. Then the only thing we can keep is the change, if any, that we make in essence?

Mr. O. No, first you must make changes in personality.

Q. But that won't last.

Mr. O. It is the only thing we can do. Only very few people can work on essence. It is not exactly an advantage to the people who can because it is very difficult for them, but it may happen.

Generally we work on personality, and this is the only work we can do, and if we work it will bring us somewhere.

MARCH 15TH 1940

MR. O. There was some question referring to recurrence. I just want to say something which may give you material for thinking. Why I always avoid speaking about this is for two reasons: first, we can only talk about the theory, we have no real facts about it; and secondly, we do know that in connection with work, laws referring to recurrence change. It is necessary to understand these things. I wrote in the 'New Model' long ago that even in ordinary life people are very different in relation to recurrence. Some people may have exactly the same recurrence, some people may have different variations or possibilities, and some may go up and others may go down, and many other things. But this is all without relation to the work. I mean, when one comes nearer to the possibility of work, it is possible in a certain way, although only theoretically, to study three successive recurrences. Suppose the first is when one comes near to the possibility of meeting with some kind of ideas of higher mind; second, when one comes definitely in contact with C influence, and the third which will result from that. And what is interesting is that after the second, the possibilities of recurrence diminish very much. I mean in ordinary conditions they looked unlimited, before one came to definite ideas; but from the moment one comes to definite ideas, which we put as C influences, the possibility of recurrence diminishes. That is what must be understood. If we understand that, we will be able to speak about it with a certain reason, a certain possible amount of usefulness, otherwise it is all theoretical talk, quite useless if we take all on the same plane.

Q. Do you mean that after coming in contact with C influences the number of chances diminishes?

MR. O. Yes, because C influence cannot be wasted. B influence is practically unlimited; that means, thrown into life, and one can take it or not take it; it does not diminish. But C influence is limited. You must know already why it is limited. Now try to answer this question, why C influence is limited. Answer this question to yourselves and you will understand why the possibility of receiving C influence must be limited, because if one does not make use of it, what is the use of wasting it?

Q. Does it mean if we worked in the right way?

Mr. O. No, it does not mean that at all. It means only that if we don't work in the right way we will lose the possibility of recurrence; it means nothing more.

Without this additional feature which I gave, it is quite useless to speak about recurrence even as a theory. It would be quite useless talk if we took everything on the same level.

Q. Where does this thing come from which recurs?

Mr. O. It is you. You recur, I recur, he recurs, they recur. There is no need for theoretical divisions. When we speak about recurrence, we think about our recurrence, not about somebody else's recurrence. Where it comes from we don't know, and we can spend our whole life on theoretical definitions, we can even get quite good definitions, but it will not change anything and it will not help our psychological understanding of the idea. I am now trying to establish certain principles which will give us practical understanding of the idea. We could find many words, but words will not lead anywhere.

Have you found the answer, why C influences cannot be wasted? Think about that. If you answer this question you will answer many other questions. And this you do know—put two and two together.

[Many guesses, all wrong.]

Q. Is it because if such a thing would be liable to recur, again and again you waste it?

Mr. O. This is implied but this is not the answer. Certainly, if it is wasted, and again wasted, what is the use? But there is something you don't see in all this, and this is the key to the whole thing that you must find. It is very simple, there is nothing mysterious. It is not a puzzle that you can guess the solution of; it is a question of thinking.

Try to think like this. Take an ordinary school. A boy goes to school and every year begins to learn the same thing. He learns something for a whole year, then he goes home and forgets everything, and has to learn the same thing again, and again he learns for a whole year, and again goes home and forgets, and again comes back and learns the same thing. What will they tell him at school? This is why schools are never repeated; that is why there is no recurrence for schools. And this is what people want, they say they want to learn the same thing again. But next time you must be in a higher school. If you cannot go to a higher school there will be no other school on this level, because you have already passed that.

Q. Would you meet the school through C influence?

MR. O. You meet the school through B influences. School means C influence.

Q. You cannot go into a higher class unless you pass an examination.

MR. O. Quite right, but you can pass the examination and forget everything. It happens very often.

Q. But you have learnt how to learn, a little.

MR. O. Sometimes, and sometimes not. You learn how to learn and learn how to forget.

Q. It seems to me from what you have said that this C influence is transmutation, power to transmute, and anything less than that is not C influence.

MR. O. Quite right. You are very near, but you can take C influence simply as a certain amount of knowledge.

Q. Knowledge that can be used?

MR. O. No, that again is definition. I said knowledge; definitions will not help. It is strange how you don't see it, how you don't catch it, what it means simply. Transmission of knowledge means C influence, it means a certain work, it does not happen by itself, it means somebody's work, and somebody's work cannot be wasted. If it brings results then it can be continued, but if it brings no result, then certainly it will stop—it is quite natural. What I mean is that it explains why the possibility of recurrence must be limited. If one does not profit—suppose one comes to a school and does not profit by being in the school, then certainly one cannot come again and again to learn the same things; one must make something of it—then it is another thing. Try to understand it, it is very simple, but without understanding these principles it is impossible to speak about recurrence. All ordinary talks, based on mathematics or anything else, they make it too uniform, and recurrence cannot be uniform. You remember, we spoke very often about materiality of knowledge and about the fact that one has very little chance even to begin, because many circumstances are necessary for that. But you must understand that, when one begins to get a certain knowledge, chances become smaller and smaller, because if one does not use it, then it will be more and more difficult to get, quite naturally. And the same thing applies to every day, every year, to all our life—this is what must be understood. This thing about recurrence is useful because it refers to this life. If we don't do something to-day, how can we expect to do it to-morrow? If we can do it to-day, we must; nobody can put it off till to-morrow, because to-morrow we could do something else, and so on. We always think we have time.

Q.   Does it mean that if we don't listen to what you say to-day, we won't hear it again?

Mr. O.   Or maybe you will be here, but I will not be here—how can you know?

Q.   Can we only make progress through you?

Mr. O.   No, you are quite free to find any other place—you are not bound at all. If you know somebody else with whom you can make progress, certainly you must use him. One must not lose any opportunity if one has an opportunity.

Q.   I meant—are you the only medium here?

Mr. O.   No, nobody can be the only one. If you know another way, there is another opportunity, but if you don't know of another opportunity, that is another question. If you know nobody but me, then you must try to get it from me, but if you know somebody else, you can get it from somebody else —quite clear? Only remember one thing—it cannot be a theoretical study. Theoretical study is not sufficient. There are so many wrong things in our mind, that it is necessary to bring in a certain order, even theoretical. But it is no use spending all the time on theories, we must learn practice, we must learn how to do the most important things for us.

Q.   There is no means of knowing for oneself whether one has used C influences, is there?

Mr. O.   One cannot get C influences from oneself. Certainly, one must know, this is one of the first things one has to know, whether one has heard something or not. You remember how we spoke about valuation?

Q.   In the idea of recurrence things happen again. But do schools necessarily appear in the same places? Perhaps in my last recurrence this system never came to England.

Mr. O.   You see, that is the difficulty about recurrence, because people either don't know about it, or, when they hear about it and begin to think about it, they think in the ordinary formatory way, that is, ordinary logical way, or very often they think quite illogically, or worse. But even if they think logically, they haven't enough material; they don't know enough to think about it. It is necessary to understand first of all that we speak about a theory, and secondly, that this theory must be sufficiently full—there must be sufficient material in it. When we think about recurrence, we think that everything repeats, and this is exactly what spoils our approach to it. As I said once before, the first thing to understand about recurrence is that it is not eternal. It sounds absurd, but really it is so, because it is so different in different cases. Even if we take it theoretically, purely people in mechanical life, even their lives change. As I have pointed out in the 'New Model', only certain people in certain conditions, quite frozen conditions of life, have their lives repeating exactly in the same way, and maybe for a long time. In other cases, even in ordinary mechanical life things change. If people are not so definitely kept by circumstances, like great men who have to be great men again and nobody can do anything about it, and they themselves can do nothing against it—with people in exalted positions nothing changes. But more ordinary people can have different variations in their lives, but again, not for ever. Never think that anything is for ever. It is a very strange thing that it seems as though people who have no possibilities either owing to certain conditions, or to their own insufficient development, or to a pathological state, could have their lives repeated without any particular change. But in the case of people with theoretical possibility, their lives can reach certain points, and either they meet with some possibility of development, or they begin to go down—one or another. They cannot go on remaining for ever in the same place, and from the moment one begins to meet with some real possibility, it means that one begins to come to the end of purely mechanical accidents. Then one is able to see the possibility to do something, or to lose it and then go down. Just think about it and perhaps you will be able to formulate questions about it.

Q. When we try to change our being, is essence as much affected as personality?

Mr. O. We have to work on personality, but essence is affected if we really change something.

Q. The one virtue of the state of sleep seems to be that as it is at the bottom of the scale we cannot fall any further.

Mr. O. Oh, yes we can.

Q. Future in the work seems a little like walking on a tightrope. Can one hope to attain another level of stability later?

Mr. O. Every state has many different forms, and so has the

state of sleep many different forms. There may be sleep with possibility of awakening, sleep with less possibility of awakening, and there may be sleep with no possibility of awakening, and so on.

Try to think about what I said about recurrence. It is a very good exercise for the mind, because it is very difficult to think rightly about it.

APRIL 2ND 1940

Q. In reference to recurrence I can understand that a spiral may lead us out of our present circle, but was the present circle derived from a previous spiral?

MR. O. This is quite arbitrary and I don't think I can speak about spirals from the point of view of the system. But if we do speak about spirals in relation to recurrence, then, in ordinary recurrence there is no spiral at all, it is all on the same level. Recurrences may differ from one another in small details, one may be inclined one way and another more inclined another way—but it is only a small deviation and so there is no spiral. The idea of spiral begins from the moment of escaping from constant repetition of the same things, or from the moment of introducing something new. This should be understood first of all.

Q. MR. O. spoke some time ago about the paradox that things could not have happened differently, but at the same time at different moments several possibilities must exist. Is the solution that in order for things to happen differently it is necessary to see the possibilities, and the ability to do this must depend on change of being which can only be achieved after a long period of repeated small efforts?

MR. O. There are two things necessary to understand about this. First: things are in a different relationship to the possibilities; some things, although they have not yet happened and we may think that they could happen in one or another way, are in reality predestined—nothing can be changed because such big causes are moving these things that, although they have not yet happened, they can happen only in one way. Second: in relation to some other things it is not so strict. There are many gradations and, together with some things that can happen only in one way, there may be other things, which have not yet happened, which can happen this or that way. Suppose to-day is decisive, or yesterday was decisive, or a moment a thousand years ago was decisive; it is necessary to remember that things can stand in different relations. We don't know what will happen in a year's time; we think they will go this way or that way, but in reality things are different. Some things can be changed to-day, but some can no longer be changed to-day. It is necessary to understand this as a principle, to understand why things are different and what is different about these things. You can answer like this: sometimes you can find the cause. Suppose you see things going on in exactly the same way for a long time—then you cannot expect a sudden change without some particular reason. Other things are comparatively new—a certain tendency has just appeared, and if it has just appeared, it may easily disappear. But if a tendency has been going in the same direction for a long time it is difficult to see the possibility of change. That is the only way we can discuss it —you cannot know anything definite about it. One principle you must understand in relation to this—things are never the same. If you say that some things can be changed, and apply it to everything, you will be wrong, because things are never in the same relation: in one case it will be one thing and in another case, another thing.

Q. May the possibility of variation in people's recurrences mean that people born in one recurrence might not be born in the next?

MR. O. That is possible only in some cases, but we cannot go into details of this kind. One thing you must understand definitely about it, that as long as people are quite mechanical, things can repeat and repeat themselves. But if people become more conscious, or if the possibility of becoming conscious appears, their time becomes very limited. That is what must be understood; they cannot expect an unlimited number of recurrences if they have already begun to know something or to learn something. The more they learn, the shorter becomes their time. It is the same principle as that which applies to one life. You remember, it was said that in the work, in relation to one life, time is counted. For those who are in the work time is counted, and the more seriously they work, the more strictly is their time counted. If one works very little, he may continue a year, two years in the same relation to the same idea; he can misunderstand something for one year or two years, and does not lose much because there is still a third year. But if one has already begun to work, he cannot have three years, because every day is an examination and he must pass one examination in order to come to another examination. That must be understood, and the same principle can be applied to recurrence.

Q. If personality dies with us, what effect can attempts to weaken it have in future recurrence?

MR. O. There is no need to be very dogmatic about it, but when we speak about recurrence, we speak of something that recurs, and that 'something' which recurs keeps in itself traces of all tendencies, all the created tendencies. If the tendency of weakening personality has been created, then it will continue; and if the opposite tendency has been created, a tendency to strengthen personality, again it will continue. It is quite right that personality dies, but if this 'something' recurs then the same causes will produce the same effects. If certain new tendencies have been created, they also will have their own effect.

Q. What is it that wants recurrence so much and yet fears it?

MR. O. That I don't know—it is material for your own study. Certainly, to the ordinary idea of death one prefers the idea of recurrence. At the same time one fears it, because, if one is really sincere with oneself, one realizes that things are repeated in this life. If one finds oneself again and again in the same position making the same mistakes, one realizes that to be born again will not help if one continues to do the same things. But a change can only be the result of effort. No circumstances can produce change. That is why all ordinary beliefs in the change of external circumstances never lead anywhere: circumstances may change, but everything will remain the same.

Q. Is the result of work on oneself to weaken tendencies in essence?

MR. O. Which tendencies? Sometimes they are in essence and sometimes in personality, but I would not formulate it as 'essence' and 'personality'. I would simply say—to weaken certain tendencies and strengthen other tendencies, to weaken mechanical tendencies and strengthen conscious tendencies. That is the only formulation possible—all other things would be out of place.

Q. Am I living exactly the same life again? Was I reborn when I was born in 1915 and will I again be born in 1915?

MR. O. Always in 1915—that is the only thing you cannot change. And certainly we are bound to have lived before—we could not have come out of nothing, only we don't remember. Even those who think they remember something, remember only as children. But in most cases they forget.

Q. Is it right to think that we can't go on living for ever (i.e. dying and being born)?

MR. O. Quite right. People with a quite mechanical life have a long time, and people who become conscious have a shorter time. That is the only difference. It looks very unjust, but at the same time mechanical people can get into very unpleasant circumstances. Suppose through external accident connected with historical events, such as wars or something like that, somebody dies very young and continues to die young every time, then no change can come. Only a very, very exceptional combination of circumstances can introduce some change in this case.

Q. A recent experience has caused me to think that much of emotional suffering lies in false personality. How can I remember this when identification with the suffering is very strong?

MR. O. Only by self-remembering. Suffering is the best possible help for self-remembering if you learn how to use it. By itself suffering does not help people's development, as some people think. One can suffer life after life and it will not give one a grain of result. But if one learns to use the opportunities which suffering provides, then suffering can help development. Suffering is the best thing to remember yourself. The moment you feel suffering, try to remember yourself.

Q. How can I use possibilities when I identify so much?

MR. O. Try to observe—you don't always identify in the same way—sometimes you identify so that you can see nothing else, at other times you can see something. If you can realize that you can identify more or identify less, it means that after some time you may identify not at all, or much less. If things were always the same, there would be no chance for us. They are never the same, they always vary in degree of intensity, and that gives the possibility change.

Q. It seems to me that personality, physical body and appearance are too impermanent to recur.

MR. O. Yes, but all that was created by certain causes and, as the causes will be the same, naturally they will produce the same effects.

Q.   If a person ceased to be born in one particular period what happens to all the other lives associated with him?

MR. O.   This is one of the very difficult problems. As far as we can say anything about this theory, it must be that one cannot start being born at once. This also is a process like everything else. One fades out little by little, and this fading out does not produce any big effect; some people can fade out and others will have to remain, such as people connected with historical events and things like that. They are in a most unpleasant position; they may become quite dead and just turn round and round. Most of them are quite dead.

Q.   Is it not possible for great people in historical movements to escape from life?

MR. O.   Yes, but, as I said, in most cases it is too late for them to escape; they are dead already, they are almost losing their bones on the way, but they have to continue to exist and turn round. That is one of the mysteries of life—that it is governed by dead people.

Q.   I feel I cannot have done exactly the same as before and think of the possibility of any change.

MR. O.   You do exactly the same: you do not remember yourself, and if you do not remember yourself now, then again next time you will not remember yourself, so it will be the same. The possibility of change begins only with the possibility of beginning to remember yourself now. In the system recurrence is not necessary. It may be interesting or useful; you can even start with it, but for actual work on yourself the idea of recurrence is not necessary. That is why we have not heard it from this system. It came from outside, from me, from literature. It does fit, it does not contradict the system, but it is not necessary because all that we can do we can do only in this life. If we don't do anything in this life, then the next life will be just the same, or maybe with slight variations but no positive change. That is what must be understood first of all.

Q.   I should like to know why time is limited for anyone who worked but not for one who hasn't.

MR. O.   For one who has not begun to awake, time is not counted because it does not exist. Everything repeats, always the same thing and then the same thing again. You can take it like this: knowledge is limited, but they don't take any knowledge, so for them it is not. Then you can make a comparison with an ordinary school. It is not possible to remain always in the same form. One must either make progress or go.

Q. I don't see how it is possible to remember a previous recurrence from what I understand about memory. I thought that memory was dependent on the contents of centres which are in personality. How can personality remember recurrence?

Mr. O. You cannot remember if you do not remember yourself here, in this recurrence. We have lived before. Many facts prove it. Why we don't remember is because we did not remember ourselves. The same is true in this life. Mechanical things we only remember that they happened. Only with self-remembering can we remember details. Personality is always mixed with essence. Memory is in essence, not in personality, but personality can present it quite rightly if memory is sufficiently strong.

Q. In a case when an accident affects one's whole life, does it recur?

Mr. O. Even this may happen; the same kind of accident may repeat itself. We speak only about a theory, but a theory may be better or worse, nearer or further from possible facts. In mechanical life even things which happen do not bring any practical change. Things are important only when a man begins to awake, either through a school or by himself. From this moment things become serious. So do you ask about mechanical recurrence or about the beginning of awakening? Remember this principle of school-work: if people work little or work badly, they have more time. If they begin to work seriously, then time is counted for them. They have less time. The same is true of recurrence. School-work means influence C. Influence C is conscious both in its origin and in its results. Influence C can be wasted as everything else can be wasted, but it should not be.

Q. Did you mean that if we don't work this time we shall not meet a school next time?

Mr. O. A school of any kind, even of a very elementary kind, is not under the laws of recurrence. Schools are more free as compared with things in life. Wars, revolutions, are like lamp-posts; conscious things are like the light from passing cars. If you go out, you will always see the same lamp-posts but you are not likely to see the same cars.

Q. Is it that opportunity never comes twice?

Mr. O. The same opportunity—no, it would be waste of time.

When people meet with certain opportunities, they become responsible for the energy spent on them. If they don't use it, it never recurs. Lamp-posts stay fixed; cars don't stay, they are not for standing still, they are for moving. It is useful to think that the same opportunities may not occur next time. We expect things to be the same, but they may be different. It depends on other people. Other people may begin earlier. For example, I began these lectures in 1921, but next time I may begin them in 1900. You will be prepared only for 1921, but in 1921 there may no longer be any opportunity for you. This is just an example for thinking about.

Q. It is very difficult to think about preparing for meeting the system earlier.

MR. O. You can prepare nothing. Only remember yourself, then you will remember things better. The whole thing lies in negative emotions: we enjoy them so much that we have no interest in anything else. If you remember yourself now, then you may remember next time.

2
Negative emotions

NEGATIVE EMOTIONS I

MR. O. I want particularly to remind you about this idea of negative emotions and the state of negative emotion. It is really the second important point in the system. The first important point is about consciousness. And the second important point is about negative emotions.

If you remember what was said in the beginning about consciousness and the absence of consciousness, you must all have realized one thing in observing functions. You must have realized that, ordinarily, whatever we do, whatever we think, whatever we feel, we do not remember ourselves. We do not realize that we are present, that we are conscious, that we are here.

But at the same time you must already know and understand that, if we make sufficient efforts for a sufficiently long time, we can increase our capacity for self-remembering. We begin to remember ouselves more often, we begin to remember ourselves more deeply, we begin to remember ourselves in connection with more ideas—the idea of consciousness, the idea of work, the idea of centres, the idea of self-study, the idea of schools.

But the question is how to remember oneself, how to make oneself more aware. Then, if you come back to the idea of negative emotions, you will find that this is the chief factor which makes us not remember ourselves. So the one thing cannot go without the other. You cannot struggle with negative emotions without remembering yourself more, and you cannot remember yourself more without struggling with negative emotions. If you remember these two things, you will understand everything better. So try to keep these two ideas, which are connected, in mind.

Now about how to struggle with negative emotions. First of all it is necessary to realize that there is not a single useful negative emotion, useful in any sense. Negative emotions are all equally bad and all a sign of weakness. Next, you have to realize that we can struggle with them, they can be conquered and destroyed because there is no real centre for them. If there were a real centre for them, then there would be no chance; we would remain for ever in the power of negative emotions. But luckily for us there is no real centre. It is an artificial centre that works, and this artificial centre can be destroyed and lost. And we will feel much better if it is. Even the realization that this is possible is very much; but we have so many convictions, prejudices and even principles about it, that it is very difficult to get rid of the idea that negative emotions are necessary and obligatory. As long as we think they are necessary, unavoidable, and even useful for self-expression or many other things—we can do nothing. It is necessary to have a certain mental struggle to realize that they are quite useless, that they don't have any useful function in our lives and yet at the same time that all life is based on negative emotions. This is what nobody realizes.

Q. But it seems to me there are circumstances that simply induce one to have negative emotions.

Mr. O. This is one of our strongest illusions, when we think that negative emotions are produced by circumstances. All negative emotions are in us, inside us.... We always think our negative emotions are produced either by the fault of other people or by the fault of circumstances. We <u>always</u> think like that. This is our chief illusion. Our negative emotions are in ourselves and produced by ourselves. There is absolutely not a single unavoidable reason whereby somebody else's action or certain circumstances should produce negative emotion in me. It is only my weakness.

Q. Then, if your best friend dies, you should be optimistic?

Mr. O. Death of a friend or grief of some kind is suffering, not negative emotion. It can produce negative emotion only if you identify with it. Suffering can be real; negative emotion is not real. And, after all, suffering occupies a very small part of our life but negative emotions occupy a big part—they occupy the whole of our life. And why? Because we justify them. We think they are produced by some external cause. When we know they cannot be produced by external causes, most of them disappear. But this is the first condition: we must realize that they cannot be produced by external causes if we don't want to have them. They are generally there because we permit them, explain them by external causes; and in that way we don't struggle with them. This is the important point.

Q. Is there any reason why we are so anxious to keep negative emotions?

MR. O. Habit. We are accustomed to them; and we cannot sleep without them. What would many people do without negative emotions?

Q. Do we make negative emotions much worse by imagining them?

MR. O. They cannot exist without imagination. Simply suffering pain is not a negative emotion, but when imagination and identification enter, then it becomes negative emotion. Emotional pain, like physical pain, is not negative emotion by itself, but when you begin to make all kinds of embroidery on it, it becomes negative emotion.

Q. To struggle with negative emotions themselves we have to observe more and work against the strong identification with the emotion?

MR. O. Yes. Later we will speak about methods for struggling with emotions, because there are many and very definite methods, different for different emotions, but first you must struggle with negative imagination and identification. This is quite sufficient to destroy many of the usual negative emotions—in any case, to make them much lighter. You must start with this, because it is only possible to begin using stronger methods against negative emotions when you can struggle with identification to a certain extent, and when you have already stopped negative imagination. That must be stopped completely. It is useless to study further methods until that is done. Negative imagination you <u>can</u> stop; and even the study of identification will already diminish it. But the real struggle with negative emotions begins later, and it is based on right understanding, first of all, of how they are created, what is behind them, how useless they are and how much you lose because of this pleasure of having negative emotions. When you realize how much you lose, then perhaps you will have enough energy to do something about it.

Q. From what you say it seems to me you are presupposing we have one 'I', higher than the others, who can do this?

MR. O. Not higher, but some intellectual 'I's are free from emotional centre and can see things impartially. They can say,

'I had this negative emotion all my life. Did I get a penny? No, I only paid and paid and paid. That means it is useless.'

Q.   When you are in the middle of having a negative emotion can you stop it by just thinking?

Mr. O.   No, but you can prepare the ground beforehand. If, for a long time, you can create a right attitude, after some time it will help you to stop the negative emotion in the beginning. When you are in the middle of it you cannot stop it.

Q.   But surely there are times when one's own feelings may not be negative, yet, for some perfectly just reason, one is indignant or angry. . . .

Mr. O.   There are no just reasons. Once and for all you must understand there are no just reasons for being angry. And anger is not in the reason, it is in you. Negative emotions are not in external reasons, they are in you. When you understand this, you will begin to think about it rightly. As long as you think that external reasons exist, it means you have not begun yet.

Q.   Why does one feel negative emotions more strongly and more frequently in the company of some people than with others?

Mr. O.   People who are full of negative emotions and identification produce similar reactions in other people. One must learn to isolate oneself in such cases by means of self-remembering and not identifying. Isolation does not mean indifference.

Q.   Are negative emotions always connected with identification in some way?

Mr. O.   Always. Negative emotions cannot exist without identification and negative imagination. These two things are the psychological basis of negative emotions. The mechanical basis is wrong work of centres.

Q.   I can sometimes manage not to express a negative emotion to begin with, but it goes on trying to come out.

Mr. O.   That means you only stopped the external manifestation and you must try to stop the cause of it. I don't mean the emotion itself, but the cause of the expression. There is a difference. Emotion is one thing, expression another. Try to find the difference.

Q.   Where does the expression of negative emotions begin? Often the emotion persists in spite of efforts to exclude imagination and identification—for example, disappointment. Should it stop if one makes the right observations and efforts to overcome imagination and identification, or may it persist in spite of all this? If it persists does it mean one is still expressing it?

MR. O.   It is different in different cases. Many things are mixed together here. You must understand that if you speak about not expressing negative emotion, you must speak only about not expressing negative emotion. If you speak about causes of emotions or reasons, then you must speak only about that and say nothing about not expressing. Only one thing at a time.

Q.   Is it only by observing that one can understand that the cause of an expression of negative emotion is different from the cause of the emotion?

MR. O.   I did not say to compare. I said speak about one thing. I exactly said not to ask such questions, not to think about two things at the same time. If you want to speak about cause of expression of negative emotion, speak about cause of expression. If you want to speak about cause of the negative emotion, speak about cause of the negative emotion. But not about the two things at the same time.

Q.   If I can refrain from expressing a negative emotion, the results are extreme irritation and subsequent vulnerability to all outside things.

MR. O.   Certainly, if you keep expression shut up you feel irritable. This means you identify. You try to keep identification and destroy expression. You must begin by destroying identification.

Q.   Is it possible that efforts to control negative emotion make one tired?

MR. O.   No. Such efforts give us much more energy—they cannot tire. You can become tired if you only suppress expression. But I never said suppress. I said, 'Do not express; find reasons for not expressing'. Suppression can never help, because sooner or later the negative emotion will jump out. It is a question of finding reasons, thinking rightly.

Q.   Changing attitude?

MR. O.   Quite right. Because expression of emotion is always based on some kind of wrong thinking.

Q.   I should like to get more help about tackling negative emotions.

MR. O.   It must be your own effort, and first of all you must classify your negative emotions. You must find which negative emotions you have chiefly; why they come, what brings them, and so on. You must understand that your only control over emotions is by mind—but not immediately. If you think rightly for six months, then it will affect negative emotions, because they are based on wrong thinking. If you begin to think rightly to-day, it will not change negative emotions to-morrow. But negative emotions next January may be changed if you start thinking rightly now.

Q.   When I think about negative emotions, I do understand very clearly that they are in ourselves, and yet, soon after, I still continue to be negative and continue to express negative emotions. Is it simply because I am not one?

MR. O.   First, because you are not one, and second, because you do not try in the right way. It is a question of long work, as I said, and it cannot be changed at once. If one has constant negative emotions, recurring negative emotions of the same kind, one always falls in at the same point. If one observed oneself better one would know that this was coming, or had come, and if one had thought rightly beforehand one would have some resistance. But if one has no right attitude, if one does not think rightly, then one is helpless, and the negative emotion happens again at the same time, in the same way and so on. . . .

The first thing one has to do is to learn not to express it, because when one expresses a negative emotion, one is in its power. One can do nothing at that moment. First of all one must learn not to express negative emotion. When one learns that, then one can try not to identify, to create right attitude, and to remember oneself.

About this question of negative emotions I want you to understand that the stopping of expression of negative emotion and the struggle with negative emotions are two quite different practices. Trying to stop the expression of negative emotion comes first. You can do nothing about the negative emotions themselves until you have already learned to stop the expression of them. When you have acquired a certain control of non-expression of negative emotion, then you can study negative emotions themselves. First, you must understand how wrong they are, how useless they are, and then you must understand that they cannot exist without identification. When you have realized this you must try—I didn't say you can do it at once, it will take a long time, but you must try—to divide them into three categories. First, the more or less ordinary, everyday negative emotions, which happen often and are always connected with identification. Certainly, you must observe them and you must already have a certain control over expression of them. Then you must start dealing with them by trying not to identify, by avoiding identification as often as you can, not only in relation to these emotions but in relation to everything. If you create in yourself the capacity of not identifying, that will affect these emotions and you will notice how they disappear.

The second category do not appear every day. They are the more difficult, more complicated emotions depending on some mental process—suspicion, hurt feelings and many things like that. They are more difficult to conquer. You can deal with them by creating right mental attitude, by thinking—not at the time when you are in the negative emotion, but in between, when you are quiet. Try to find the right attitude, the right point of view, and make it permanent. If you create right thinking, that will take all power from these negative emotions.

Then there is the third category, much more intense, much more difficult, and very rare. Against them you can do nothing. These two methods—struggle with identification and creating attitudes—do not help. When such emotions come you can do only one thing: you must try to remember yourself—remember yourself with the help of the emotion. That will change them after some time. But for this you have to be prepared; it is quite a special thing.

These are the methods of dealing with negative emotions. As even negative emotions can be different, you cannot use the same methods against all of them. In all cases you must be prepared. As I said in the beginning, it will be difficult to conquer them or struggle with them, but you will learn through time. Only, never mix this with the expression of negative emotion. That comes first. It is given almost at the first lecture, and before you can do anything else you must learn to control the manifestation of negative emotion. As long as you cannot stop expression, it means you can do nothing about the emotions themselves. But if you learn to control expression, then you can start. But remember you can do nothing when you are in a negative emotion; you can only do something about it before and after.

Q. I would like to know more about why you speak about negative emotions and the expression of them as quite separate subjects.

MR. O. Because different knowledge is necessary for that. The idea of not expressing negative emotion begins in the first lecture. At the very first moment of self-observation one is told to observe and try not to express negative emotions, and for a long time one has to work on that. Then, later, many other explanations and practices are given, and after a very long time you come to the study of emotions themselves and the study of methods of changing emotions. So you cannot put them together, they are quite different things. But you must understand that after some time of coming to talks, lectures and so on, you begin to forget the chronology of the ideas, and it is very useful to remember the order in which they come.

NEGATIVE EMOTIONS II

Q. I still cannot understand why all causes of negative emotions are in myself. I think there must be some causes that come from outside.

MR. O. If you observe yourself, you will see. Causes outside remain the same, but sometimes they produce negative emotion in you, sometimes not. Why? Because real causes are in you. There are only apparent causes outside. If you are in a good state, if you are remembering yourself, if you are not identifying, then nothing that happens outside (relatively speaking—I don't mean catastrophes) can produce negative emotion in you. If you are in a bad state, identified, immersed in imagination or something like that, then everything just a little unpleasant will produce violent emotion in you. It is a question of observation.

Q. But I don't see how some things could fail to produce negative emotion, for instance, other people's behaviour.

MR. O. But they are machines. Why should the behaviour of machines produce negative emotion? If a machine hits you, it is your own fault; you must not be in the way of the machine. You may have a negative emotion, but it is not the fault of the machine; it is your own fault. Negativeness is in you. Other people do not have as much power over you as you think, it is only the result of identification. You can be much more free if you do not identify, and sometimes you are more free. That is why I say it must be observed. If you observe well, you will see that sometimes you identify more, sometimes you identify less; and because of this, sometimes you are absolutely in the power of negative emotions and sometimes you have a certain resistance. It may take a long time to learn how to resist negative emotions, but it is not impossible; it is possible. You must understand one thing about negative emotions; we are too much afraid of them, we consider them too powerful. We can show resistance to them if we persist and do not consider them inevitable and omnipotent.

Q. I could see myself losing my temper when talking to somebody recently, and although I tried to struggle with it, I was not successful. How can I control temper?

MR. O. This is an example of mechanicalness. You cannot control your temper when it has already begun to appear. It cannot be otherwise, it is already too late; it has already jumped out. You can control such things as manifestations of temper, for instance, only in one way. It takes a long time. Struggle must begin in your mind. You must first find your way of thinking on a definite subject. Suppose you have to meet a certain man, and suppose he irritates you. Your temper shows itself. You don't like it. How can you stop it? You must begin with the study of your thinking. What do you think about this man—not what you feel when you are irritated, but what do you think about him at quiet moments? You may find that in your mind you argue with him; you prove to him that he is wrong; you tell him all his mistakes; you find that, generally, he behaves wrongly towards you. This is where you are wrong. You must learn to think rightly; you must find the way to think rightly. Then, if you do, it will happen like this: although emotion is much quicker than thought, emotion is a temporary thing, but thought can be made continuous; so whenever emotion jumps out, it hits against this continuous thought and cannot go on and manifest itself. So you can struggle with the expression of negative emotions, as in this example, only by creating continuous right thinking. And to explain in two words what right thinking is, is impossible; it is necessary to study it. If you remember what I said about parts of centres, you will come to that, because in most cases and most conditions in ordinary life, people think only with the mechanical part of the intellectual centre. This is not sufficient. It is necessary to use the intellectual part of the intellectual centre.

Q. Is it because lower parts of centres interfere with each other that we cannot be in higher parts?

MR. O. You cannot put this as a cause. Identifying is the chief cause.

Q. Is the simplest way to avoid identification by self-remembering?

MR. O. It is the only way, because they are two sides of the same thing, the one requires the other. But you always forget about identification and about self-remembering. Trying to self-remember and trying not to identify is the chief means of passing into higher parts of centres.

Q. Can conquering negative emotions, like fear, create energy?

MR. O. Very much so. This is one of the strongest means of collecting energy. All possibilities of development are contained in conquering negative emotions and transforming them. A man with negative emotions will never do anything.

Q. Into what kind of things can negative emotions be transformed?

MR. O. No, it is better to say they must be conquered. If you like, they are transformed into some kind of emotion mixed with very much understanding—an emotion of higher parts of centres. Almost any negative emotion we have now can be transformed into emotion of higher parts of centres. But this needs understanding, conviction that it is necessary, and decision to do it.

Q. Is it negative emotions that prevent us from getting into those emotional states?

MR. O. Yes. We have quite enough money, but we spend it all on unpleasant things. If we save a sufficient quantity we can use it in the right way. Power to use comes with quantity.

Q. But is fear really a negative emotion?

MR. O. In most cases it is a negative emotion. Real fear is in instinctive centre, but this is, comparatively speaking, very rare. In most cases fear is imaginary—the fear is in you.

Q. Did you say pain was a negative emotion?

MR. O. Pain belongs to instinctive centre. It is a very useful thing—it warns us of danger.

This division of emotions into emotions of instinctive centre and emotions of emotional centre is very important—you will find it only in this system. Emotions of instinctive centre and emotions of emotional centre are quite different and they are never fully separated one from the other in any other system. And without this separation you cannot know anything. Instinctive emotions, both positive and negative, are all useful.

We are in a very strange state, because positive emotions don't belong to our ordinary emotional centre but to higher emotional centre, and negative emotions don't belong to this ordinary centre but exist in an artificial centre. So our emotional centre is neither positive nor negative, and higher emotional centre has no negative emotions. Negative emotions are some kind of artificial creation. How are they created? The emotional centre borrows material from the instinctive, and with the negative part, of the instinctive centre and the help of imagination, it creates negative emotions. They can be destroyed exactly because they have no real centre. This is very difficult work, but you must realize that as long as negative emotions exist no development is possible, because development means development of all that is in man. Negative emotions cannot develop—it would be very disastrous for us if they could. So, if one is trying to create consciousness, one must at the same time struggle with negative emotions.

Again, when speaking about negative emotions, the question arises what to do with emotions that are not negative and may even be pleasant. If you can have such emotions, even quite personal emotions like friendship or affection, without identification, and they do not pass into and become negative emotions, then I always say that there is no harm in them from the point of view of this system, although other systems find them equally wrong, which is an exaggeration. But if pleasant emotions produce negative emotions, then certainly they cannot exist at the same time as development. Either you keep them, or you develop, but you cannot have both together. Certain particular kinds of negative emotion must be destroyed before one can even think of any serious development.

Q. Did I understand you to say that negative emotions are a wrong use of instinctive centre?

MR. O. No. Negative emotions are created from material taken from instinctive centre. This material legitimately belongs to the instinctive centre and is wrongly borrowed from it.

Q. Why is it that negative emotion appears to affect the functioning of instinctive centre to such a great degree?

MR. O. Negative emotion affects all centres. Centres are so connected that you cannot have a strong or violent negative emotion (and with the help of identification they all become strong) without affecting all centres. You cannot have negative emotion and at the same time do something else right or even think rightly. You eat wrongly, you breathe wrongly, walk wrongly, work wrongly—everything.

NEGATIVE EMOTIONS III

Q. MR. O. once said that certain negative emotions make serious work impossible. Does that mean they must be absolutely exterminated before one begins, and what does he mean by serious work?

MR. O. By serious work I mean not only study but change. First you must study certain things, then you work to change them. But, as even study cannot go without a certain change—because these two processes of study and change are not fully divided—a more serious study than just at the beginning can be called serious work. With certain negative emotions serious work is practically impossible because they will spoil all results; one side of you will work and another side will spoil it. So after some time, if you start this work without conquering negative emotions, you may find yourself in a worse state than you were before. It already happened several times that people made continuation of work impossible for themselves, because they wished to keep their negative emotions. There were certain moments when they realized this, but they did not make sufficient effort at that time, and later the negative emotions became more strong.

Q. Could we hear more about right attitude as a weapon against negative emotion? It must mean more than just not identifying.

MR. O. Certainly, it means more; it means right thinking on a definite subject. For instance, take one thing: almost all our personal negative emotions are based on accusation; somebody else is guilty. If, by persistent thinking, we realize that nobody can be guilty against us, that we are the cause of everything that happens to us, that changes things—not at once certainly, because many times this realization will come too late. But after some time this right thinking, this creating of right attitude or point of view can become a permanent process, then negative emotions will only appear occasionally. Exactly by being permanent this process of right thinking has power over negative emotions—it catches them in the beginning.

Q. I find that much of my time is passed in a negative state, not very definite, and I don't seem able to do anything about it.

MR. O. Yes, but you must have realized that it is generally connected with some kind of identification or imagination.

When you find different manifestations of this negative state you can struggle with it, because this struggle is in the mind. You can refuse some points of view and accept other points of view, and very soon you will see a difference.

This is connected with a very big question, because from one point of view we are so mechanical, we can do nothing, but from another point of view there are in us—perhaps not many, but there are several things which we can begin to do. We have certain possibilities in us, only we don't use them. It is true you cannot 'do', in the sense that you cannot change what you feel at any given moment, but you can make yourself think about a subject at a given moment. This is the beginning. You must know what is possible and begin from that, because possibility to 'do' will increase very quickly. You can make yourself think about a subject in a certain way, or you can make yourself not think.

You do not realize what enormous power lies in thinking. I do not mean that as a philosophical explanation of power. The power lies in the fact that, if you always think rightly about certain things, you can make it permanent—it grows into a permanent attitude. You may find some inclination to wrong emotional manifestations of some kind. Just at that moment you can do nothing, you have educated in yourself the capacity of this kind of reaction by wrong thinking. But if you start from right thinking, then after some time you will educate in yourself the capacity for a different reaction. Only, this method has to be understood and this understanding must be quite deep. You can apply this method to many different things. This is really the one thing you can do. You can 'do' nothing else. There is no direct way to struggle with negative manifestations because you cannot catch them; and there is no way to prevent them except by being prepared beforehand for them. But a passing realization that they are wrong will not help; it must be very deep, otherwise you will again have an equally difficult process to prepare the ground for another manifestation. You do not realize how much you lose by these spontaneous manifestations of a negative character. They make so many things impossible.

Q.   Even if I begin to think rightly I find imitation starts when I hear somebody else grumbling and I begin too. . . .

Mr. O.   The fact that you begin to think rightly will not change anything straight away. It is necessary to think rightly for a long time then results will come, but not at once. It is a question of

months or years to create right attitudes. By creating right attitudes you consolidate the fact that you have really and seriously
decided not to give way to negative manifestations. We do not
realize how much we lose in this way. We lose exactly what we
want to get.

Q.   But how is it possible to arm oneself when one <u>knows</u> one is
going to be in the presence of something which always produces
negative emotion?

MR. O.   I have already answered that. But first of all you must
stop the habit of expressing negative emotions. Only after that
is it possible to speak of something else. That is why it is already
explained in the first lectures, at the same time as you hear about
self-observation, that you must learn not to express negative
emotions. As long as you continue to express negative emotions
without any attempt to stop them, nothing can be done. And
everybody knows how not to show what they feel. I do not
mean in exceptional cases, but in ordinary cases. Negativeness
is all based on identification, imagination and on one particular
feature, namely, allowing oneself to express it. You always
believe you cannot stop it and therefore feel it is quite right if
you show what you feel. So first you must get rid of this illusion.
You <u>can</u> stop the manifestations of negative emotions. If you
say, 'I don't want to,' I will believe you, but not if you say, 'I
can't'.

Q.   I cannot think of any way of thinking that is not dependent
on associations.

MR. O.   Quite right. But one can try new associations, or one
can go on thinking by old associations without any attempt to
change them. The idea is to try new associations by introducing
new points of view.

Q.   I have been struck by the limitations of our thinking
capacity. What do they depend on?

MR. O.   Only when you have examples of a better kind of
thinking in yourself, using higher parts of centres, having more
consciousness, only then will you see in what these limitations
consist. We know our mind is limited, but we do not know in
what it is limited. When you know these two ways of thinking
and are able to compare them, then you will know where the
difference lies and it will be possible to speak about causes. For
instance, I can tell you what is lacking in our thinking, but if
you have no observations of your own, it will mean nothing to
you. First, each thought is too short—it ought to be much

longer. When you have experience of short thoughts and long thoughts, then you will see.

Mr. O. I notice from the questions that people do not understand how new things come. The difficulty of thinking about them is this: we are accustomed to think in absolutes—all or nothing. But it is necessary to understand two things. First, that anything new comes at first in flashes. It comes, then it disappears. Only after a certain time these flashes become longer and then still longer, so that you can see and notice them. Nothing comes at once in a complete form. Everything that can be acquired comes, then disappears, comes again, again disappears. After a long time it comes and stays a little so that you are able to give a name to it, to notice it.

Secondly, we must see how we deceive ourselves when we think in the ordinary way: that we can 'do', that we are not guilty, that all the others are guilty and so on. We must change this way of thinking, we must understand how little we possess.

Q. Is it better always to say, 'I am guilty'?

Mr. O. This is equally wrong. It would simply be an excuse for not thinking, a ready solution. We must think every time.

Q. By what means can we prolong these flashes?

Mr. O. By repeating the causes that produced them. I don't want to give an example, because it will lead to imagination. All I will say is that, for instance, by certain efforts of self-remembering one can see certain things that one cannot see now. Our eyes are not as limited as we think. There are many things they can see but don't notice.

Q. Is it necessary to perceive things differently before we can think differently—to perceive things in relation to each other instead of as separate wholes?

Mr. O. We cannot perceive differently until we think differently. We have control only over thoughts; we have no control over perception. Perception does not depend on our desire or decision, it depends particularly on state of consciousness, on being more awake. If one awakes for a sufficient time, say for one hour, one can see many things one does not see now.

NEGATIVE ATTITUDES

MR. O. It would be very good if you could study the question of negative attitudes in the same way as you studied negative emotions.

We have given a sufficiently long time to the study of the psychological side of the question of negative attitudes, but there are many other sides to this question. But I think we must try to see how this question of negative attitudes connects us with many other possibilities. You see, this question of negative attitudes is a kind of bridge, a kind of introduction, which leads us now to the next chapter of our studies. Until now the centre of gravity of our work—at any rate the centre of gravity of the practical work—was in ourselves, in self-study, self-remembering, and all that. At the same time, at the very beginning it was explained that the right study of man must go parallel with the study of the universe, and certainly we got some ideas in relation to the universe—things like the Ray of Creation, cosmoses, hydrogens and so on—only on very general lines; also we have the idea of laws under which man lives. In the diagram on magnetic centre we spoke about the influences under which man lives, influences A, B and C. Influences C come at a certain moment to very few people.

Then we spoke about what these influences A, B and C mean. This is connected with the idea, explained in the beginning, that man is a machine controlled by external events, things that are around him. But we did not specify these things, we took them just as influences. Now we must come to the study of these influences, we must learn to divide things into classes, and the practical side will be how to control these influences, how to be receptive to certain influences, and not be receptive to influences you do not want—this is, so to speak, the 'plan'.

What I call the 'new chapter' refers to the study of life. Until now the centre of gravity of our study was in ourselves; this will continue, but it is necessary to begin to study external things and try to understand, try to form a right opinion about external things. We will not be able to go further, or to go far, if we cannot learn to discriminate between external events. In relation to ourselves we have learnt to do this to a certain extent—at any rate we must be able to see what is good and what is bad (taking good and bad in a simple sense). If we take work as our aim, the aim of awakening, or being free or something like that, then from this point of view we can see that 'bad' is what prevents our work, 'bad' is what takes our energy from our work or hinders our work, and 'good' is what gives us energy and helps our work, and what is favourable to our work.

Now we must learn to study external events, events on a big scale, and find what is good and what is bad from the point of view of possible evolution. If we find in external events what helps evolution, that immediately brings us to the question: how can individual evolution, i.e. evolution of a small number of people, affect the general state of people. We heard about the esoteric circle, then the intermediate circles and the mechanical circle. And if we look at things as they are, if we try to think about external life, if we ask ourselves in which state it is, how we can regard it from the point of view of esoteric circle, then we shall certainly see that the state of humanity is very far from favourable. Because, from one point of view, we know that everyone cannot be in the esoteric circle. But at the same time there may be definite influences of esoteric circle in life; and here we can say positively that such influences do not exist in our life. Life is going by itself. And in what state is esoteric circle itself? We do not know; it is just theory. But the fact is that in life we cannot see any signs of definite control of things by the esoteric circle.

These principles of which I speak now must be understood from quite different sides. During the years when we have studied the general structure of the universe on a large scale, and man, we made very useful realizations; now we must find all these realizations which we made before. I mentioned 48 laws, man-machine, influences A, B and C, and there are many other ideas which you must think of for yourselves, and find which ideas connect us with this question of our position in the midst of external things. Roughly speaking, man's situation is this: he is a machine, and he is governed by some kind of currents coming from the big machines which surround him. What are these big machines? All big events, wars, revolutions, civilizations, religions, science, art, inventions of the last century, all these things are producing different influences on man, and he lives under these influences.

In connection with this I will mention only one point which it is necessary to understand, one point from which it is useful to look at this question. You will remember, it was explained about centres, from this point of view, that we cannot control our functions, i.e. our thoughts, emotions or movements, because, at best, man's will is only sufficient to control one centre, and the other centres will be opposed to this will. Suppose I know all I should know, and suppose I decide to think in a new way. I begin to think in a new way; but then I sit in the ordinary posture, or smoke a cigarette in the usual way, and I again find myself in the old thoughts.

The same about emotions; one decides to feel in a new way about something, and then one thinks in the old way and certainly negative emotions come in the same way again, and so one has no control. Really, in this sense, the position is almost hopeless.

Then, in connection with schools it was explained that the possibility exists only in schools, i.e. that under such organized work, centres can be developed and controlled simultaneously. And it was explained that, for the control of moving centre, organization is necessary and someone else's will is necessary. You will remember, we spoke about stop exercises, and all this. But what is the situation of people who do not know these schools? Intellectually we admit that schools must exist somewhere, but we do not know where. It was explained very definitely—and this must be taken as a very definite fact—that studying or working on moving centre is impossible without a teacher who knows specially this side of the work, who is specially prepared for it and who has had special experience in this work. And even in schools there are many other questions, for instance, the question of age, even if one does find a school. If a man is young, he can begin to work on moving centre, but if he is older it becomes more difficult, because moving habits are very strong and it is difficult to reach their origin, and so it becomes almost impossible.

So the question now arises: does this mean it is absolutely impossible to attain anything without a school, or is there a possibility? Later we will come to this, and see that the possibility exists, and this possibility is necessarily connected with the question we are now talking about. It is impossible to produce a simultaneous action in two centes—the thinking and the emotional centre. The moving centre will always be in the way. Moving centre will unconsciously work in the interests of mechanicalness, because moving centre is accustomed to work in a certain way, and it will keep all centres back. So we must accept that as one of the conditions under which we work. And really this is one of the 48 laws.

When we know it, then we can see our situation. And we have to work on the emotional centre and the thinking centre. We must remember all we learnt about that, and about negative emotions. We must remember all that is understood now about negative attitudes. We must add to that that our attitudes are kinds of wires which connect us with events, and certain currents produced by the nature of these attitudes go by these wires; and the nature of the current determines which kind of influence we receive from a given event. A certain big event produces an influence on us, but this influence can be changed by our attitude. And this is the only way by which we can counterbalance the influence of moving centre. Because otherwise we can work for thirty years or more and remain just in the same position. We will learn, know and understand more, but every moment we shall catch ourselves in the same negative attitude and the same negative emotion. There is no means of changing this just by our own energy. But if by changing our attitude towards some external influence we change the character of the influence in that way, that can balance the work of centres and help us to pass an interval between this note in which we find ourselves and the note in which we wish to find ourselves.

I cannot explain it sufficiently to-day; it is a big question and we will return to it. Please think now and ask all the questions you can and try to remember that now we have to think on these lines. What can help in this work? Only knowing more, knowing more about oneself, knowing more about things.

It is necessary to realize one very important new thing about negative work of emotional centre and negative work of intellectual centre. And thinking on this point we can see that all the work we have done before, all these talks, all these theories were necessary in order to be able to speak as we can speak now. If I had said the same things to new people, they would have understood things in a wrong way.

What I want to say is this. In the beginning, when it was first mentioned about negative parts of centres, negative part of the emotional centre was taken as quite a legitimate thing. Negative part of the intellectual centre was also taken as a necessary part of it. Then, when you go further and begin to study different kinds of emotions, you realize that the negative part of the emotional centre is not only useless, not only wrong, not only all the evil depends on it but, what is even more important, it need not exist, there is no necessity for it to exist. Very much was said about this before, so I will not repeat it. It is much more difficult to understand that the same thing refers to the intellectual centre. Negative part of the intellectual centre is also not necessary. But that needs more mental gymnastics to realize. It can be understood if one realizes that we do not know what positive attitudes are, exactly in the same way as we do not know what positive emotions are.

And here we come to a very interesting thing from my point of view. I want to say that these centres are not centres at all, these centres with which we live. About formatory centre it was explained that it was only a registering apparatus, and it was said definitely that it was not a centre. Ordinary emotional centre is also not a centre; it is some kind of sensitive organ but it does not deserve the full name of centre, because, after all, centres are only three: one emotional, one intellectual, and one moving-instinctive-sexual. Higher emotional and higher intellectual differ from the ordinary thinking and emotional centres, first, in their speed, and second, because they have no negative parts, there is no 'No' in them. 'No' is exactly the thing that keeps our centres working at a low speed. A centre cannot work properly if it has 'No' in it. Real centres, i.e. higher centres which work without 'No' we cannot understand. Why cannot we understand them? Because we think in a centre with 'No' in it; so we cannot understand what it means to think or feel without 'No'.

I want to remind you of one thing, not in connection with 'Special Doctrine', but in another book. When we read the chapter called 'Experimental Mysticism', I drew your attention to some interesting experiences when in a certain state I thought about certain things. Quite unexpectedly I realized then, that about certain things I could think and about certain other things I could not think, because they did not exist. It does not mean that I had a negative attitude towards them. I could not make myself think about them—they were simply non-existent, without any feeling of negativeness. I asked myself at the time different questions; certain questions I could analyse and was able to find something in them; but to other questions there was no answer because they were like an empty place—words without any meaning. This is an example of how a certain centre—we do not know which—in any case some kind of thinking centre, can work without 'No'. A real centre can see what exists and what does not exist, and it would think only about existing things; non-existent things simply would not exist for it.

Again, our ordinary mind does not see how to live without negation; all forms of negation play such an important part in our thinking that we cannot believe that one can think without 'No'. This partly points the way and partly shows the difficulty of the way. But this is knowing. And it is necessary to know; only knowing can help in this way.

Q. Did I understand you to say that these wires are our negative attitudes?

MR. O. Not necessarily negative.

Q. If we change these attitudes we shall be capable of receiving different external influences?

MR. O. Yes.

Q. And we must try to differentiate between A, B and C?

MR. O. First of all, speaking about events, we must study external events, not only internal things. Until now we were saying that all causes are in us; now we will try to find causes in things outside. for instance, if we think about the state of evolution in which mankind is in relation to esotericism, we will see many things which are in the way of possible evolution, and other things which have certain uses, that may help. We must try to create a certain standard, or better to say a kind of understanding about external things; this means that we must not judge them by personal sympathies or antipathies or from whether we like them or not, but try to judge them from the point of view of their relation to this possible evolution. In other words, we must regard them from the point of view of the increase of the power of esotericism. Because the evolution of mankind means the increase of the power of the esoteric circle over life.

But in relation to 'influences' it is necessary to understand that at every given moment one is surrounded by many many big moving things, and they affect one whether one knows it or not—they always affect. One can have very definite attitudes towards these, one can have very definite attitudes towards wars, revolutions, events in social life, political life, art, or one may be indifferent, or negative, or chiefly negative or chiefly positive; but in any case positive on one side means negative on another side—it does not change anything. People are affected by these things; and what they call a positive attitude does not really mean a positive attitude, it simply means liking certain things. A really positive attitude is something quite different. Positive attitude can be defined better than positive emotion, because it refers to thinking. But a real positive attitude includes in itself understanding of the thing itself and understanding of the quality of the thing from the point of view, let us say, of evolution and those things that are obstacles. Things that are against, i.e. if they don't help, they are not considered, they simply don't exist, however big they may be externally. And by not seeing them, i.e. if they disappear, one can get rid of their influence. Only, again it is necessary to understand that not seeing wrong things does not mean indifference; it is something quite different from indifference. Because people who are indifferent certainly don't see things, but things affect them just the same.

Q. You said that positive attitude includes in itself understanding.

MR. O. For instance, as I said, in this particular state which was described in the chapter on 'Experimental Mysticism', I asked myself different questions and I found that certain things I could analyse and certain things I could not, <u>because they did not exist</u>.

It is necessary to think about things using the ordinary emotional and ordinary thinking faculty and trying to find in what relation things stand towards evolution, what <u>we</u> call evolution, i.e. increase of the influence of inner circles and growth of the possibility for the right kind of people to acquire the right kind of knowledge.

Q. Do you mean in this sense that we have to try to place things like politics, education or religion, and see which helps evolution?

MR. O. To understand their weight. You remember, it was explained about words. Words have different weight, and it is necessary to feel their weight, to be able to weigh them.

Q. You put politics very low, I suppose?

MR. O. I don't put them anywhere. There are politics and politics.

You must understand that we find ourselves before a very difficult problem. We must be able to find out what is good and what is evil, and we must not shirk this task. Until now, with the help of the work, we were able to define good and evil in relation to ourselves; now we must come out of our shell and try to look round ourselves, using the same methods and the same principles. If we use one type of principles for ourselves and another type of principles for external things, then certainly we will be in an impossible position, we shall never get anything out of it.

Q. Is it possible then to use the same methods for ourselves and outside events?

MR. O. Certainly, the same principles. But, again, it is necessary to remember on this occasion something of what you learned before; something which will show you the way that is possible and the way that is impossible. You must remember what was said about cosmoses—one cosmos does not represent the universe, but three cosmoses represent the whole universe. The universe and separate cosmoses are not analogous to one another.

Q. When you say 'development of man', do you mean individual man?

MR. O. What is the difference? The principle is the same; what is good for the development of one man is equally good for the development of ten men, and what is good for ten is equally good for two hundred—just the same.

Analysis of events can be based on the idea of influence C, influence B and influence A. Influences A are things based on a quite accidental mechanical combination of forces. Influences B are things which have a certain amount of conscious intention in their origin, but which very quickly change, distorting and corrupting, being distorted and being corrupted, or in some cases remaining more or less in pure form, although a mechanical form. And influences C are things conscious in their origin and conscious in their action.

Having established this, we can ask ourselves: how many of the third kind do we see? And we must say that we never see them. If we are looking for something, we meet only with certain manifestations of influence B; and every kind of influence B is surrounded by all possible dangers and all possible kinds of forces trying to destroy it. Many kinds of influence B disappear under our eyes, so to say; things that could be found ten years ago, or even less, cannot be found now.

It is quite possible that we live in a very interesting time—it is impossible to say it with certainty, because in practically every period, every time, people think 'this is an extraordinary time'.

There is no time in history when people did not think 'this time is very unique'. But at the same time there exist certain big events in our time that never were there before. For instance, can you put your finger on this thing and tell me which is the most extraordinary thing of our time?

Q.   Things go so much quicker?

MR. O.   But why? Really, time keeps on to be the same.

Q.   Instability?

MR. O.   Just the same, always the same. There may be more stability now, we don't know; but it is not the cause, it is the result if it is instability. Why do you think instability is peculiar to our time, and why more stability in the time of Caesar?

Q.   Inventions? Scientific discoveries?

MR. O.   Yes. But do you understand what has changed? Take two hundred years ago and now. What amount of force was used then and what amount of force is used now? These forces enter more and more into life, and inventions are absolutely without any plan, and so we don't know what may be invented to-morrow. This is very noticeable on a practical scale, because often now after three years an invention may be scrapped, whereas twenty years ago a piano or something else would last for a lifetime.

Q.   Did you say that the changing of negative attitudes could make up for the lack of special work on moving centre?

MR. O.   Yes, but you must remember that this is very far ahead. But if we really learn how to create right attitudes towards things, then we will be able to change the quality of influences which we receive; and then they will outbalance this bad influence of automatic moving centre. This is the only thing that can outbalance it.

Q.   This increase of inventions means increase of A influences?

MR. O.   No, it does not mean increased A influences. If you like, it can be put like that, but what is important is the increase of force which is used. People use now such great quantities of energy which they could never have used before, and this energy can be turned one way or another way. This is what, in my opinion, makes our time unique. There was never such a time in history, although certainly five hundred years ago people also thought their time was unique. Really, looking through history we cannot see times similar to ours.

Q.   So if conscious man appeared, he could. . . .

MR. O.   Conscious man cannot appear by himself. Conscious

man can 'do' only through other people, people prepared to accept his guidance.

Q.   But how does the question of inventions alter the possibility of evolution for man?

Mr. O.   It makes it possible that soon there will be nothing to evolve. Suppose somebody invents something to destroy the earth, all life on earth; we are not far from it!

Q.   Are we already beginning to destroy ourselves?

Mr. O.   I am not speaking about facts; I speak about principles, about uncontrolled inventions. And if they go further and further, it is impossible to say what will be invented next, and where we shall go to with these inventions, and what force will stop them. I do not mean that it could be stopped or changed; I gave it merely as an illustration that, maybe, we live at an interesting time.

Q.   If more energy is being used. . . .

Mr. O.   It means forces can be used for one thing or another.

Q.   It is used for mechanicalness rather than for evolution. . . .

Mr. O.   I don't speak about evolution. But suppose people carry dynamite bombs in their pockets. God knows what might happen! I mean nothing more. And these inventions have another side: machines, especially big machines, make people work in a certain way; or things happen in a certain way, because of machines which can only work in a certain way and have to be fed. More and more machines are invented for more and more different purposes, and all these machines have to be fed. I don't mean fed with fuel, I mean they must be kept functioning.

Q.   It is curious that these inventions are designed to conserve a person's energy.

Mr. O.   What means conserve? Really it means use more. They are supposed to save men's energy in manual work, but machines also need work on them, feeding them and keeping them clean. Really they do conserve energy, but they give the possibility of using more energy.

Q.   Did you say there were some influences we ought to be more receptive to?

Mr. O.   Certainly. There are different influences, some harmful and some useful, and certainly it would be good if we could know which influences are harmful and which are useful.

Q.   I have been trying to think which are useful influences.

Mr. O.   If you just think about it and don't try to be too clever, you will be able to see which are useful and which are harmful. Certainly, if we try to be too clever we shall not see which is the right and which the left side.

Q. Is it possible to divert this energy?

MR. O. Yes, it is possible to become unreceptive.

Q. What I have wondered is, what kind of individual will grow out of all this noise?

MR. O. With long ears probably!

Q. Or with no ears! Do human beings adapt themselves to external circumstances?

MR. O. Judging by the existence of negroes they do; they are better adapted to sun than we are. In any case in known history there is no perceptible change in organs or functions. But again you will say there never was such a noise!

Q. I would have thought in an age like this, when machines are getting bigger and bigger and more human in their functions, it would be bad for esoteric ideas, because the more man can make a machine that does the work of five or six men, the more he feels he can bend forces to his own ends and is master of the forces; and this takes away the idea of any possibility of change in himself.

MR. O. Quite possible; but the chief thing here is not so much using machines. Machines make people serve them, and really machines control the movements and the life of human beings— the place where they live, the food they eat. . . . Certainly they control them, because machines keep them for themselves. But the important thing is invention itself.

You know, we take so many things, such as railways etc., for granted now, that we forget how new they really are; we do not notice how such things change during a comparatively short period, visible to ordinary eye. We can see how things change, and at the same time the direction of inventions is not controlled and cannot be controlled. It is absolutely chance or accident; no one decides which inventions are useful or necessary, and nobody can say even from which point of view to look at them, because immediately people begin to think, they begin to argue, and each person will think that his idea is the most useful. Someone may say quite easily that a small bomb which can destroy the population of London is the most useful thing to carry in one's pocket! Somebody else will say that cure for consumption is most useful, and a third will say that the most useful thing would be coloured photographs. So how can people come to an agreement about which is the best invention, and what is useful and what is useless?

Q. I must say I don't understand where all this extra force comes from. Do people spend the force on inventions instead of spending it on looking for evolution?

MR. O. Which evolution?

Q. Is there really more force or is there the same force turned in another direction?

MR. O. There is more force. Forty, or even thirty, years ago you could not drive in a carriage of seventy horses—now you can.

Q. This phase of inventions seems to have sprung from prosperity in America.

MR. O. No, you cannot put it so definitely.

Q. Certainly many things are developments of inventions of twenty or thirty years ago.

MR. O. Always like that.

Q. What is important for us is to understand, to be passive, to be quiet, and hush our negative attitudes and negative emotions, and listen sharply to all things that go on around us?

MR. O. No, no. We must learn and know; we must not listen vaguely; we shall hear nothing if we don't know what to listen to. So, in this case, it is simply a process of thinking, putting things together—all the things we already know, principles—and to be able to see facts when we are ready to talk, and see them from a new point of view. To think in a new way is a very difficult thing, but the old way of thinking is kept up not only by postures or negative emotions; it is kept up by habits of thinking, attitudes, and by influences of things. Suppose we have a certain attitude towards something, and this thing itself tries to keep up this attitude in us by all possible means; if we change it, if we direct it, then we make a big step.

RIGHT AND WRONG ATTITUDES

Q. I feel that I am prevented from thinking practically about the ideas by a destructive attitude which starts by trying to find difficulties and objections. What is the best method of weakening this attitude?

MR. O. By studying. As a matter of fact, this is interesting as observation, because many people, not necessarily only those in the work, live only on objections; they only think themselves clever when they find an objection to something. When they don't find any objection, they don't feel themselves to be working, or thinking or anything.

Q. I remember hearing you speak about right attitudes as a weapon against negative emotions. Did you mean negative or positive, accepting or rejecting?

MR. O. It is not a question of rejecting, it is a question of understanding. When I spoke of right and wrong attitude in that connection, I spoke about right and wrong attitude to emotions themselves, because we may have right or wrong attitude to our negativeness—it is different in different cases. There can be no generalization. But now I speak about attitudes in themselves. We must have positive attitudes in some cases and negative in others, because sometimes lack of understanding is caused by having wrong attitudes. Some people can have a negative attitude towards everything and anything, and some people try to cultivate a positive attitude towards what should have a negative attitude. To understand certain things you must have negative attitudes; other things you can understand positively, so to speak. But too much of positive attitude can also spoil things. Here I use the words 'positive' and 'negative' in the ordinary sense of approve or disapprove.

Q. Aren't one's attitudes governed by emotions?

MR. O. Try to understand attitude apart from emotion. It can be independent. It is really a point of view. To a certain extent, this is under our control. If a point of view is right, there is one effect; if it is wrong, another effect. Points of view may be of very different kinds.

Q. Do you mean point of view on life and things?

MR. O. Think for yourself. Try to find out what attitude or point of view means.

Q. Can one define attitude or point of view in relation to the work?

MR. O. Certainly—or in relation to something else. One can have attitudes in relation to everything.

Q. How can one change one's attitudes?

MR. O. First, by studying oneself and life on the lines of this system. This changes attitude. This system is a system of different thinking, or rather of different attitudes, not merely of knowledge. Then, a certain valuation is necessary; you must understand the relative value of things.

Q. Is it possible always to have a right attitude towards ordinary life?

Mr. O. Certainly it is possible to have right attitude, but the attitude is not always the same, and that is the difficulty. It is the same principle as that which we discussed in connection with different kinds of action. There can also be different attitudes. For the moment we will take only two: positive and negative—not in the sense of positive and negative emotions, but referring to the positive and negative parts of intellectual centre, that is, the part which says 'yes' and the part which says 'no'. These are the two chief attitudes.

We must understand that we have no control, that we are machines, that everything happens to us. But simply speaking about it does not change these facts. To cease being mechanical requires something else. First, a change of attitude is necessary. One thing over which we have a certain control is our attitudes—our attitudes towards knowledge, towards friends, towards the system, work, self-study and so on. It is necessary to understand that we cannot do things, but we can change our attitudes.

It is very important to think about attitudes because very often we take a negative attitude towards things we can understand only with a positive attitude. Right attitude is necessary for right understanding. For instance, it may happen that people accidentally take a negative attitude towards something connected with the work. Then their understanding stops and they cannot understand anything until they change their attitude. But towards many things in life it is necessary to have a negative attitude in order to understand them. There are things that can be understood only with a positive attitude, and there are things that can be understood only with a negative attitude.

Q. With regard to right attitudes, I often have a feeling that it is not fair if I do not hear the opposite argument.

Mr. O. Maybe, maybe not. Argument is one thing and negative attitude is another thing.

Q. Can you explain more why certain attitudes are necessary in order to understand a thing?

Mr. O. Try to think about it; try to see for yourself why certain attitudes are necessary for understanding. There are many, many things in life that you cannot understand unless you have a sufficiently good negative attitude towards them. Very often, when people begin to speak about different things, they get nowhere because they do not have a negative attitude. If you look at them positively, you will never understand anything. So sometimes a negative attitude is a very useful thing. On the other hand, the moment you have a negative attitude towards things that refer to the work, to rules of work, methods of work, you cease to understand anything. You can understand, according to your capacity, only so long as you are positive.

Q.   Isn't having an attitude to something only substituting another word for identification?

MR. O.   Certainly not. Attitude means point of view. You can have a point of view on things without being identified. Very often, identifying is the result of a wrong attitude.

Q.   Do we have a positive attitude towards false personality?

MR. O.   Yes, always. We like it and glorify it, think it is the best part of us.

Q.   If we had a negative attitude towards it, would we begin to see it?

MR. O.   We will begin to understand it when we have a negative attitude towards it.

Q.   Is there not a danger of negative attitude having a negative emotion attached to it?

MR. O.   Great danger, yes, but if you do not identify with the negative attitude then the emotion cannot come. As a matter of fact, we have many negative emotions because we do not have a sufficiently negative attitude towards negative emotions. That may seem paradoxical, but if you find right examples you will see that it is like that.

Q.   Do you mean that to get wakefulness one must hate indolence?

MR. O.   No. Hate means negative emotion. I am speaking about negative attitude.

Q.   Is it wrong attitude that makes us justify?

MR. O.   Yes, that is it.

3

Self-remembering

SELF-REMEMBERING. AUGUST 1939

MR. O. Out of all that you have heard up to now, and all the observations you have made before, you must make certain deductions. If you return to the beginning, when we first spoke about consciousness and absence of consciousness, you must all have noticed one and the same thing in observing functions. You must have realized that whatever we do, whatever we say, whatever we think, whatever we feel, we never remember ourselves.

The expression, 'remember oneself' is taken specially, intentionally, because in ordinary conversation we very often say: 'He forgot himself', 'he did not remember himself', or 'he remembered himself in time'. As a matter of fact, we never fully remember ourselves. We never remember ourselves in time. We never realize that we are present, that we are conscious, that we are here.

This must be understood; and at the same time, it must be understood that, if we make sufficient efforts and for a sufficiently long time, we can increase our capacity for self-remembering, we begin to remember ourselves oftener, we begin to remember ourselves deeper, we begin to remember ourselves in connection with more ideas—the idea of consciousness, the idea of work, the idea of centres, the idea of self-study, the idea of schools; we begin to remember ourselves in connection with all these ideas.

So one of the first points is: how to remember oneself, how to make oneself more aware. And then you will find that negative emotions are one of the chief factors which make us not remember ourselves. So one thing cannot go without the other. You cannot struggle with negative emotions without remembering yourself more, and you cannot remember yourself more without struggling with negative emotions. If you remember these two things, you will understand everything better. So whenever you think about this, try to keep these two ideas, which are connected, in mind.

Q.   Since self-remembering is so important, could you give some indication as to how to approach it?

Mr. O.   The first and most important thing is to understand that we don't remember ourselves, and what it means, and how much we lose by this. When we realize how much we lose by not remembering ourselves, we will have a strong impulse to remember ourselves when we can. This is the only real way to understand. We must first remember we don't remember ourselves; second, how much we lose by that; third, how much we will gain if we get self-remembering.

Q.   There seem to be different degrees of self-remembering; I mean, degrees that one notices oneself.

Mr. O.   Yes, there are several degrees, but we always speak about the next degree, we cannot speak about several degrees at the same time; but I don't think you speak about different degrees, but about more emotional and less emotional.

Q.   There seem times when you are aware only mentally. . . .

Mr. O.   Self-remembering always becomes emotional. What you speak of is only the beginning. You can try to remember yourself through the mind, but if you <u>really</u> remember yourself, even for a short time, it becomes emotional. It is not degree. It is one thing. It is necessary to try more and more.

Q.   Would it be possible to remember oneself with emotional centre leaving the intellectual centre to go on with what it is doing?

Mr. O.   As a matter of fact, real self-remembering begins when you remember yourself with emotional centre. But that happens after many other things—when one has acquired a certain control of emotional centre. And the beginning, what is possible for us, is trying not to express negative emotions. Then we must study negative emotions and learn how to struggle with them; and the only way is to struggle with identification. After long work on these lines, you acquire a certain control of emotional centre, and then only will it be possible to speak of how to use it for one or another purpose.

Q.   What is the difference between self-remembering and self-observation?

Mr. O.   It is best when they go at the same time. But in the beginning, learning to self-remember, it will be sufficient if you are aware of yourself. But if at the same time you are aware of something else, your surroundings, people, your aim, ideas, the more the better. But first yourself, because in ordinary life people can be aware of anything else but themselves, and that is of no value. In the beginning people divide these two processes. The aim of self-remembering is only to be aware of oneself. With self-observations you also observe different facts besides.

Q. But self-observation is entirely mental, isn't it?

MR. O. It must be mental, yes—but again, it may be different.

Q. Can you observe yourself emotionally?

MR. O. No, you cannot really, but it may come. At present you have no control of emotional centre so you cannot; but it may come, and an emotional element must come into the observation of certain things later.

Q. How is it possible to recognize self-remembering?

MR. O. First it must be understood by mind, what it means and what it would mean to have it. And then one can be at different distances from it. Suppose one is never sure, but the distance between that state and our present state changes, and after some time you realize in your mind what self-remembering is, and one day you can say it is five thousand miles away, and another day only three thousand miles—there is a difference.

Q. I try to find out what is self-remembering. . . .

MR. O. Try to understand what is not self-remembering, because this is easier. We are always in this state and we never notice it. So begin with not-remembering.

Q. The difficulty about this work is that no idea can be completely clear to me.

MR. O. It is impossible to make it clear with formatory thinking and words. People think they understand a thing when they can give a name to it, but they don't realize that this is artificial. When you can feel a thing, and when you can verify it by higher consciousness and higher mind, then only can you say it is really true and really exists. And schools don't deal with ordinary intellectual ideas, and that is why nobody in Europe (I take it that we can trace it for the last two hundred years or so), with all its elaborations and all its science, could come to the idea of self-remembering and the possibility of self-remembering. And that means it is not clear without higher centres; it means that without higher centres one cannot come to the truth. Schools are the work of higher centres; they give us something which we cannot attain by ourselves, because we can use only the ordinary mind. And ordinary mind has definite limits it cannot jump over. It can accumulate material, forget it, accumulate again and forget again, and reduce this system to just nonsense by following too straight in one direction.

Q.   Is the object of self-remembering the gradual discovery of permanent 'I'?

MR. O.   Not the discovery. It is preparing the ground for it. Permanent 'I' must grow. It is not there. But it cannot grow when it is all covered with negative emotions and identification and all that. So you begin by preparing the ground for it. But first of all it is necessary to understand what self-remembering is, why it is better to self-remember than not to self-remember, which effect it will produce, and so on. It needs much thinking about.

You can get many things, but only emotionally, not in any other way. The more emotional you are, the more you can get. When you find yourself in the state of coming to higher emotional centre, then you will be astonished to find how much you can understand at once—and then you come back to the normal state and you forget it all. It is a very strange thing that if by persistent self-remembering and by certain other methods you come to higher emotional centre for a short time, you will be surprised how much you understand at one time—but you will not be able to retain it. If you write it all down, it will have no sense when you read it with intellectual centre later.

Q.   Is it possible to self-remember while you are doing other things?

MR. O.   Yes, it is possible. It is necessary to create a certain particular energy or point (using it in the ordinary sense), and that can be created only at a moment of very serious emotional stress. All the work before that is only preparation of the method. But if you find yourself in a moment of a very strong emotional stress, and if you try to remember yourself then, then it will remain afterwards, and then you will be able to remember yourself. So only with very intense emotion is it possible to create this foundation for self-remembering. But that cannot be done if you do not prepare yourself for that. Moments may come—and you will get nothing out of them. These emotional moments come from time to time, and we don't use them, because we don't know how to use them. But if you have tried to remember yourself sufficiently hard, and if self-remembering in a moment of emotional stress is strong enough, it will leave a certain trace, and that will serve for self-remembering in the future.

Q. What is the preparation you are speaking about?

MR. O. Self-study, self-observation, self-understanding. You can change nothing yet or make a single thing different. It all happens in the same way, but there is already a difference—the fact that you see many things you have not seen before, and many things already begin to happen differently. It does not mean you have changed anything—they happen differently.

Q. But which is the most important for us to do now?

MR. O. All that we speak of is equally important—self-remembering, not identifying, not considering, self-study, study of centres, everything. There is no one thing better than another. Everything is necessary.

Q. Self-remembering is much more difficult in some life circumstances. Should one avoid them?

MR. O. It is a mistake to think that life circumstances, that means external circumstances, can change anything or affect it. This is an illusion. As to whether to avoid them or not—try to avoid them, or try to take them as a part. But if you manage to avoid them, you will see that it is exactly the same; there may be exceptions, but the general balance remains the same.

Q. I can't, by any effort I make, reach a state at all like the states that come accidentally. Is there any effort that one can make?

MR. O. Yes, but you say it comes accidentally. If it is what I mean, it comes as a result of your efforts, previous efforts, only it comes not at that time. But if you hadn't made efforts it wouldn't come accidentally. The more efforts you make, the more you have these 'accidental' moments of self-remembering, of understanding, of being emotional and things like that. It is all the result of effort. Only we cannot connect cause and effect in this case; but the cause remains and it will produce its effect. Probably we cannot connect because of many small things—identification, imagination, or things like that. But the cause is there; and it will find a moment and bring results. We must never expect immediate results. It is necessary to work for a long time and create some kind of permanent standards in order to have these immediate results. And even that comes only in very emotional states. If we could, by will or desire or intention, become more emotional, then we would see many things differently. But we cannot. We are very low emotionally and that is why most of the work we do now, even if we really do it, can have no immediate results. But something always remains; it is not lost; no effort is lost; only it must be followed by other efforts, and bigger efforts. So one of the first questions is how to become more emotional, but we cannot do that. The second question is how to use emotional states when they come—and that is possible; this is what we must prepare ourselves for. Emotional states, emotional tension comes, but then we lose it in identification and things like that. But we could use it.

Q.   Is the way of using it to continually recollect the taste of it?

MR. O.   No. I mean use. If you try to remember yourself in an emotional state—you will see for yourself, it is a matter of observation—that will give you a different power of thinking, a different power of understanding. You can understand things quite differently. If the emotion is very strong, and if you remember yourself at the time, you will even see things differently; you will see many things you cannot see now. But that cannot be described because it must be a personal experience.

Q.   Sometimes after I have tried to self-remember, I have a feeling about inanimate objects, like tables and chairs, as if in some way they had a sort of awareness or consciousness which was them, but afterwards it always seems so incredible that I can't believe it.

MR. O.   Discount the possibility of imagination. Say like this: you feel something new in things. But when you begin to explain this, you begin to imagine. Don't try to explain. Just leave it. Sometimes you can feel strange things in that way, but explanations are always wrong, because you feel with one very good apparatus, and explain with a very clumsy machine which cannot really explain. It very often happens like that.

Q.   Is there any way of dealing with rather vague, dull, negative states that come from feeling tired or cold?

MR. O.   Yes, many ways, but supposing even that it is so dull that you can do nothing at the given moment, if you have made efforts before in a better state, that will help. In any case you mustn't identify—you must remember that it will pass, that it is not normal—and that helps.

Q.   I say to myself that it is just that I am tired and so on, but no enthusiasm comes.

MR. O.   Nothing can be done. You have to do what is absolutely necessary at that time and only know that it will pass. We cannot always be the same. Sometimes you can struggle with it and sometimes not, but you must not identify with it, must not believe that it is permanent. Because emotionally we always believe in things—emotional centre does not know to-morrow—everything is present, everything is permanent for emotional centre. So you must not identify with this feeling: you must know that it will change.

Q. Can we only make efforts through our intellectual function?

MR. O. Efforts may be different, but in the beginning we can be guided only by that, only by understanding. So for a long time all the work must be concentrated on understanding. When you understand things better, many other things become possible.

THE SLY MAN AND THE DEVIL. MARCH 2ND 1939

Q. Could you tell me the exact difference between two men on their death beds, one of whom has learned the art of self-remembering and one of whom has never heard of it?

MR. O. No, it needs an imaginative writer to describe this. There are so many different possibilities—the men may be so different and there may be different circumstances. It cannot be described like that.

Q. Is self-remembering the development of the capacity to remember at will?

MR. O. Not to remember but to be aware of yourself. Remembering is only a word used because there is no other word. But in all languages there exists this ordinary expression—you forgot yourself, you did not remember yourself, I remembered myself, and he remembered himself. This is just in an ordinary sense, but I think it is connected with some of your questions about the state of self-remembering. About what you said about self-remembering and a dying man, I think I had better tell you a story. It is an old story, told in the Moscow groups in 1916, about the origin of the system and the origin of the work, and about what self-remembering is. It happened in an unknown country at an unknown date that a sly man was walking by a café and met a devil, and the devil was in a poor state, a very poor state, both hungry and thirsty and all that, and the sly man took the devil into the café and ordered coffee for him and asked him why he was in such a poor state. The devil said that there was no business. He used to buy souls and burn them to charcoal, because when people died they had very fat souls that he could take to hell and the devils were all pleased, but now all the fires were out in hell, because when people died there were no souls. So the sly man said perhaps they could do some business. 'Teach me how to make souls, and I will give you a sign to show which people have souls made by me,' he said, and he ordered more coffee, and the devil said he should teach them to remember themselves, not to identify and so on, and after a time they would grow souls. So the sly man began to work, and he organized groups and taught people to remember themselves, and some of them began to work seriously and tried not to identify and things like that. And then they died, and for a long time it went like that, that when they died and came to the gate of paradise St. Peter was there with his keys on one side and the devil was on the other side, and when St. Peter was ready to open the gate to devil said, 'Can I just ask one question—did you remember yourself?' And they said 'Yes, certainly,' and then the devil said, 'Excuse me, that is mine'. This went on for a long time in this way, until somehow they managed to communicate to the earth what was happening at the gate of paradise, and people came to the sly man and said, 'What do you teach us to remember ourselves for, since, when we say we have remembered ourselves, the devil takes us?' But the sly man said, 'Did I teach you to say you remembered yourselves? I taught you not to talk'. Then the people said, 'But it is St. Peter and the devil,' and the sly man said, 'But have you seen these people, St. Peter and the devil, at groups? Very well, don't talk. But some people don't talk and they manage to get into paradise. I did not only make an arrangement with the devil, I also made a plan to deceive the devil, but if people talk. . . .'

CONSCIOUSNESS. JANUARY 16TH 1940

Q. Can we think of self-consciousness as an intensified form of self-remembering?
MR. O. You can think what you like, but it does not help anything. It is necessary to do something about it. If we spend our time in finding new names for things we don't possess, this will not help us. People have tried for thousands of years in that way, without result.

ALARMS. JANUARY 16TH 1940

Q. I find that when I discover a method to make myself remember myself, this works for a few times and then wears off.

MR. O. You must always change them; these things don't work for long—it is part of our state. Take it as a fact; there is no need to analyse it. The more new and unexpected things are, the better they will work. This is connected with the fundamental principle of the whole mental and physical life. Generally speaking, we observe in the ordinary sense only changes of our associations. Permanent associations we don't feel; we notice only changes. So when you become accustomed to them, you have to make some kind of alarm; and then you get accustomed to that and it does not work any more. If you make the alarm-clock sound permanently, then you will notice it only when it stops.

CONSCIENCE—CONTRADICTIONS. JANUARY 16TH 1940

Q. I think it would be useful if someone could show me some of my contradictions.

MR. O. You must find them. If you don't want to see them, nobody can find them for you. And first you must be sincere with yourself.

Q. I cannot quite understand what is meant by conscience meaning that all our emotions can be felt at the same time.

MR. O. If you have no experience (I don't mean complete, but coming nearer to that), then it is very difficult to explain. But I am sure you have had this experience, but at the time you did not notice them, and you cannot reconstruct. It means that we can have contradictory feelings about the same thing. It does not mean all emotions that exist in the world, but one separate thing, either person, situation or thing, or certain work—it does not matter—one moment you can feel one thing about it, and another moment you can feel something quite different. And sometimes moments come when you can feel all your emotions on the same subject at the same time. But you must wait till you notice it, you cannot invent.

Q. A state of self-remembering would help towards it?

MR. O. Yes, effort to self-remember would help in this direction.

17. 1. 40

Q. We were told to think about conscience and why we could not think of all our emotions at the same time.
MR. O. Don't connect these two things. If you use them in the same phrase, they lose all meaning.

CONSCIENCE. JANUARY 26TH 1940

Q. How can I connect conscience with not being able to feel all my emotions at the same time?
MR. O. Conscience is a very strange thing. In the ordinary sense it can be understood very well. It can be in ordinary people. It is an emotional feeling of truth. But in ordinary people it has to work under very great difficulties and against false personality all the time, so it occurs only very rarely.

SELF-REMEMBERING. 1944

Q. Is remembering oneself and asking the question of oneself 'Who am I?' the same thing?
MR. O. No. Understanding the idea of self-remembering is connected with idea that one cannot remember, and all one's life one never noticed this.
Q. If we could self-remember we would be what you call awake, wouldn't we?
MR. O. Quite.
Q. Then we'd be self-conscious?
MR. O. Maybe different degrees—and different lengths of time. Things don't all come at once. But it begins with realization that we don't remember.

LAUGHTER. MARCH 7TH 1945

MR. O.   Do you remember I said last time that laughter helps at this point where self-remembering begins?

Q.   Is it because laughter helps you to relax?

MR. O.   No, it helps you to self-remember in a certain way.

Q.   People who laugh the most seem the least aware.

MR. O.   No, it doesn't mean that all laughter is good.

Q.   Is that related to a sense of humour?

MR. O.   I speak of manifestation, not cause. If one is hit by a stick and one laughs, result is the same.

Q.   Isn't it easier for some people to laugh than others?

MR. O.   And for some people quite useless. They laugh and laugh—and get nothing.

Q.   Can you explain those hydrogens in relation to the centres?

MR. O.   I think that was first said about hydrogens . . . Intellectual centre works with H48. Moving and instinctive with H24, higher emotional with H12, and higher mental with H6.

Q.   Then according to that diagram, without extra effort these centres wouldn't work?

MR. O.   A certain amount is produced with the help of laughter, for instance. Sol 48, for example, develops further up to si 12. It may be not effort, it may be accidental. In any case, a certain amount of H6 can be produced.

CONSCIOUSNESS AND FUNCTIONS. JANUARY 16TH 1940

Q.   How can I get into the intellectual part of moving centre?

MR. O.   You cannot put such questions separately. All control of functions depends on the state of consciousness; the more conscious you become, the more right things you will do for one purpose or another purpose. The fact that you ask such questions separately shows that you don't see how everything is connected. You can do one thing and leave other things; and control of functions is acquired through increasing the intensity of consciousness—which means awakening. As long as you are fully asleep, you have no control at all—things may happen or not happen.

Q. Do our functions affect our states? Although my state changes I have not been able to find any reason why it does.

MR. O. There are many reasons you can find: they may be in functions, they may be in many things, but you must understand that that refers only to change of state of consciousness in ordinary state—more asleep, less asleep.

Q. Would a man who is beginning to awake develop a sense of inner duality?

MR. O. Is that an observation or not? If it is an observation it is one thing; but if it is just philosophy, it is another thing, and it is quite useless. It will not help if you decide one way and things happen in another way. You must deal with to-day, not with a possible to-morrow.

17. 1. 40

Q. Everything that I was interested in in the work I very soon began to feel negative about, and began to feel it a frightful grind. How to avoid this trap?

MR. O. Well, it is a beautiful state for self-remembering—you can use it. The more negative you are, the better you can remember yourself—if you realize that you can get out. It must remind you, otherwise you will remain in a state of negative emotions all the time.

4
Identification

Q. I think I have not got the right idea about identification. It means that things control us and not that we control things?

MR. O. Identification is a very difficult thing to describe, because no definitions are possible. Such as we are, we are never free from identifying. If we believe that we don't identify with something, we are identified with the idea that we are not identified. But you cannot describe identification in logical terms. You have to find a moment of identification, catch it, and then compare things with that moment. Identification is everywhere, at every moment of ordinary life. When you begin self-observation, some forms of identification already become impossible. That's why your friends will find you dull, because they are with one thing one moment, with another thing at another. They will say you are not interested in anything, that you are indifferent, and so on. In ordinary life almost everything is identification. The origin of the idea, the origin of the word, is very interesting. Certainly the idea exists in Indian and Buddhist literature. Generally it is called 'attachment' or 'non-attachment'. But, you see, I read these books before I met the system and did not understand what it meant. Only when I heard the system explanation much later, I began to see what it means. It is a very important psychological feature that penetrates the whole of our life, and we don't notice it because we are inside it. It is useless to try to find definitions. Find some examples. If you see a cat with a rabbit or a mouse—that is identification. The mouse can also be identified in some other way. Then find analogies to this picture in yourself. Only, you must understand that it is there every moment, not only at exceptional moments. Identification is an almost permanent state for us, it is the chief manifestation of false personality, and because of this we cannot get out of the false personality. You must be able to see this state apart from yourself, separate it from yourself, and that can only be done by trying to become more conscious, trying to remember yourself, trying to be aware of yourself. Only when you become more aware of yourself are you able to struggle with manifestations like identification and lying and with false personality itself.

Q. I find when I am identified it is nearly always with things inside me.

MR. O. Perhaps you are right; perhaps you are not right; but it does not matter. You can think that you identify with one thing and really you are identified with quite a different thing. It doesn't matter at all. It is the state of identification that matters. In the state of identification you cannot feel right, see right, judge right, and the subject of identification is not important: the result is the same.

Q. So the way to overcome identification. . . .

MR. O. That's another thing. It is different in different cases. First it is necessary to see; then it is necessary to put something against it.

Q. What do you mean by 'put something against it'?

MR. O. Just turn your attention to something more important. It is necessary to learn to distinguish important from less important, and if you turn your attention to more important things, you become less identified with unimportant things. You must realize that identification can never help you. It only makes things more confused and more difficult. If you realize even that—that alone may help in some cases. But people think that to be identified helps them, they do not see that it only makes everything more difficult. . . .

This is exactly our ordinary thinking. We think identification is necessary when actually it only spoils things. It is not a thing which has useful energy in it at all, only destructive energy.

Q. Is identification mainly emotion?

MR. O. It always has an emotional element—a kind of emotional disturbance, but sometimes it becomes habit, so one does not even notice the emotion.

Q. Is there a state between self-remembering and identification?

MR. O. Different sides of the same thing. Not remembering is identification. If one is not identified one must remember oneself to a certain extent, perhaps even without knowing it. There are many different degrees.

IDENTIFICATION AND ENERGY

Q. Is there some way in which I could be helped to want to work? Will 'wanting more' increase my power to work. Or is even that not sufficient?

MR. O. But who will do that, if only one 'I' is interested and other 'I's are not interested? You say 'I' as if you were something different, separate, from these 'I's. One 'I' may decide but another 'I' will wake up and will not know about it. This is the situation and you must try to do all you can; don't dream about things you cannot do. Nobody can help you to want to work, you must want yourself, and you must do what you can. In this way your wanting will increase; but if you don't do what you can you will lose even that and work less and less. If you do what you can, you will want more and more. How can we increase this power to work? Only by working; there is no other way. If you learn to make small efforts it will give small results; if you make bigger efforts you will get bigger results.

It is necessary to put more energy into things—I mean into your self-study, self-observation, self-remembering and all that. And in order to put more energy it is necessary to find where energy is going.

You awake every morning with a certain amount of energy. It may be spent in many different ways. A certain amount is necessary for self-remembering, study of the system and so on. But if you spend this energy on other things, nothing remains for that. This is an important point. Try to calculate every morning how much energy you intend to put on work in comparison with other things. Even in relation to time, for instance, you will see that you give very little time to work—if you give any, or some—and all other time to quite useless things—good if it is to pleasant things, but in most cases they are not even pleasant. And as a result of this lack of calculation, this lack of elementary statistics—we don't even understand why, with all our best intentions, our best decisions, after all we do nothing. But how can we do anything if we don't give any energy, any time to it?

You must give a certain amount of time and a certain amount of energy, then very soon you will see results. In every kind of work or study there is a certain standard—whether you give enough energy or not enough energy. It may be that you give some energy, but just not enough. If you give a certain amount of energy and just not enough, you will never have any results. You will simply turn round and round and you will be approximately in the same place.

Q. Can one make a store of energy?

MR. O. Absolutely necessary. All the future depends on this store. But you cannot begin to think about storing energy before you learn to stop leaks. And there is no question of not being able to stop leaks. We spend our energy in the wrong way, on identification and negative emotions. All considering, lying, idle talk, expressing of negative emotions, these are open taps from which our energy runs out. Stop these leaks and then it is possible to store energy.

Q. Can one suddenly change the energy of anger into something else? One has tremendous energy in these moments, but one does not know how to use it.

MR. O. By not identifying. One has tremendous energy and it works by itself and makes one act in a certain way. Why? What is the connecting link? Identification is the link. Stop identification and you will have this energy at your disposal. How can you do this? Not at once. It needs practice. Practice at easier moments. When emotion is very strong, you cannot. It is necessary to know more, to be prepared. If you know how not to identify in the right moment, you will have great energy at your disposal. What you will do with it is another thing. You may lose it again on something quite useless. But it takes practice. You cannot learn to swim if you fall into the sea during a storm. You must learn in calm water. Then, perhaps, if you fall in, you will be able to swim.

Q. So if you are identified it makes it more difficult to be conscious?

MR. O. Impossible. They are direct opposites. Either you are identified or you are conscious. You cannot be both. This is one of the difficulties that comes later because people have some favourite identifications which they don't want to give up and at the same time they say they want to be conscious. The two things cannot be together. You cannot have both together. There are many incompatible things in life, and this is one of the most incompatible.

Q. In struggling against identification, is it necessary to know why one is identified?

MR. O. One is identified not for any particular purpose but in all cases because one cannot help it. How can you know why you identify? You identify because you cannot help it. But you must know why you struggle. This is the thing. If you do not forget this you can be ten times more successful. Very often we start to struggle and then forget why.

There are many forms of identification. But first it is necessary to see it. It is a process, not a moment. We identify all the time. The first step is to see it; the second, to struggle with it in order to become free from it.

Q. When one is required to sympathize with other people's troubles, how can one determine at what point one becomes identified?

MR. O. If you learn to observe yourself, you will find that the moment imagination enters, identification begins. So long as you deal with facts, you may keep away from identification, but when imagination starts you are lost.

Q. How can one avoid the reaction which comes after feeling very enthusiastic?

MR. O. This reaction comes as a result of identification. The struggle against identification will prevent this from happening. It is not what you call enthusiasm which produces the reaction, but the identification. Identification is always followed by this reaction.

Q. Is a bored man identified with nothing?

MR. O. Boredom is also identification—one of the biggest.

Q. With what?

MR. O. With oneself. With false personality. With something in oneself.

Q. Is identification always a manifestation of false personality?

MR. O. False personality cannot manifest itself without identification, the same as negative emotions. Negative emotions cannot exist without identification—and many other wrong things in us as well—all lying, all imagination. One identifies, first of all, with one's imaginary picture or imaginary idea of oneself. One says: 'This is I' when actually it is not 'I' but one's imagination. And lying—one cannot lie without identification. It would be very poor lying and nobody would believe it. So it means that first one must deceive oneself and then one can deceive other people.

Q. Why cannot one stop identification?

MR. O. I cannot answer why. But, for instance, thinking about the system, about ideas, principles and rules, helps to be less identified.

Q.   You mean we have not only to identify with what we are doing, but also not to identify with ourselves?
Mr. O.   It is not so much a question of what to identify with. You must remember that identification is a state. You must understand that many things you ascribe to external causes are really in you. Take fear, for instance. Fear is independent of things. If you are in a state of fear, you can be afraid of an ash-tray. In pathological states this often happens, and a pathological state is only an intensified ordinary state. You are afraid, and then you choose what to be afraid of. This is why it is possible to struggle with those things, because <u>they are in you</u>. Instinctive emotions are different. Instinctive fear may be quite right; bad taste or a bad smell are facts. But negative emotions are based on imagination. You bring yourself to a state of envy—jealousy—fear—and then look for subjects.
Q.   You said that if one could stop identification altogether one could stop negative emotions. Does it mean that all negative emotions are connected with identification?
Mr. O.   Yes, they are all based on identification, they cannot exist without it. But you can stop identification—not altogether, but for short moments. If you stop it for half an hour, then you can study. There is a possibility to identify less, and then negative emotions become less important.
Q.   I find I can sometimes get out of a feeling of negative emotion by allowing myself to get identified with something pleasant.
Mr. O.   You use the word 'identified' in a wrong sense. You cannot say, 'if I allow myself to get identified'; you can only say, 'if I allow myself to get interested in something'. It may work for some time, but if you become identified, it will be just the same thing from a practical point of view. Only, in a pleasant thing you <u>can</u> be interested without being identified; in an unpleasant thing you <u>cannot</u> be interested without being identified.
Q.   Sometimes I feel very frightened—that I don't know what I am doing and what I want. I allow myself to get very negative.
Mr. O.   First, you must not allow, and second, you must, when in a state of doubt, remember to try and bring up other 'I's which have a certain valuation. This is the only way to conquer doubts.
Q.   Can we have any understanding with identification?
Mr. O.   How much can you understand in deep sleep, and

what else is identification? If you remember your aim, realize your position and see the danger of sleep, it will help you to sleep less.

Q.   How can I get rid of identification?

Mr. O.   By realizing that you are asleep. Until you realize you are asleep nothing else can happen; only then will you want to awake. When you realize that you are asleep, that everybody is asleep, then you realize that the only way out is to awake— nothing else.

Q.   If one has the realization of sleep and being asleep. . . .

Mr. O.   There is no 'if'. 'If' is already dream. All dreams begin with 'if'. Try to think about this.

Realization of sleep is the only one thing. It is necessary to find ways to awake, but before that you must realize that you are asleep. Compare sleep and waking. All ideas of the work begin with the idea of sleep and the possibility of waking. All other ideas, life ideas, may be clever, elaborate, but they are all ideas of sleeping people produced for other sleeping people. Sleep is the result of many things: division of personalities; different 'I's; contradictions; identifications and all that. But the first thing of all—just pure, without any theory—is the realization of sleep.

Q.   How can one find what one can do about it that one doesn't?

Mr. O.   One can do nothing. Even the realization that one can do nothing again shows about sleep. What can one do in sleep? One can only have different dreams—bad dreams, good dreams—but always in the same bed. Dreams may be different, but the bed is the same.

Q.   I mean, I can go through days without finding any possibility of effort.

Mr. O.   Certainly. But you can realize yourself differently, see things differently. Change can only begin from this.

Q.   I find it astonishing the way my understanding of things can fluctuate. Certain ideas have great meaning one day and the next mean nothing at all.

Mr. O.   Quite right. You must remember always about sleep and the possibility of awaking. In ordinary life, ordinary conditions, everyone is asleep and you are asleep. You awake for moments only when you think about work; it is only partial awakening and very small, very rare. You are not different from other people. You are equally asleep. This will show you your way—I mean, the realization of that, when the realization becomes stronger.

Q. Sometimes when I think I have been a little nearer recognizing sleep, it has left me very unemotional; I feel heavy and clogged.

MR. O. Yes, that means realization, but not in the right place. The deeper it goes the more you will feel.

Q. There are times when I feel that things have much more value than is ordinarily the case. Is there any way of using the memory of such moments to try and recapture the feeling?

MR. O. Self-remembering only; this is the only weapon we have, the only means. If we try to remember ourselves, if we succeed in that, immediately we begin to see new things and begin to understand things and so on—that means, we become more awake. And what can strengthen that? Only the realization that we are asleep, that we are so seldom conscious during the day. If, in the evening, you look through the day, perhaps you realize that everything happened, and not a single moment you looked from aside and saw how things were happening, and that you were in the middle of things. And days and weeks may pass that way, so what can you expect? The only way to change things is by becoming more awake; there is no other means.

This system is good in many ways, but it gives too many ideas, and people identify with these ideas and fall asleep in these ideas and talk about one thing or another thing. It is necessary to concentrate on one fact—sleep and waking, and the possibility of waking. If you just think about it, realize it and feel it, then the chance appears. Until you come to this realization, there is no chance. You can talk about this system in the same way as you talk about everything else, and that will be all.

IDENTIFICATION WITH DISAPPOINTMENTS. JANUARY 17TH 1940

Q. I have been feeling more dissatisfied than usual with myself and the lack of results obtained from my efforts. Will MR. O. do something to help me individually to wake up or what is it that is needed?

MR. O. I can do nothing. I am doing all that is possible in the given circumstances and position. You must do more, and first of all you must not let yourself identify with these negative feelings and disappointments, and things like that. It is one of the worst possible things.

Q. How do you stop that?

MR. O. Think about something cheerful. There are many things in the system. You can take any subject and compare your own individual questions, how you thought before and how you think now, and you will see that you gain one thing, and another thing, and a third thing.

That will help you to struggle.

ATTITUDES. FEBRUARY 3RD 1938

Q. Is having an attitude to something only substituting another word for identification?

MR. O. No. Attitude means point of view. You can have a point of view on things without being identified.

5
Being, knowledge and influences

Q.   How can we recognize the unreality of ourselves unless we
see the real one to compare with?
MR. O.   No, that we cannot do. We can see it when we try to
change something. Certainly, many things would be much easier
if we could experiment with the next stages. But we cannot.
Even in this state there are many degrees. When we compare
them, we can understand the possibility of lower and higher
degrees. Attention means different parts of centres. In some
parts we cannot have attention, in others we cannot be without
attention. This is material for observation.
Q.   When we secure attention, is there the beginning of real
'I'?
MR. O.   No, but it is preparation of material for it.

Sometimes questions come which you should be able to answer
yourself. For instance, about helping people. Try to ask yourself,
how people can help others? In what sense? Suppose you think
that the most important thing is to awake. How can you try to
awaken people who don't want to awake? Nothing happens if
you try. First, they must wish to awake. People cannot be awakened by force without their own desire. This is one of the most
important ideas connected with esotericism. It is exactly the
point where one has free choice, otherwise there would be no
value in awakening if one could be awakened artificially. The
nature of the things that can develop is such that they cannot
be given, they must develop. Some things can be given, some
cannot. They can be developed only by man's own efforts. By
the very nature of these things there can only be one's <u>own</u> will,
they can only grow out of one's <u>own</u> efforts. Nature can make
a painter, but not pictures. It is the same thing.
Q.   What is desire to awake due to?

Mr. O.   Man lives in mechanical life under different kinds of influences. Most of them are created in life itself, others are created in the inner circle and then are thrown into life. People live under both these kinds of influences. Among ordinary influences man finds ideas that come from a different source, but have the same form as other influences and cannot be distinguished from them outwardly. It depends on man whether he discriminates between these two kinds of influences or not. If he does, those influences of the second kind come together and make a magnetic centre. Centre—in the sense that these influences are all together and act together in a certain way—turning him, producing a certain influence on him. This is the origin of interest in this kind of ideas. With the help of the magnetic centre man can recognize another kind of influence, influence C. (Influences A are those created in life, influences B are those created in the inner circle and then thrown into life.) If there is no magnetic centre, or if it is too weak, or if there are two or three magnetic centres, man will not recognize influence C. What is C influence? These are influences conscious not only in origin but also in action, school influences.

Q.   How can one have several magnetic centres?

Mr. O.   I know a man who had twelve.

Q.   What is the formation of magnetic centre?

Mr. O.   These influences live together. They have a different density from A influences. They collect together.

Q.   What do you mean about twelve magnetic centres?

Mr. O.   When people believe in too many different theories.

Q.   Is it better to have only one magnetic centre?

Mr. O.   Only one is any good. Two means turning round. . . . If there is more than one, it is the [? devil].

Q.   Can a good magnetic centre be deceived?

Mr. O.   It may be considered good and yet be satisfied with false influences.

Q.   Is false C an accident?

Mr. O.   All is accident. It depends on magnetic centre whether man will recognize C or not. It cannot be fate, it cannot be will. So meeting C influences must be either accident or cause and effect.

Q.   Is magnetic centre an accident?

Mr. O.   Not quite. It is a combination of many causes.

Q.   If you are acting on C influences, would emotional centre be working with H12?

MR. O.   Not at once. We must have this fuel in sufficient quantity. Our emotional centre works on H24, because we cannot afford H12. It is too expensive, and if we have it, we immediately throw it away on negative emotions.

Q.   Can influences act only on personality?

MR. O.   Personality is mixed with essence.

INFLUENCE C AND MAGNETIC CENTRE; FOUR WAYS
AND OBJECTIVE WAY; BEING AND KNOWLEDGE.
SEPTEMBER 12TH 1935

Q.   I think it was said that magnetic centre is outside the Law of Accident?

MR. O.   I never said that magnetic centre was outside the Law of Accident. I said that if a man with magnetic centre meets with influence C, in the point of meeting (in the magnetic centre) he becomes free. In all other sides of his life he is just the same as before, under the Law of Accident. But influence C is conscious and it falls on magnetic centre. In this way at this point it is not under accident.

Q.   Is it only in relation to schools that magnetic centre operates?

MR. O.   Yes, it is in the Fourth Way. In religious way a different kind of magnetic centre is necessary. A magnetic centre that brings one to a Yogi school or a monastery is different from the magnetic centre that brings you even to a possible group that leads to the Fourth Way. With a religious magnetic centre one would not be able to work here; people would not have enough initiative. In the religious way they must obey. In this way people must have a broader mind; they must understand. In Yogi schools and religious way for a long time one can do without understanding, just doing what one is told. Here, result is proportionate to understanding. A fakir needs no magnetic centre. He can become a fakir by accident; he begins to imitate instinctively, and this, with time, makes him a fakir. There is no emotion and no intellect in it.

Q.   And the result is evident in oneself?

MR. O.   Certainly. If it is the result of consciousness, how can it be unconscious?

Q.   I was thinking of smaller results.

MR. O.   Smaller results—smaller consciousness. It may be at first only flashes, then longer periods of consciousness. All other things come through that.

Q. Does not general experience of life give consciousness?

Mr. O. As a rule not. We see that usually people lose consciousness in life; in their young days they have glimpses of consciousness, and later they lose them. There are exceptions, but we speak about rules. Exceptions are very rare.

Q. A greater understanding of the system means using higher part of intellectual centre?

Mr. O. Higher parts of all centres. You cannot understand the system by mechanical or emotional parts.

I want to give you a right way of thinking about life experiences. There are three traditional ways, and the Fourth Way which may take many forms. This system belongs to the Fourth Way. These four ways are called subjective ways. Take this simply as a name now. These ways are supposed to produce certain effects. But the same things can be got without any ways, just in life. This is called the objective way. Such possibilities as one gets in subjective ways can be had also without these ways. But it is very rare and takes, a long time. Subjective ways are short cuts. Theoretically, you can get all in objective way, but, in practice, life is too short for that. There are people who acquire a stable being in the objective way. But we are looking for short cuts, for the possibility of doing something consciously about it, not of waiting.

Q. Take music—one can get much from music.

Mr. O. This is only one line, it does not concern the general being. It would be a very one-sided development. We speak of change of being only when it means all sides. Suppose by music one can develop one side. But music, art, is not development. It is only capacity to use one part. Great artists may be insignificant people.

Q. Is there any relation between being and knowing?

Mr. O. A very important relation; they are closely connected. In a certain state of being only certain knowledge is possible. If you want to know more, you must change being. What does your present state of being mean? First, it is your state of consciousness—long periods of sleep-walking with a few glimpses of another state. There is no unity; one is in the power of negative emotions, and so on. One can, in this state have an enormous amount of knowledge that cannot change being, and a very little amount of knowledge that can. Many questions that people ask themselves cannot be answered in this state. If we want to answer bigger questions not as a theory, we must change our being. Then perhaps we will know. What is definite, is that now we cannot know. When knowledge and being differ too much, it produces bad results. If one could develop being without knowledge, it would be useless. Or, if by luck or a trick one could have more knowledge without change of being, it would also be useless for we should not be able to use it.

Q.   You say that by luck or accident we can acquire knowledge beyond our being, or vice versa. Will that help if it happens after one starts work in a school?

Mr. O.   If one knows everything, one would not come to a school. No, that is another thing. I said that one can change being without a school, but that happens very seldom. But I can say that if one gets being or knowledge so to speak undeservedly, it is generally incomplete and worse than nothing, with the exception of very rare cases in objective way. But usually that needs three hundred years. It happens so seldom that it is no use speaking about. Certain examples of wrong ways will be explained later, because in understanding the wrong way we can understand better the right way. For instance, efforts can be made on the basis of fear. A monk, by being afraid of the devil, may create being. But it will not be right being, for it will be based on a negative emotion.

Q.   Isn't almost all effort actuated by fear?

Mr. O.   No, then it is not right effort. Right effort is based on understanding, not on fear. If a house is burning and you run away, it is not because of fear.

Q.   Anyone who knew the truth would seem mad to others.

Mr. O.   It would be very stupid of him to talk about truth to everybody, to people who don't want to know the truth. Why think that a man who knows truth would be an idiot?

Q.   I was thinking of Mysteries. Religion allows you to have certain beliefs. . . .

Mr. O.   Beliefs are not knowledge. In our state of being we can have beliefs, but we cannot know. Why? We don't understand that limitations lie in our state of consciousness. Perhaps even in another state we cannot know—we cannot be certain—but we may. If we go below, we can see that in sleep we can know less than in waking sleep. So knowledge is proportionate to state of awakening.

SNATAKA—TRAMP—LUNATIC—KHAS-NAMOUS

MR. O.   Right questions, right problems are to think about being and how to change being, how to find the weak sides of our being and how to find ways to fight against them. . . .

What is interesting, and what I should like to speak about, is the division of men from the point of view of the possibility of changing their being. There is such a division.

In short, it can be put like this: in relation to possibilities of development, possibilities of school-work, people may be divided into four categories, not parallel to any other division, quite separate. Again, belonging to one or another or a third category is not permanent; it can be changed in ordinary conditions—I mean, one can be in one category and think about oneself as belonging to another category. There is very much imagination about all that, and in ordinary life one does not really know and take into account these categories. But, at the same time, it must be understood that one can come to the work only from one category; not from another, or from a third. The fourth category excludes all possibilities. This division means only one thing—speaking in general—that people are not in exactly the same position in relation to possibilities of work. There are people for whom possibility of changing their being exists; there are many people for whom it is practically impossible, because they brought their being into such a state that there is no starting-point in them; and there are people who already, by different means, different methods, destroyed the possibility of changing their being.

So, though people may be born with the same rights, so to speak, they lose their rights very easily.

In Indian and Buddhist literature there is a very well defined type of man and type of life that can bring one to change of being. Unfortunately, it is very difficult to translate the word. It is the word 'snataka' or householder. 'Householder' means simply a man who leads an ordinary life. Such a man can have doubts about ordinary things; he can have dreams about possibilities of development; he can come to a school after some time—either after a long life or at the beginning of life, he can find himself in a school and can work in a school. It is the first category.

The two other categories of people are called either 'tramps' or 'lunatics'. But 'tramp' does not necessarily mean poor people;

they may be rich, but still they are tramps in their attitude towards life. 'Lunatic' does not mean deprived of ordinary mind; they may be statesmen, professors and so on.

These two categories will not be interested in a school. Tramps, because they do not value anything; lunatics, because they have false values. So they will never go to a school.

First it is necessary to understand these three categories from the point of view of the possibility of changing being. When you understand these three categories and find them in your own experience, among your acquaintances, in life, in literature and so on, when you find examples and understand them, then you will be able to understand the fourth category of people whom I call 'vacuums', who destroyed in themselves, in different ways, all possibility of development. In ordinary conditions, in ordinary life, in ordinary times, they are just criminals or actual lunatics—nothing more. But in certain periods of history—in times like these, for example—such people very often play a leading part; they may acquire and become very important people. But we must leave them for the moment and concentrate on the first three categories.

Q.   Is this possibility of growth of being connected with willingness to obey certain laws and principles?

MR. O.   Not necessarily. This is on monk's way, for instance. There you have to begin with obeying. But there are other ways that don't begin with obeying, but with studying and understanding. General laws you cannot disobey, because they make you obey. You can escape from some of them only through growth of being; not in any other way.

Q.   Does it follow then, that people who have connection with a school, however slight, belong to those who can change their being?

MR. O.   Certainly, if they are interested in school and are sincere in their attitude towards school, it shows that they belong to those who can. But you see, in each of us there are features of tramp and lunatic. It does mean that if we are connected with a school we are already free from these features. They play a certain part in us, and in studying being we must detect them and know in which way they prevent our work, and we must struggle with them. This is impossible without a school. As I said before, tramps can be not only rich, but they can be very well established in life and still remain tramps. Lunatics can be very learned people and occupy a very big position in life, and still they are lunatics. If you take tramp and lunatic only literally, then it is not sufficient.

Q. Is one of the features of a lunatic that he wants certain things out of proportion to other things in such a way that they will be bad for him as a whole?

MR. O. 'Lunatic' means having false values. Lunatics cannot have right discrimination of values. A lunatic always runs after false values. He is always formatory. Formatory thinking is always defective, and lunatics are particularly devoted to formatory thinking: that is their chief affection in one, or another, or a third way. There are many different ways to be formatory. For instance, I gave an example of formatory thinking half an hour ago. I said that some people say that war is not necessary, because all disputes and difficulties can be decided by conferences, negotiations and things like that. If you formulate it like that and don't add that negotiation is possible only at certain periods and not always—if you think it is always possible, then it is formatory and quite wrong. It is not always possible. A right principle can be made quite wrong by making it absolute; and formatory thinking makes everything absolute.

Q. I never thought before of this trying to find tramp and lunatic in oneself. Is the tramp side a sort of curious irresponsibility that is prepared to throw everything overboard?

MR. O. Quite right. Sometimes it can take very poetical forms. 'There are no values in the world'—'Nothing is worth anything'—'Everything is relative'—those are favourite phrases.

Q. It seems to me then, that the rules which we have in this work would give us special opportunities for seeing the tramp.

MR. O. Some of them, yes. But really tramp is not so dangerous. Lunatic is more dangerous—false values and formatory thinking.

Q. What is it that determines which category a man belongs to?

MR. O. A certain attitude towards life, a certain attitude towards people, and certain possibilities that one has. That's all. It is the same for all three categories. The fourth category is separate.

About this fourth category, I will give you just a few definitions from which we can start later. In the system this category has a definite name, consisting of two Turkish words. It is 'Khas-Namous'. One of the first things about a 'Khas-Namous' is that he never hesitates to sacrifice people or to create an enormous quantity of suffering, just for his own personal ambitions. How 'Khas-Namous' is created is another question. It begins with formatory thinking, with being tramp and lunatic at the same time.

Q. So any change of being in the fourth category would be impossible?

MR. O. Yes, because such a man has already become a vacuum. Another definition is that he is crystallized in the wrong hydrogens. 'Khas-Namous' category cannot interest you practically, because you have nothing to do with them; but you meet with the results of their existence and so on. But this is a special thing; there will be special conversations.

For us it is important to understand the second and third categories, because we can find in ourselves features of them both, especially the third. In order to struggle against the second, certainly school discipline is needed and inner discipline in general; one must acquire discipline, because there is no discipline in the tramp. In the third, there may be very much discipline, only in the wrong way—all formatory. So struggle against formatory thinking is struggle against lunacy in ourselves, and the creation of discipline and self-discipline is struggle against the tramp in us.

As to the characteristics of a man in the first category—to begin with he is a practical man; he is not formatory; he must have a certain amount of discipline, otherwise he would not be what he is. So practical thinking and self-discipline are characteristics of the first category. Such a man has enough of these for ordinary life but not enough for work, so in work these two characteristics must increase and grow.

Q. Is there the possibility of the first man in everybody?

MR. O. Not everybody. I already said that there are some people who have lost the capacity for practical thinking or the capacity for development. Then they are full category two or three according to what it is they have lost.

Q. You mean from birth?

MR. O. That we don't know. We cannot speak about that. We speak only about results. We know that in the work one must have the capacity for practical thinking and practical attitude, and one must have sufficient discipline to accept school discipline.

Q. What do you mean by practical thinking?

MR. O. Just what is called practical thinking in ordinary

language, namely, the capacity to calculate things in different circumstances; nothing more. This same capacity he can apply to ideas of the work, school principles, rules, everything.

Q.   It seems that people in the category of lunatics or tramps are further from any appreciation of truth than the householder?

MR. O.   There is no guarantee of that. Only the potentialities are different, not the facts. As facts go, they can be exactly on the same level in relation to that, but their potentiality is different. Like many other things, people don't differ as manifestations go; they don't differ one from another among mechanical people. But possibilities are different. One can become different, another cannot; one can become different only if a miracle happens, another can become different by his own effort and with certain help. There are different possibilities.

Q.   You say we all have parts of tramp, lunatic and householder. . . . ?

MR. O.   Try not to think about it in these terms. Find your own words—what is meant by 'householder', what is meant by 'tramp', what is meant by 'lunatic'. Try to understand it without using these words. These words are not a description, they are only a hint of certain possibilities.

Q.   If one does not like self-discipline, is this a description?

MR. O.   Not a description; only one feature. First of all the tramp has no values; everything is the same; good and bad do not exist for him; and because of that, or in connection with that, he has no discipline. The lunatic has false values; he values what has no value and does not value what has value. These are chief characteristics, not description. The householder has at least certain values from which he can start—a certain practical attitude towards things. He knows that if he wants to eat he must work.

Q.   About this fourth category of man who has destroyed all possibility of development, does that situation arise in him because of some form of extraordinary selfishness?

MR. O.   Yes, in most cases. But this is not really the practical point. It is useful to know about this category because these people play a great part in life in general. But they are already there; we can neither help nor destroy.

We must think about our own selves, our attitude, and chiefly about our understanding. Because if we understand, it is already better; we accept them easier, and know their way.

Q. What is the significance of the idea represented by these words: tramp, lunatic, householder?

MR. O. From the point of view of the possibility of changing being, man can be divided into these three categories: some who have values and a practical attitude to things; others who have no values and no practical attitude to things; a third category who have wrong values. That is important, because in each of us, even if we find we have some practical attitude and certain values, an important part of us also has no values or has false values.

Q. What can help us get more discrimination?

MR. O. Divide in yourself mechanical from conscious, see how little there is of conscious, how seldom it works and so on, and how strong is the mechanical—mechanical attitudes, mechanical intentions, mechanical desires and all that.

NOVEMBER 15TH 1945

Q. How would you characterize the evil done by Khas-Namous? Would that be unconscious?

MR. O. That's too complicated. You cannot begin in that way. This is a kind of perverted school. It is very rare. . . though certainly it grows. Khas-Namous has to make himself by destroying conscience. In us it is asleep. But killing it is the beginning of making Khas-Namous.

Q. If evil is not a force, what is it?

MR. O. This is not a right question. You can say, 'What is it?' But if you say, 'If it is not a force, what is it?' this makes it impossible. But evil can only come from our unconscious actions. So, not to be evil we must avoid unconscious actions. In continuation, it can be said that there is no conscious evil.

CENTRE OF GRAVITY. JULY 7TH 1942

MR. O. Let us speak about what it means to create moon in oneself. You will never be able to answer this in one phrase, because this is a symbolical expression. Symbols in the form of diagrams or symbolical expressions are used for very definite purposes. A symbol expresses many ideas at once. If it meant one idea only, the answer would be simple. But a symbol is used to avoid long descriptions and to put many ideas in one sentence.

How to decipher a diagram or symbolic expression? In order to decipher a symbol, it is necessary to know the order of ideas in it. For instance, when we speak of the enneagram, we learn that this is a general plan of each cosmos. Then we are told that it shows the relation of the Law of Three and the Law of Seven. Then we learn that one cosmos is to another as zero to infinity. To answer one of these questions, we must answer the question before it. So we must know the questions in order.

Now if we ask, what means to create moon in ourselves: first, what is moon? What is moon's function in relation to man, individual man? What will happen if this function of moon disappears? Will it be beneficial or the opposite? We know, for instance, that moon controls all our movements. If moon disappears we will not be able to make any movements—we will collapse like a marionette whose strings have been cut.

We must realize that all this refers to being. What are the features of our being? The chief feature of our being is that we are many, not one. If we want to work on our being, make it correspond better to our aim, we must try to become one. But this is a very far aim. What means to become one? The first step—which is still very far—is to create a permanent centre of gravity. This is what it means to create moon in ourselves. Moon is a permanent centre of gravity in our physical life. If we create a centre of gravity in ourselves we do not need moon.

But first we must decide what the absence of permanent 'I' means. We will find here many features about which we have been told. But these must be established definitely by observation. Then we must begin a struggle against these features which prevent us becoming one. We must struggle with (1) Imagination, (2) Negative Emotions, (3) Self-Will. Before this struggle can be successful, we must realize that the worst possible kind of imagination, from the point of view of obtaining a centre of gravity, is the belief that one can do anything by oneself. After that, one must find the negative emotions which prevent us doing what we are told in connection with the system. For it is necessary to realize that self-will can only be broken by doing what one is told. It cannot be broken by what one decides oneself, for that will still be self-will.

What is self-will? Self-will is self-will. That is a dictionary word. But self-will is always struggle against another will. Self-will cannot manifest without opposing itself to another will.

Let me repeat. Work on being is always struggle—against what you like doing, or what you dislike doing. Say you like roller-skating and you are told to remember yourself. Then you must struggle against roller-skating. What more innocent than roller-skating? But you must struggle against it and things like it. Every day and every hour there are things we cannot do, but there are also things we can do. So we must look at a day, and see what we can do, and don't do. There can be no rule, 'You must remember yourself'. If there were you would have a right to say 'I cannot', (though, if you said that, it would mean you did not want to, or not enough). But if you are told to do something or not to do something. . . say you are asked to attend as many meetings as you can. Then you miss one lecture, two, three. It means you do not want anything, you do not want to work.

You have sufficient knowledge. Now it is necessary to push work on being. We always escape from what we are told to do or what is suggested. We miss these things. Think about self-will. One can only work against self-will by doing what one is told.

Q. If the suggestions come from oneself?

MR. O. I speak of suggestions by me only.

Q. What have you told us not to do?

MR. O. That must be in your memory.

Q. But don't we have to make the first decision to work, to come here for instance?

MR. O. Quite. But it is still necessary to realize that the worst imagination is to think that you can decide what to do.

Q. Am I right in understanding that if one is to progress in this system everything else in life must become complementary to this?

MR. O. Take 'if' from your question and you will see it does not exist.

Q. That would be permanent centre of gravity, wouldn't it?

MR. O. I said about permanent centre of gravity that it was very far. In St. Petersburg an example was given about a man walking towards a certain place and having this aim. One thing remained right, and that was direction. But following this direction he might find other places on the way. He can also start in the wrong direction, in which case, each new aim will take him further from his original aim.

Q. Would you repeat again the second thing about negative emotions?

MR. O. You must find the negative emotions which prevent you hearing what is said and following it. Either you dislike me that day, or somebody else, or the weather. And then you feel justified in doing nothing.

Q. Would you repeat about self-will? How to account?

MR. O. Try to count how many things you don't do in a day, which you could do; things from which you excuse yourself.

Q. And then, after we have counted them, what to do about them?

MR. O. Simply do. All the things you have heard. What else?

Q. What is the purpose of struggling against self-will?

MR. O. You remember how we started. The aim was to create a centre of gravity, create moon in ourselves. We cannot do that through self-will.

Q. Perhaps it is the moon that pulls us round.

MR. O. The moon is indifferent. It helps us to do any movement, without discrimination. If we have permanent centre of gravity it will help us to do only certain movements.

Q. How is it possible to find the 'I's that prevent you from doing the things that you are told to do?

MR. O. The first time you find you did not do something that was suggested, find the cause. And the second time, find another cause—and so on.

Q. Is not the cause very often inertia and mental laziness?

MR. O. These are only words. Perhaps if you look better, or take a field-glass, you will see something else.

Q. Is self-will the expression of the 'I' dominant at the moment?

MR. O. Yes, at one moment it is an expression of one 'I', at another moment of another 'I'.

Q. What else is imagination on our part?

MR. O. Many things. Observe. One can imagine that one is working, for example.

Q. Does the lack of energy to make effort keep us from working?

MR. O. Imagination. We always have enough energy to do something. Take one day, and see all the things you could do and didn't even attempt.

Q.   Taking that one day and studying one's imagination, negative emotion and self-will, would that be an activity?

MR. O.   No, no. That is not an activity—all that refers to this work is one activity. Avoiding it, shirking it, is crime.

Q.   Can a person, instead of giving up some of his strong 'I's, use these to further his real aim?

MR. O.   I said one cannot do much oneself. If he was told to do that, all right. But if he invented, it is probably an escape.

Q.   Why do we have self-will given to us?

MR. O.   How do you know it was given us? I think we invented it.

Q.   How can we determine what we can do and can't?

MR. O.   By trying. And then we may say: 'How strange, I never thought I could do that'.

Q.   If the moon controls all our movements, is that one of the things that makes us mechanical?

MR. O.   No, that does not make us mechanical. The moon controls our movements because we are mechanical.

Q.   What would you call the opposite of a permanent centre of gravity?

MR. O.   Absence of permanent centre of gravity. What is the opposite of a man with a hat? A man without a hat. Nothing more.

Q.   Then we have no centre of gravity now?

MR. O.   All lunatics have a centre of gravity. One thinks he is Napoleon, that is his centre of gravity. Another thinks he is Mohammed—centre of gravity. Another, he is God—centre of gravity.

Q.   Ordinary people don't have it?

MR. O.   No, ordinary people think they are Napoleon one minute, Mohammed another minute, God a third minute. No centre of gravity.

Q.   And only with the help of school-work can one get centre of gravity?

MR. O.   Try to do it without school-work. You can only come to school-work when you have tried everything else and found you can do nothing. Then we can talk.

Q.   How literal is the statement that the moon controls all our individual movements?

MR. O.   Verify.

Q.   The making of effort is what you call struggle—like the effort to come here every night. But if one is not aware of struggle?

MR. O.   That means it happened. Four kinds of things can happen to us—by accident, cause and effect, fate and will. Struggle must be by will, intention. And you must be aware of your intention. You cannot make effort and not be aware of it. Will would be if you wanted something, and decided, and acted and achieved what you wanted. That is what is important.

Q.   I thought I heard it said that if a man studies groups of 'I's, he will understand how groups of 'I's help each other.

MR. O.   What is important in this case is will-action. At first we were told about three things only—will, fate and accident. Then we came to the conclusion that there must be a fourth class, corresponding to Karma. Only this word had gained many wrong associations from theosophy. So we used 'cause and effect', meaning in this life and referring to yourself only. Because certainly from another point of view the whole world is based on cause and effect.

Q.   In those four categories, will is not often used, is it?

MR. O.   Will has to be used. We are never ready for work, but we must work all the same. If we are ready, then we are given other work for which we are not ready.

Q.   That comes in for No. 5 man.

MR. O.   We have will of No. 5 man in school ideas, originally. These ideas could not come from people like ourselves.

BEING AND KNOWLEDGE

Q.   I should like to know more exactly what is meant by being. I understood it is something more permanent as opposed to a sort of shifting collection of 'I's.

MR. O.   Don't make it so complicated. All of you is your being. Knowledge is separate. You can visualize separately all that you know, but all that you <u>are</u>—that is your being. In this division you consist of two things: what you know and what you are. What you are is your being and what you know is your knowledge.

From the point of view of development the idea is that work on knowledge without work on being is not sufficient. You have not only to acquire a certain knowledge, but you must also learn how to work on your being and change your being. Knowledge is limited by being. In the state in which you are, if you get more knowledge you will be able to use it, to understand it, to connect it. Development of knowledge alone is not sufficient, for at a certain moment it has to stop, and instead of leading you forward it will lead you backwards, because if your acquiring knowledge is not followed by change of being, all knowledge will become distorted in you.

Q.   What part does being play in the attainment of knowledge?

MR. O.   Being is your state. In one state you can acquire certain knowledge, but if another state develops you can acquire more knowledge. If you are divided into different 'I's all contradicting one another, then it is very difficult to acquire knowledge because each part will acquire by itself and understand by itself, so you will not have much understanding. If you become one then certainly it is easier to acquire knowledge, and you remember it and understand it. Being means state, inner conditions, all together, not separate.

Q.   Does not our being grow with knowledge?

MR. O.   No, being cannot grow by itself. Knowledge, even very good knowledge, cannot make being grow. You have to work on knowledge and on being separately, otherwise you will cease to understand the knowledge you acquire.

Generally speaking, we know more about our knowledge than we know about our being. We know how little we know about ourselves; we know how, at every moment, we make mistakes about everything; we know how we cannot foresee things, how we cannot understand people, how we cannot understand things. We know all that and realize that it is all the result of our insufficient knowledge. But, although in ordinary thinking we understand the difference between objects, we do not understand the difference between people's being. It is useful to take a piece of paper and write on it what constitutes our being. Then you will see that it cannot grow by itself. For instance, one feature of our being is that we are machines; another—that we live in only a small part of our machine; a third—this plurality that was spoken about in the first lecture. We say 'I' but this 'I' is different every moment. One moment I say 'I' and it is one 'I'; five minutes later I say 'I' and it is another 'I'. So we have many 'I's all of the same level and there is no central 'I' in control. This is the state of our being. We are never one, and never the same. If you write down all these features, you will see what would constitute a change of being, and what can be changed. In each particular feature there is something that can change; and a little change in one feature means also a change in another.

Being is what you are. The more you know yourself, the more you know your being. If you do not know yourself, you do not know your being. And if you remain on the same level of being you cannot get knowledge.

Q.   In order to work on being, is it necessary for us to occupy all our time during the day, not to have any spare time?

MR. O.   You begin with the impossible. Begin with the possible. Begin with one step. Try to do a little, and results will show you. There is always a limit, you cannot do more than you can. If you try to do too much, you will do nothing. But, little by little, you will see that right thinking, right attitudes are necessary. It needs time, because for so long people have been in the power of negative emotions, negative imagination and things like that. But little by little these will disappear. You cannot change everything at once.

We must always think about the next step—only one step. We can understand our being as a little more collected than it is now: that we can understand. When we have understood that, we can think of it as still a little more collected—but not completely, not finally.

Q.   Shall we be able to judge the change of our being without deceiving ourselves?

MR. O.   Yes, but before you are able to judge the change, you must know your being as it is now. When you know most of the features of your being, you will be able to see changes.

Q.   On what does the difference in level among ordinary sleeping people depend?

MR. O.   On reliability. There are more reliable people and less reliable people. This is also true in the work. Unreliable people cannot get anything.

Q.   Do we all start on the same level?

MR. O.   More or less, but there are variations. The chief thing is reliability.

Q.   How does one develop one's being?

MR. O.   All that you have learnt, all that you have heard about the possibility of development, it all refers to being. Development of being means awakening first of all, since the chief feature of our being is that we are asleep. By trying to awake we change our being; this is the first point. Then there are many other things: creating unity, not expressing negative emotions, observation, study of negative emotions, trying not to identify, trying to avoid useless talk—all this is work on being. Certainly you acquire certain knowledge in that way but it is put separately if it is simply intellectual knowledge. Being is power—power to do; and power to do is power to be different.

KNOWLEDGE AND BEING

MR. O.   From all the lectures that have been read, and from everything we have heard and been told about this system, it is very clear that without schools there is no means of acquiring real knowledge—objective knowledge, that is, knowledge that comes from higher mind.

Such knowledge shows us how to study man, how to study the universe, and also how to study the one in relation to the other.

With objective knowledge it is possible to know the real world by making use of the principles of relativity and scale and by knowing the two fundamental laws of the universe: the Law of Three and the Law of Seven.

The approach to objective knowledge is through the study of an objective language. You remember, I said that the study of this system begins with the study of a new language, and I gave you several examples: centres, divisions of centres, division of man into No. 1, 2, 3, 4 and so on. These are all expressions of this language.

The next step is the study of oneself, the study of the human machine, and the understanding of man's place in the universe. This knowledge of oneself is both an aim and a means.

But if a man wants to develop, knowledge alone is not sufficient; he must work to change the level of his being. Only, change of being is so difficult that it would be nearly impossible if knowledge were not there to help him. So knowledge and being must grow side by side, though the one is quite separate from the other.

In school, the conditions are such that from the very first steps work progresses simultaneously along two lines, along the line of knowledge and the line of being. And some understanding of school principles and school methods is necessary to make work on being possible.

Neither knowledge nor being separately can give right understanding, because right understanding is the 'resultant' of a simultaneous growth of knowledge and being.

Growth of knowledge means a transition from the particular to the general, from details to the whole, from the illusory to the real. Ordinary knowledge is always a knowledge of details without knowing the whole, a knowledge of the leaves, or the veins and serrations of the leaves, without knowing the tree. Real knowledge not only shows the given detail, but the place, the function and the meaning of this detail in relation to the whole.

Q.   If knowledge exists on different levels, then we can only have the knowledge belonging to our level?

MR. O.   Quite right, but if we had all the knowledge that we could get on our level, then our level would change. The point is that we don't have all the knowledge which is possible on our level—we have too little.

Q.   Is knowledge only given in direct connection with work?

MR. O.   From the very beginning you are given certain ideas and told certain things about the human machine; for instance, about the four functions, about different states of consciousness, about the fact that we live in a state which goes up and down, sometimes nearer to self-consciousness, sometimes nearer to sleep. When you heard this you were also told to prove it for yourself. If you only hear about such things, or read about them, it remains simply words. But when you begin to verify for yourself, when you understand each function in yourself and find out your own feeling about them, then it becomes knowledge. And being is quite separate. In your present state you can make all possible efforts and yet feel there is more to be got out of your knowledge, but your being is not sufficient. So it is necessary to work on being, make it stronger, more definite. Then from the same words you can extract more knowledge.

Q.   But doesn't a certain amount of knowledge in a man increase his being?

MR. O.   No, it cannot. Even a great amount of knowledge will not increase being by itself. Work on increasing knowledge and increasing being is different work—different effort is necessary.

Q.   If understanding is the resultant of knowledge and being, I cannot see how the two combine.

MR. O.   Any understanding, any moment when you understand something, is a combination of knowledge and being.

Understanding is the result of experience: a certain experience in being and a certain experience in knowledge.

Q.   It is still not clear to me what you mean by being and state of being.

MR. O.   All that is not acquired in the way of knowledge is in your being. Many things enter into being. We can be more divided or more whole, more asleep or less asleep. All that shows being. One may lie more or lie less, dislike lying or like it, have a feeling of mechanicalness or not. Generally, state of being means a greater or lesser consecutiveness of actions. When one thing contradicts another too much, it means weak being. We do not realize that if a man is very inconsequent, it makes his knowledge very unreliable. Development of one line only, either of knowledge or of being, gives very bad results. There are some very insufficient schools, controlled by people who should not control schools, which develop only one side and give very bad results.

The two sides of a man must develop. Being includes all our force to 'do'. Knowledge is only auxiliary; it can help. But in order to change our being, first—and this is where knowledge comes in—we must realize and understand our state. As we begin to understand the state of our being, at the same time we learn what to do with ourselves, that we have to remember about different 'I's, struggle with useless functions like lying, imagination, negative emotions and so on.

Q.   What did you mean when you said that development of either knowledge or being alone gives bad results?

MR. O.   It may help you if I tell you how I first heard about it. In the first case, if knowledge develops beyond being, the result is called a 'weak Yogi'—a man who knows everything but can do nothing. In the second case, if being develops beyond knowledge, the result is a 'stupid saint'—a man who can do everything but does not know anything.

Q.   Are B influences any help towards the growth of being?

MR. O.   You should know already that without absorbing a certain amount of B influences you cannot come to C influences. I am often asked why I have no groups for children. It is because people must have enough experience, they must first try different things and be disappointed in them. Otherwise they will take the system on the level of B influences, they will lower it, they will not be able to feel it as different from anything else they can read or hear about. They must first have experience of B influences to know whether the system is something ordinary or not ordinary.

If you try to compare this system with others, you will find that it is in the importance of this idea of being that it differs from other systems, philosophical or otherwise. Other systems are concerned about knowledge, or about conduct. They assume that, such as we are, we can know more or behave differently. In religious systems 'faith' and 'conduct' are generally regarded as being voluntary. One can be good or bad—it is arbitrary. This is the only system that has the idea of different levels of being. On our present level of being there is one knowledge, one conduct, one faith, all determined by being. But first comes knowledge—how little we know. You begin to study yourself; you realize that you are a machine but that you can become conscious. The machine starts on a certain level of being. All it can or cannot do is dependent upon this level. Try to understand what is meant by being, by levels of being, change of being. Other systems regard knowledge or moral conduct as independent of being. In this system the most important and most characteristic idea is the idea of being. This system says that everything—forces, energies, different kinds of activity, they all depend on the level of being. We cannot know more because of our level of being. At the same time the slightest difference in the level of being opens up new possibilities for knowledge and for doing. All our powers are determined by our level of being.

Q. I understood we were all on the same level.

MR. O. Yes, in comparison with man No. 4. But there are people who are further away from the level of man No. 4 and others who are nearer to it. As in everything else, there are degrees. There is a big distance between the two levels, but there are intermediate states. It is the same in ourselves: each of us can be different at different moments.

Q. Could you explain more about the degrees that exist between us and man No. 4. I want to understand.

MR. O. This is a right question. And you can understand by observation of other people and yourself. There are degrees. There are men No. 1, 2 and 3 who are not interested at all in the possibility of development or in acquiring knowledge or in anything like that. Then there are those who have the possibility of a certain understanding, but it moves from one thing to another—it is not a directed interest. Then there may be directed interest, the beginning of magnetic centre, the growth of magnetic centre, meeting with school—there may be many schools of one or another kind, and one may pass through many wrong schools. Then one meets the work. Again there are different degrees. Many things were explained about that. Man No. 1, 2 and 3 can be quite different—he may be nearer to possibilities, further from possibilities, or even without any possibilities.

Q. You spoke about other systems and moral conduct. Am I right in thinking we cannot understand objective right and wrong without knowing the purpose of the whole?

MR. O. Which whole? First we must establish on which level we are speaking and on what scale. Even humanity is a very large scale.

Q. The scale of humanity must fit organic life.

MR. O. Probably, but not necessarily.

Q. Then there is no objective right and wrong.

MR. O. Why not? Organic life is an auxiliary cosmos. What may be right in the interests of a smaller cosmos may be wrong in a higher cosmos, or indifferent. But this is purely theoretical. When we discuss it we must leave big things and come as near as possible to ourselves. First we must connect it with three lines of work. The first line is study; struggle with useless functions like identifying and negative emotions. All that helps the first line is right. In the first line everything you get is only for yourself. This is the principle. On the second line you cannot have all to yourself, you must give to other people. The circle becomes larger; the right and wrong become bigger. You have to learn not only to understand but also to explain. And you will soon see that you can only understand certain things by explaining to others. The third line is the idea of school. The circle is still larger. It relates to the outside world. Then good and bad become what helps or hinders on a larger scale. This is the way to think.

The first line concerns only yourself.

The second line concerns people in the work.

The third line concerns all the outside world and all the present and the future of the work.

You see how it becomes larger? There are many things to discuss here. It also simplifies things. All the time we have a point of application.

I particularly draw your attention to the study and under-

standing of the idea of three lines. It is one of the principles of
school-work. If you apply it, many things will open up for you.
This system is full of such instruments. If we use them, they
open first one door, then another door.

FRAGMENT FROM A MEETING (N.D.)

If we think about this question of different influences under
which man lives, we will see that what is important for us is to
distinguish between influences created in life itself and influences
whose source stands outside of life. It is necessary to <u>understand</u>
about them; the whole thing depends upon this understanding
and also on the capacity to discriminate between the two kinds
of influences. The difficulty lies in separating them. If, in
receiving the two kinds of influences, a man does not separate
them, that is, if he does not see and feel their difference, then
their action on him will also not be separate; they will act on
him in the same way, on the same level, and produce the same
results.

But if a man discriminates, then the results of the influences
whose source lies outside life, collect within him; he remembers
them together, feels them together, and, after a certain time,
they form a magnetic centre in him which begins to attract to
itself kindred influences, and in this manner magnetic centre
grows.

A man can start work only if he has a magnetic centre. If you
take people in life—some of them have a magnetic centre, others
have not. If a man has the right kind of magnetic centre, it may
help him to get into contact with the third kind of influences—
direct influences. Without understanding about the three kinds
of influences, one cannot see the relationship of school-work to
life and why school-work is limited, why only a few people can
do it.

There are many different sorts of influences A, but they
are. . . .

INFLUENCES (A FRAGMENT FROM A MEETING. N.D.)

MR. O. . . . the past reach us? They don't live long; they have
their short life with the exception of two or three which are

surrounded by such a tangle of mechanical adaptations that they really become influences A. They survive only in this form.

Q.   Who would destroy them?

MR. O.   Everything, all forces, all mechanical forces, because in their nature they are opposed to mechanical forces, and certainly mechanical forces destroy them.

Q.   Do you know of any circumstances which are favourable to influence B flourishing?

MR. O.   We can imagine it but we don't know them. Can we see such a state of things that influence B is not destroyed, but exists and does its work? It is not necessary to invent anything; it is sufficient for us to see how things are.

Q.   If we knew how to divert the energy, everything would be useful, I suppose?

MR. O.   No, this is another question; at the same time it is quite true that everything can be made useful; so this is not only diverting energy, it is already creating suitable currents turned into right influences. This is still further.

You see, all views of things are no good; they don't lead anywhere. It is necessary to think differently, to think in a new way, and to see things differently. And that means seeing things we don't see now, and the last is perhaps the most difficult, because we are accustomed to see certain things. It is a great sacrifice not to see things we are accustomed to see. We are accustomed to think that we live in a more or less comfortable world; certainly there are unpleasant things like revolutions, wars, but on the whole it is a comfortable world, a well-meaning world. It is most difficult to get rid of the idea of a well-meaning world. And then, certainly, we must understand that we don't see things at all; we see as in Plato's allegory of the cave—we see only the reflections of things which take place behind our back; and the things we see have lost reality. It is parallel to the cave; so very often we are controlled not by the things themselves, but by our idea of the things, our view of things, our picture of things. This is the most interesting thing. Try to think about it and then we will talk next time.

B INFLUENCES. JANUARY 17TH 1940

Q. Remembering why I came into the work, I also remember how I came. If things just happen, why do they appear linked as if there is a guiding purpose all through?

MR. O. That was explained about B influences. You see, if you came to the system, this or similar system, if you are not prepared you will not stay, like many people—they just come and then go away because they cannot touch anything, which means they are not prepared. In a sense this preparation is accidental, but at the same time people in exactly the same circumstances—one becomes prepared and another is not prepared, which shows something in one's nature. But influences themselves are accidental, they cannot be intentional. I mean they are intentional in their origin but accidental in the world.

6
Aim

DOING THE IMPOSSIBLE—CHANGE OF BEING—
EMOTION AND EFFORT

Q. We have been told that real work on being requires a realization of how to get right understanding. You also said we must understand what we want.

MR. O. There are several reasons for that. Understanding is the strongest force we have which can change us. The more understanding we have, the better the results of our efforts.

Q. I find it quite impossible to judge of any alteration in the level of my being. I can perceive understanding, but not change of being.

MR. O. Understanding depends on the level of being. I see that you don't understand what level of being means. As I explained in the first lecture, one of the first features of our being is that we have many 'I's, an organization of work, a direction of work. This will mean change of being.

Q. What degree of being do you want from us?

MR. O. Understanding. It is impossible to determine the degree in words.

Q. If we are machines, how can we change our being?

MR. O. You cannot wait until you change. There is one very important principle in the work—you never have to work in accordance with your forces, but always beyond your forces. This is a permanent principle. In the work you always have to do more than you can. Only then can you change. If you do only what is possible you will remain where you are. One has to do the impossible. You must not take the word 'impossible' on a big scale. But even a little means much. You have to do more than you can, or you will never change. This is different from life—in life you only do what is possible.

It is necessary to understand that the only aim is change of being. The aim is to reach higher states of consciousness and to be able to work with higher centres. All the rest is for that, in order to achieve that. It is necessary to do a thousand things that seem to have no relation to it, but they are all necessary, because we live below the normal level. First we must reach the normal level, and second, we must try to develop new things and possibilities.

Then again, people often say they have worked for a long time and see no results. But, to gain even a little, work must be of a different intensity. It is like learning a language. If you learn ten words a day, in ten or fifteen years you will still be in the same place—you will learn something and forget something. Work needs permanent effort, very big effort, and continual effort. A long time is required for preparation, and certain things, like work on obstacles, need a long time—it is slow work. But you have to think not only about obstacles but also about aim, and this demands a different effort.

Q.   What does it mean—trying to do the impossible?

MR. O.   Changing your state—self-remembering. In order to move from this dead spot you have to do more, make more effort than in ordinary life. People forget this, or think they can do this work with the same, or even smaller, effort than in life. This is really impossible. Effort has many different sides. Sometimes the effort not to do something, or to do it differently, is greater than the effort to do something. Efforts may be different, but in the beginning we can be guided only by mind and by understanding. So for a long time all work must be concentrated on understanding. When you understand things better, many other things will become possible.

Q.   How can one make the right effort in relation to self-remembering?

MR. O.   By trying to understand what it is, why you want to do it. The more you put into it, the more you understand about it, the better the result will be. When you realize how much you lose by not remembering yourself you will have a strong impulse to remember yourself when you can. If you realize that you don't remember yourself and what it means, and if you realize what remembering yourself would mean, and when that is connected up with what you lose by not remembering yourself and what you would gain by remembering yourself—then the more you understand, the more effort you will make.

Q.   When I feel something emotionally in the work, I soon destroy the whole thing.

MR. O.   Only identification is destructive. Emotion can only give new energy, new understanding. You mistake identification for emotion. You don't know emotion without identification.

Q. Is there any way to increase one's understanding?

Mr. O. Not one way; there are thousands of ways. All that we have spoken about from the first day until now is about ways of increasing understanding. But chiefly you must struggle with obstacles, with the things which prevent you from understanding. Only by removing these obstacles will you begin to understand more. But obstacles, with the exception of the general description of identification and so on, are individual. You must find your own. You must find what is in your way. Generally, you will find it is one or another form of identification, but individually, for you personally, it may have a different taste. Another person's difficulty may look very simple to you, but your own difficulties look very difficult and as though you can do nothing—until you wish to. But it is not impossible. Nothing impossible is demanded of you. Only you must be persistent and act in a certain way, and remember what has been said.

Q. Before coming to the work I was full of little enthusiasms and so on. I see that many of them were based on imagination, but now I have almost no feeling at all. It seems a very flat feeling, and I can't believe that other people are like that too.

Mr. O. Unfortunately they are. This is one of the biggest problems—how to make oneself more emotional—because we cannot go far on intellect. It is only effort—effort and remembering different lines of the work, trying not to identify, trying to remember oneself, trying this and that—effort, effort. . . . At the same time, this is a very big problem, because there are so many things against it. . . . But if you make sufficient effort, you will become more emotional. The more effort you make, the more emotional you will become. But the fact that this is a constant question that everybody asks—or if they don't ask, they feel this problem—shows that one does not make enough effort.

Q. You say more effort is needed. Do you mean effort to feel emotion or effort to work?

Mr. O. It cannot be put like that. It is effort to work, simply. You cannot make effort to feel emotion. No effort will help in that.

Q. You said there were many things against us in making efforts to be emotional.

MR. O.   You cannot make efforts to be emotional. This is quite wrong. You cannot make efforts to be emotional, <u>but you can make efforts</u>. If you are doing something, you can do it without effort, trying to do as little as possible, or you can put much effort into it. Emotion can appear only as the result of a certain pressure. In ordinary conditions, in ordinary life, it only happens; something happens and brings you to an emotional state. The question is how to produce emotion, how to make ourselves emotional. And I may say that in our present state there is only one thing—effort. But not effort to produce emotion. There is no such effort. But, very strong continuous effort in any work you do will make you more emotional after some time—not at once, certainly. But a certain period of effort on different lines will certainly increase your emotions.

Q.   Why should making efforts be so very difficult? I suppose it is partly because until we have some control over negative emotions we haven't enough energy?

MR. O.   No. Control of negative emotions is a far aim. We cannot wait for that. Efforts may look difficult because we are not prepared in our mind. We don't think rightly about them. We don't even accept mentally that it is necessary to make efforts. That creates the biggest difficulty. The necessity for making efforts comes as a shock—as a new thing. We are not prepared for that.

DESIRE TO WORK AND MANY 'I'S

Q.   I want to find the way to make a decision to work from which I cannot draw back.

MR. O.   This is one of our greatest illusions, that we can make decisions. It is necessary <u>to be</u> in order to make decisions because, as we are, one little 'I' makes decisions, and another 'I', which does not know about it, is expected to carry them out. This is one of the first points we have to realize, that, as we are, we cannot make decisions even in small things—things just happen. But when you understand this rightly, when you begin to look for the causes, and when you find these causes, then you will be able to work and, perhaps, you will be able to make decisions, but for a long time only in relation to work, not to anything else.

The first thing you have to decide is to do your own work,

and to do it regularly, to remind yourself about it, not to let it slip away. We forget things too easily. We decide to make efforts—certain kinds of effort and certain kinds of observation—and then just ordinary things, ordinary octaves, interrupt it all and we quite forget. Again we remember, and again we forget, and so on. It is necessary to forget less and remember more. It is necessary to keep certain realizations, certain things that you have already realized and understood, always with you. You must try not to forget them.

The chief difficulty is <u>what</u> to do and <u>how</u> to make yourself do it. To make yourself think regularly, work regularly—this is the thing. Only then will you begin to see yourself, that is, to see what is more important, what is less important, where to put your attention, and so on. Otherwise, what happens? You decide to work, to do something, to change things—and then you remain just where you were. Try to think about your work, what you are trying to do, why you are trying to do it, what helps you to do that and what hinders you, both from outside and inside. As I have often said, it is even useful to think about external events, particularly at the present time, because they show you how much depends on the fact that people are asleep, that they are incapable of thinking rightly, incapable of understanding. When you see this outside, you can apply it to yourself. You will see the same confusion in yourself on different subjects, on one subject or another. It is difficult to think, difficult to see where to begin to think. Once you realize this, you start to think in the right way.

If you find your way to think rightly about one thing, that will immediately help you to think rightly about other things. The difficulty is that people don't think rightly about anything.

Q.   The thing I find most alarming in myself is the ease with which I fall into a state in which no effort is possible.

Mr. O.   Yes, but if you arrange with yourself to make regular efforts, that will help you to go on.

Q.   How can you prevent regular efforts from becoming just formal; prevent the meaning slipping out of them?

Mr. O.   Self-remembering can never become formal. If efforts of that kind become formal, that means very deep sleep. Then it is necessary to do something to awake yourself. And you have to start from the idea of mechanicalness and the results of mechanicalness.

Quite right. Everything slips away and disappears and then

you find yourself with nothing. Again you start with some kind of conscious effort. Again it slips away. The thing is, how to prevent it from disappearing like that. In our ordinary way of thinking and feeling there are many mechanical tendencies, and these mechanical tendencies always turn us in their usual way. We want to think in another way, we want to be different, to work in another way, feel in a new way—but nothing happens, because there are many tendencies which turn us back. It is necessary to study these tendencies and try to throw light on them, to see them. Take this constant use of the word 'I' when you have no right to say 'I'. You can say 'I' in speaking about yourself only in relation to your work for a definite aim—self-study, study of the system, self-remembering, things like that. Only then can you say 'I'. In other things—certainly there is no other language—but you must realize that this is not 'you' really, but only a small part of you. When you learn to distinguish this difference, when it becomes almost habit (not habit in the ordinary sense, but when it becomes constant), then you will feel yourself in the right way. But if you always say 'I', and don't distinguish, that helps these mechanical tendencies and strengthens them. And what a quantity of things there are which we do that really we don't want to do at all! And that takes all our energy, and nothing remains for real work.

Q. Is constant changing of 'I's the result of habit?

MR. O. Yes, but it is all change in the same place, turning round in the same place. It is not change really. . . . We want to produce change, but change can only be the result of constant effort. Ordinarily, mechanically, it is all just turning round.

Q. Can one find responsibility in oneself?

MR. O. Certainly. But in relation to what? You begin certain work. You have responsibility towards that work—you should have, at least. But who? If you call everything 'I', you must know there are many 'I's; some have responsibility, some have no responsibility, because they have nothing to do with this work. There are different parts of you.

Q. What quality is it that the few people who can develop possess, that others do not possess?

MR. O. Many things, not one. Try to think again of different sides of yourself, and perhaps you will find those things; this is the only practical approach. You will find sides that work and sides that cannot, and then perhaps you will see which qualities can work and which are impossible. Generally, we can tell in

that way. It begins with capacity for valuation; if you begin
with that it is useful. Some people have real values, some have
false values, some have none at all. It is the same with different
'I's; some value real things, some wrong things, some value
nothing. You can find it in yourself.

Q.   What is it that people have that can develop, and which it
seems I have not? I always see the negative side of me, things
that stop me working.

MR. O.   Who is working? It is something in you also. Certain
'I's are interested in the work, and other 'I's don't want to
trouble. It is only a question of observation, nothing more, to
see that. Then you will see that one 'I' is connected with another
and another. One that wants to work is connected with many
others. In that way you can find many groups of 'I's in yourself.

IDEAS AND THEIR ACTUALIZATION. SEPTEMBER 3RD
1935

MR. O.   The system cannot explain everything. Many things
we know very well but continue to deceive ourselves, mainly
about words. It is very difficult to understand the value of words.
'Poor in spirit' means who does not believe in words, and 'rich
in spirit'—who believes in words. Often people say (and this
has connection with triads), 'If I do this or that, then it will be
beautiful'. They don't understand that it is impossible to do
exactly as they wish, that everything will be a little different,
and in the end everything will be different. Then they see that
it is different and say, 'Yes, but the original idea was very
good'. It was not good. It can look beautiful as an idea, but in
realization it becomes its own opposite. It will necessarily change
because of friction. There are some ideas that can pass through
triads, and others that cannot, that can exist only in the form
of one force, or half a force, or a quarter.

Q.   They cannot be actualized?

MR. O.   If they are, they become different, or their own
opposites. Take psycho-analysis or bolshevism. This is why
things generally go so wrong with people—they don't realize
that many beautiful ideas cannot be actualized in that form.
People don't realize that there are ideas quite empty, with no
content, and there are others that are very heavy. People (masses,
men 1, 2 and 3) live by these non-existing ideas. And every ten

years, if one looks back, one can see they were wrong, for already one can see results. But about one's own ideas one cannot see that it is the same class of ideas as the others were.

Q. Can you supply some test?

MR. O. Certainly. In many cases, if you look sincerely, you will immediately see that such an idea cannot be actualized. For instance—disarmament. The simplest way to see it is just to look seriously and see: can this be actualized or not? For instance, socialistic ideas—bolshevism is the only practical form of them. Why? Because there will always be opposition, and in the struggle formatory ideas of socialism become criminal, if they want to exist.

Q. Why is bolshevism turning into capitalism? Their idea was distribution of wealth. . . .

MR. O. No, this was only in brochures. They wanted power, and for that they had to abandon principles. Certainly they try to repeat as many words as they can. But socialistic ideas cannot come to actualization because there always will be opposition and struggle. If there were no opposition, perhaps there would be balance for half an hour. Struggle always changes results, except with school ideas. They only become better with struggle because they are made for struggle, and made by higher minds from results, like a novel started from the end and then brought back to the beginning. Any good novel, if there is a plot, can be written only from the end. Then things will fit in all right. Just the same here. The funny thing is that writers themselves do not always know that they write from the end. Many think they write from the beginning.

Q. In relation to one's aim—there may be unrealizable things in it?

MR. O. The system shows what is realizable and what is not.

Q. I find it difficult to keep decisions. Perhaps it is better not to make them?

MR. O. Some may eventually be actualized, some may be impossible. If you make no decisions you will never try to do anything. But you must only make possible decisions, and decisions which have to be remembered. In work, certain things are necessary. There are general demands which are obligatory for people who want to work in the system. Do your decisions refer to that or not? It is necessary to begin from the beginning and always to remember why you started. Do you want things you can get from ordinary life or different things? Is it worth while trying? About certain things you can be sure you cannot get them in the ordinary way, but there is no guarantee that in this way you will get them. For instance, the order may be wrong. There is a certain order by which to get things, which we do not know. It is quite sure that you can get some things, but there is no guarantee that you will get them. But maybe you will get something else. But even if you don't get them, the sure thing is that you cannot get them in any other way.

CROSS-ROADS. SEPTEMBER 19TH 1935

Q. A few times a year a line of action becomes particularly clear to me. What was very difficult becomes then very simple and is backed by enthusiasm. I know by experience that if I put off following this line immediately, the opportunity will not show itself again for a long time, if ever. These well marked lines of action sometimes come as a result of effort, but quite often from no causes that I can discover. What is the reason of this and how can these moments be made to come more often and last longer? I have been subject to these moments all my life and have come to think it useless to take any serious action without what would be ordinarily called inspiration.

Mr. O. I cannot say without knowing in what direction, in relation to what. As a matter of fact, it is quite right. There are periods in ordinary conditions when nothing happens, and then there come cross-roads. All life consists of streets and cross-roads. Even the turning in cross-roads may become more systematic if one has a centre of gravity. Then one thing continues to be more important and one always turns in one direction. But inspiration has nothing to do with it. It is simply realization of a moment when you can do something.

CROSS-ROADS. SEPTEMBER 26TH 1935

You must start on some concrete idea. Try to find what really prevents you from being active in work. It is necessary to be active in work; one can get nothing by being passive. . . .

We forget now the beginning, where and why we started, and most of the time we never even think about aim, but only about small details. No details are any use without aim. Self-remembering is of no use without remembering the aims of the work and the original, fundamental aim. If these aims are not remembered emotionally, years may pass and one will remain in the same state. It is not enough to educate the mind. It is necessary to educate will. You must understand what is our will. From time to time we have will. Will is resultant of desires. The moment we have a strong desire, there is will. In that moment we must study our will and see what can be done. We have no will but self-will and wilfulness. If one understands that, one must be brave enough to give up one's will, to listen to what was said. You must look for those moments, must not miss them. I don't mean create them artificially, although in a house special possibilities to give up one's will are made, so that, if you give up your will, later you may have your own will. But even people who are not there, if they watch themselves and are careful, can catch themselves at such moments and ask themselves what they are to do. Everybody must find his own case. This idea is connected with cross-roads. Cross-roads are moments when one can do. A moment comes when one can help in this work or not. If an opportunity comes and one misses it, another may not come for a year perhaps, or even longer, if one does not arrange to use organized work which may make permanent difficulties.

AIM

Q.   Can you tell me what one <u>should</u> aim at, I mean, what it is possible to acquire through the work?

MR. O.   Yes, we can speak about aims. Only, as I always say, you must have your own aims. If you give them, then it will be possible to speak with much better material.

You see, the determination and definition of aim is a very important moment in the work, and it usually happens—that is why it is impossible to speak about aims in general like that—that one defines one's aim quite rightly, in quite the right direction, only one takes an aim that is very far. Then one begins to learn and accumulate material, having in view this aim. The next time one tries to define aim one defines it a little differently, an aim a little nearer. The next time again a little nearer, and so on and so on, until one finds an aim quite close—to-morrow or the day after to-morrow. This is really the right way in relation to aims, if we speak about them without definite words.

But then, we can find that many have already been mentioned. One wants to be one. Quite right; very good aim. One wants to be free. How? Only when one acquires control of the machine. One may say, 'I want to be conscious'. Quite right. One may say, 'I want to have will'. Very good. 'I want to be awake'. Also very good. They are all aims on the same line, only, at different distances.

Q. I came to the conclusion that most of my aims are too remote, and I want to work more on the practical side.

MR. O. Yes, because before you can reach remote aims, there are many things you have to do here and now, and this is in what this system differs from almost all other systems. Nearly all other systems begin at least ten thousand miles ahead and have no practical meaning; but this system begins in this room—that is the difference, and that is what must be understood first of all.

Q. Must I always keep my big aim at the back of every small aim?

MR. O. That depends on for what purpose. You are never the same for two days in succession. On some days you will be more successful; on others, less. All we can do is to control what we can. We can never control more difficult things if we don't control the easy things. Every day and hour there are things we could control and don't. So we cannot have new things to control. We are surrounded by neglected things. Chiefly, we don't control our thinking. We think in a vague way about what we want. But if you don't formulate what you want, then nothing will happen. This is the first condition. But there are many obstacles.

Q. I have tried quite often to think what I want, but I only find a muddle of many things.

MR. O. That's it. That is what I am saying. I want you to realize how difficult it is to define. Suppose you are given full choice to have what you want: you will not know what to say. You must understand it and know it; you must be able to formulate it.

Q. If I try to control the expression of negative emotions, the result makes things better for me in ordinary life. I find that I work for immediate results, not for waking up. Is this a wrong aim?

Mr. O.   There is no question of right and wrong; there is only
the question of knowing your aim. Think about aim. Aim must
always be in the present and refer to the future.

Q.   Trying to define my aim has made me see that I don't know
what it is, and I must find out before I can get further.

Mr. O.   I am afraid you only think about it in an abstract way.
Just imagine yourself going to a big shop with many different
departments. You must know what you want to buy. How can
you get something if you don't know what you want? This is
the way to approach this problem. The first question is: <u>What</u>
do you want? Once you know this, then the next question will
be: Is it worth paying for and have you enough money? But the
first question is: 'What?'

Payment is a most important principle in the work, and it
must be understood that it is absolutely necessary. Without
payment you can get nothing; and you can get only as much as
you pay for—no more.

Payment means effort, study, time—many things.

Q.   I find that I sincerely want more knowledge, but I do not
really want to change my present being.

Mr. O.   Yes, that is a very good observation, because we are
almost all in exactly the same position. We want to get something for nothing, and that is why we have nothing. If we really
decided to go for this kind of knowledge—or even for quite a
small thing—and we went for it regardless of everything else,
then we would get it. This is a very important point. We say
that we want knowledge, but we don't, really. It is not
imagination—it does not matter what you call it; you may find
another name for it—it is a special attitude. You will pay for
anything else, but for this you are not prepared to pay anything,
and so, as a result, you get nothing.

Q.   In trying to formulate clearly what I want, the strongest
feeling is that what I want is not there.

Mr. O.   Yes, always, but this is not a formulation. Certainly
if it were there you would not want it; you would already have
it. You see, it is connected with many things. Do not think you
can solve this problem quickly. We are so accustomed to think
wrongly about many things, we don't even know how to begin
to think in the right way. It is quite true that what we want is
not there, but what is it? <u>That</u> is what we must think about—and
we are afraid to think about it. We say, 'If it is not in this room,

it does not exist'. And this is how we think in general. This is
a wrong way of thinking.

Q. I have been trying to think what I want to get out of the
work. Many 'I's in me like the work in a vague sort of way. I
feel this is holding me up.

Mr. O.   Quite right, it is very useful to know more definitely.
Again and again we must return to this question of what we
want from the work. Don't use the terminology of the system,
but find what you yourself want. If you say you want to be
conscious, that is all very good, but why? What do you want
to get by being conscious? You must not think you can answer
this question immediately. It is very difficult. But you must keep
coming back to it. And you must understand that before the
time comes when you will be able to get what you want, you
must know what it is. This is a very definite condition. You can
never get anything until you know it and can say, 'I want this'.
Then perhaps you may get it or perhaps you may not; but you
can never get it unless you know. Also, you must want things
in the right order.

Q.   What does this mean?

Mr. O.   One must study and understand the right order of
possibility. This is a very interesting subject.

Q.   Do you mean in the system?

Mr. O.   With the help of the system. But you can formulate it
in your own way. You must be sincere with yourself. You must
know exactly what you want, and then you will ask yourself:
'Will the system be able to help me to get it?' and so on. But it
is necessary to know what you want.

I have spoken about this question of aim because I advise you
to think about it, revise what you have already thought about
aim and think how you would define your aim now, after a
study of these ideas. It is useless to define an aim that cannot
be attained. But if you define an aim that one can hope to attain,
then one's work will be conscious, serious.

    If I were asked about this, I would answer that what a man
can get, what can be promised him on condition that he works,
is that after some time of work he will see himself. Other things
that he may get, such as consciousness, unity, connection with
higher centres, all come after this—and we don't know in what
order they come. But we must remember one thing; until we get
this—until we see ourselves—we cannot get anything else. And

until we begin to work with this aim in view we cannot say that we begin to work. So after some time we must be able to formulate our immediate aim as being to see oneself. Not even to know oneself (this comes later), but to see oneself.

AIM. MONDAY. JANUARY 10TH 1938

MR. O.   In one question here was mentioned idea of aim. I advise you to think about it—what you thought about aim, how, after long study of these ideas you can define your aim, and how you explain—suppose new person asks you 'What can be my aim?'—how you would describe aim for them, what he could get and what he must try to get. It is useless to describe aim that you know he cannot attain, but if you give him aim that he can hope to attain, then his work will be conscious—serious.

You remember this example (I think to latest groups I did not bring it because it needs long talk)—G. always gave this example of how aim begins in that way—suppose man walking one night, in the dark, in empty place, or road, and then he sees light somewhere and he begins to walk towards this light, and this light becomes aim, and after some time this light disappeared—either hill or something—and he sees another light, and then sees third, and it changes many times, and then he will see light just straight in front, and this will becomes his aim—all first lights are aim, but when he sees there is nothing else between himself and this light, then he will understand his aim. Suppose somebody asks you to translate in ordinary language, what will you say about this aim that comes last? Perhaps some people can manage to see this aim at once but it is very doubtful—you may suppose—but how will you describe?

MRS. C.   Isn't it always more and more growing of understanding?

MR. O.   Too general.

MRS. C.   Not so very general is it, because if you don't understand you don't see the light.

MR. O.   Very general—there is no subject. You cannot say 'more and more' or anything like that. Perhaps you thought about this definition or perhaps you did not think, but if I am asked about this I give answer like that, what one can get, or can be promised to him, certainly on condition that he works, one can be promised that after some time of work he will see himself—that is only one thing that one must get first of all—other things, we don't know the order in which they come—higher centres, higher consciousness, many other things, they can be only after that, but we don't know in which order. We know only one thing (we may know or not know) that until we get that we cannot get anything else, and until we begin to work consciously towards this aim we cannot say that we even began to work—work begins; first one learns what is possible, what is impossible, and after some time he must be able to formulate the aim that he can see himself—first one must be able to see himself.

MR. R.   Does that mean a combination of self-observation and self-remembering?

MR. O.   No, it is not like that—it is to have right picture of oneself.

MR. P.   Is it possible to have a complete picture of oneself?

MR. O.   Not complete—it is better to have something, but it <u>may</u> be complete in the beginning.

MR. P.   Is it possible to come to the point when you can see what you are?

MR. O.   Yes, certainly, this is the beginning; before you get that you cannot begin any serious work, only study, and even that only fraction of study is one thing, and that is another thing; it will not become one.

MR. E.   It is very difficult to make sure if one is telling the truth to oneself.

MR. O.   Very difficult. That is why I did not say anything about saying or knowing; I said 'see'—picture you must see, first one and then another, and another, you compare them; you cannot see all at one moment.

MR. R.   Would it correspond to the picture that is seen by others?

MR. O.   That I cannot say; when you see we can compare.

MR. W.   What is the kind of verification that one is seeing oneself correctly?

MR. O.   Repeated experience.

MR. W.   But cannot repeated experience also be wrong?

MR. O.   The capacity to deceive ourselves is so great that we can continue to deceive ourselves.

MR. W.   But I wondered if there was some check.

MR. O.   I think it is more when emotional element enters in that helps to check—it is called conscience.

Mr. P.   Doesn't it involve seeing part of one's feature?

Mr. O.   Maybe.

Q.   Do you mean that one wakes up suddenly and feels ashamed?

Mr. O.   That is emotion. It depends what one sees. later one can speak how these emotions can be used; I speak only about seeing. I speak only of what you can say to new people.

Mrs. E.   Do you mean that you will see complete mechanicalness?

Mr. O.   That is one side only—there are many sides.

Mr. C.   Is the picture one sees our different personalities?

Mr. O.   No.

AIMS. APRIL 25TH 1938

Q.   How can I learn to act differently in life so as to avoid the same limited and recurrent emotions I now feel?

Mr. O.   This is our aim—this is the aim of the whole work. This is why work is organized, why we have to study different theories, to remember different rules, and so on. What you say is the far aim. We have to work in the system first. When we learn how to act in connection with the system, in connection with organization, then we learn how to act in life; but we cannot learn first to act in life, without going through the system.

Q.   If we are all weakness and no strength, from what source do we draw such strength as is needed to even begin work on ourselves?

Mr. O.   We must have certain strength. If we are only weakness then we can do nothing. But, at the same time, if we had no strength at all we wouldn't become interested in that. If we realize our situation, we already have certain strength, and new knowledge increases this strength. So we have quite enough. Later, strength comes from new knowledge, new efforts.

DEVELOPMENT. JANUARY 17TH 1940

Q.   There is a large part of me which does not want to develop. How can I make the part that does want to develop stronger?

Mr. O.   You must do what you can, and beyond that you can do nothing. This 'I' which wants to grow will grow, but it can grow only because of your efforts; then it will somehow make other 'I's not to interfere.

Q.   How can I try to build up a real direction, a stronger aim?

MR. O.   Again the same thing—by building yourself; you can be stronger than yourself.

Q.   We are a sum total of different 'I's. How to know which 'I' to trust? How is one to know if the 'I' which has taken the decision is the right one?

MR. O.   One cannot know—that is our state. We have to deal with what we are until we change, but we work with the idea of possible change, and the more we realize the hopeless state in which we are the more energy we shall have.

Q.   Is it something in ourselves that we don't desire enough to change? If we desired enough, should we get help?

MR. O.   Yes, certainly, but I would not put it like that. You have all the help that is possible; it is your turn now to work, your turn to do something. Certainly, with different conditions, different preparation, and also different circumstances, things could be better arranged, or more even could be given. But the question is not how much is given but how much is taken, because generally only a little part is taken of what is given.

UNITY. SEPTEMBER 5TH 1945

Q.   I have understood you to say that man No. 5 is a man of unity. What is meant by unity in this case?

MR. O.   You remember the diagram with 'I', 'I', 'I', 'I', 'I'. Well, he does not have this.

Q.   What other attributes does man No. 5 have besides unity?

MR. O.   Quite enough. He has to get rid of many 'I's.

Q.   What can I do in order to attain unity?

MR. O.   Be one. Conquer all this plurality of 'I's.

Q.   How can we change being?

MR. O.   This is change of being—to be one. Not for ever. But try for five minutes, then ten minutes.

Q.   What is self-will?

MR. O.   Self-will is against unity. One is told, 'Don't do that', and one says, 'I want to do that'.

12. 9. 45

Q.   I don't understand the answer you gave me about trying to have unity for five minutes a day.

Mr. O.   Well, what else can I say? Trying not to let different 'I's interrupt and argue among themselves. If not five minutes, try four, then three. Not enough to say you can't do it. Describe process. Why not?

7
Work

MR. O.   What I want you to think about is the three lines of work, because these lectures, as I proposed them in the beginning, are now finished. I have given you all the words which are necessary for the study of the system, and I explained the position of this system in relation to other systems. You will remember that I spoke about different ways. There are four ways, or three traditional ways, Way of Fakir, Way of Monk and Way of Yogi, and the particular feature of these three ways, the difficulty of these ways, is that one has to begin with what is most difficult, which is that one has to give up everything and begin a completely new life at once. But I said that there is a fourth way which differs from these three ways first of all by the fact that one can go by this fourth way while remaining in the ordinary conditions of life, continuing one's ordinary work in life and doing almost exactly what one was doing before. From what I said it came out more or less that this system, this kind of school, belongs to the Fourth Way, that is, it has all the peculiarities and all the features of schools of the Fourth Way. Then I said that schools are different. A school depends on the level of the people who study in that school. There are schools for men No. 6 who study and wish to become men No. 7; there are schools for men No. 5 who want to become men No. 6; there are schools for men No. 4 who want to become men No. 5 and there are many lower degrees of schools for people studying what man No. 4 means and how to become No. 4, and so on. But all the schools of the Fourth Way, all degrees, all levels, have certain features peculiar to them. First, they are always connected with some kind of objective work. For instance, schools connected with the building of Gothic cathedrals in mediaeval times were schools of the Fourth Way. This must not be taken too literally. It does not mean that all cathedrals were built by schools, but that schools were behind this building. And this building of Gothic cathedrals was, for some reason unknown to us, their objective, visible aim. Behind this there existed schools with their own aims. One may know this aim or one may not know it, one may see it or not see it; it does not matter, it is there just the same.

School-work can be successful only if one works on three lines, first—one's own work, one's own study; second—work with people; and third—work for the benefit of the school itself, or for the purpose of this school-work which one may know or may not know.

So far you have worked on the first line, you have studied what I have given you, what I have explained to you, and you have tried to understand, and so on. Now, if you wish to continue, you must try to work on the second line, and, if possible, on the third line, but the third line comes later. If you find something you can do in relation to the third line you can speak about it, and I can discuss it with you. But the necessity at present is to work on the second line. You must try to think how to find more work on the first line, how to pass to work on the second line, and how to approach work on the third line. Without this your study will give no result and you will not be able to continue, because, as I said, these lectures, such as they were intended, are finished; you must try to think how to make them continue, and in what form—how to remain connected with some kind of work.

Try to talk about it and ask questions.

[Question about discussing the lectures.]

MR. O. Discussion by itself will not help much.

Q. What would it be besides discussion?

MR. O. You must think about what you need besides discussion. You need instruction, you need to be shown the way. You cannot find the way yourselves, nobody can; it is the state of a human being that he has to be shown the way, that he cannot find it himself.

But you see, to put it better, you enter into the second line of work in this way: these groups have been going on for some time; there were people before you, and one of the principles of school-work is that one can get instruction and advice in all these things not only from me but also from people who were with me before, who have been studying maybe years and years before you came. Their experience is very important for you, because even if I desired it, I cannot give you more time than it is possible for me. Other people have to supplement what I am giving you and, on your side, you must learn how to use them, how to use their experience and how to make them speak, how to get from them what they can give you.

It is partly with this idea, and partly with some other ideas that we have organized a house where some of you have already been and where some may come later. But again you cannot profit much by this house because it is so fully occupied that it cannot hold more people. Occasionally you may come and talk there, but from the point of view of the work that is going on there, it is rather difficult to arrange for more people, because there are sometimes as many as sixty people at a time. So that this house is beginning to burst already.

Experience shows that in order to get what is possible to get from these ideas a certain organization is necessary, the organization of groups of people not only for discussing things, but for working together, as, for instance, working in the garden or in the house, or doing some other work that can be invented or started. When people work together at anything, for the sake of experience, they begin to see in themselves and in other people, different things which they do not notice when they just discuss things. Discussing is one thing and work is another. Again, this is not absolutely necessary or obligatory for everybody. Many different variations are possible. Some people work better in these conditions, some work better in other conditions; for some people—this kind or organization; for other people—some other kind of organization. So in all schools there exist different kinds of organizations, and people, unless they become unpleasant or disagreeable, can always find what will suit them without unnecessary sacrifices, because sacrifices are not expected.

But you must think about it, you must realize that so far people have looked after you. People who were in groups before have looked for you, talked to you. You were looked after, but now you have to look after yourselves; you have now to think how to keep connected, how to have lectures. You will have to look after yourselves, and, later you will have to look not only after yourselves, but also after new people. That will also be part of the work, and in that way you will be connected with the third line of work.

In this connection you can begin now. School organization,

and particularly organization of groups, necessitates certain rules, because, as people come without knowing one another and without knowing what it is all about, certain rules have to be invented and imposed. For instance, one of the rules that applies to new groups (although I do not think I insisted on it in your case, because people do not listen) is that you should not talk to people outside. Experience shows that it is useless to give this rule in the beginning, because nobody obeys it. People begin to realize the importance of this rule only when this form of talk turns against them, when their friends insist on their talking while they no longer want to talk. In any case, there has been a rule until now that you should not speak; now I change that—try to speak to your friends, try to find out what they think, tell them there are possibilities of lectures, bring them here if you can. If you fail—you fail. I cannot expect much success from it, but it will be an interesting experience to hear what your friends tell you about yourselves and about the ideas.

As I have explained, this rule which prohibited you from speaking, was to help you not to lie, because when people speak about things they do not know, they naturally begin to lie. So if, after listening to one or two lectures, people begin to talk about what they have and begin to express their opinions, they begin to lie. This is very important, because one must struggle against lying and that is why this rule was enforced, in order to help you not to lie. Now you must try to speak the truth, and, at the same time, if you have anybody who might be interested, you have full permission to speak, but on the condition that you will come here when we have meetings, and tell us your impressions, how your friends took it and what they said about it, and so on. This will be interesting material and in this way you will prepare a certain number of people. Very often it happens that people can become interested but they never listen long enough. Most people are too impatient, they do not give themselves enough time. They make conclusions and decisions in too short a time.

Q.   May one use this system to understand other systems, for instance, the Upanishads?

Mr. O.   I think it is too difficult. Yes, one can, but not yet. I think you must know more about this system in order to see connections, particularly in relation to old systems which really do not belong to our time. For instance, I said that there are three traditional ways, the Way of Fakir, the Way of Monk and the Way of Yogi. But at the time the Upanishads were written there were no such ways; these divisions belong to our time only. Even two thousand years ago, about the time of Christ, or before, there was no such division. Things change, but certainly if we study this system for a sufficiently long time, and if we understand the general cosmic principles of schools, then we will be able to compare different systems and understand their language.

Q. Am I lying when I say that I understand Buddhism better since I have heard about this system?

MR. O. I am very interested to hear that, because, although I do not know much about it, from what I have read of Buddhist writings I found many similarities. But they wrote things one after another without emphasizing that one thing is more important than another. But self-understanding certainly helps to understand many things.

WORK. SEPTEMBER 25TH 1935

MR. O. I want to repeat what I said to another group. Although you came at a different time, you all began on the psychological lectures and all these are on the same level. I said that going on at this speed will need three hundred years to get some results, unless we can expand this time, for you can have three hundred years in one month. It depends on understanding. All short cuts depend on understanding. The system helps only if you help yourself; it cannot create anything. With this slow movement C influence becomes B.

Those who wish to continue, will continue. Only I warn people from the beginning that unless they make sufficient efforts it will be useless. Efforts must be organized. What does this mean? Unless you understand our work, we will not be able to help you. You can be helped only if you enter into our work. One must work on three lines. Before one can understand that, one must understand in oneself different lines of work: intellectual work—acquisition of knowledge; emotional work—work on emotions; and work on will—work on one's actions. One has no big will, such as man No. 7 has. But one has will at certain moments. Will is resultant of desires. Will can be seen at moments when there is a strong desire to do or not to do something. Only those moments are important. The system can help only those who realize that they cannot control their will. Then the system will either help them to control their will, or they will have to do as they are told. You have to think how to organize work so as to have results in less than three hundred years.

Q. You mean each must realize it for himself?

Mr. O. It is necessary to understand the aims of the work, its history; what is necessary in the future. The more one understands, the better. If you do something with understanding, you will have more results; if you do it with less understanding, you will have less results.

For instance, you must understand that you have received these ideas and came here because certain people have worked before you and have put their energy and time into it. Now you must share the responsibility. You cannot continue getting ideas without sharing the responsibility. It is quite natural. You were given these ideas without conditions. Nobody is asked to do more than he can, but one must now feel this responsibility and, if not to-day, then to-morrow one must 'do'. Do what? One must understand what to demand from oneself. We study school methods, and this is the only way to study them.

Q. Can you give an example of how to share responsibility?

Mr. O. No. It is a question of understanding what is useful: what is necessary. Then it is a question of seeing what one can do, if not now, perhaps later. It cannot be given in the form of a prescription. In old groups, before I came into them, I asked: are there any conditions for entering the work, and how do you act if a person makes promises and then breaks them? And I was told: there are no conditions. Machines are given full freedom. When people acquire sufficient knowledge and understanding to be able to accept conditions, then conditions can be put to them. The moment people become capable of having conditions, conditions become necessary. Until then there are no conditions.

I don't mean that now is the moment to have conditions, but you must expect them. You must try to understand the principles and stages of school-work. You cannot work the whole life in the same way. Later, it becomes more difficult. At the same time, difficulties are help, help to remember yourself, not to identify, etc. They are very old conditions, and you must understand that they are for help. People, as a rule, do not want conditions, do not want rules. They ask, 'Why rules?' For instance, they want to talk, and they mustn't. Keeping this rule is not pleasant. School helps by creating difficulties for mechanical manifestations. Gradually one becomes surrounded by unpleasantnesses. This is the only way school can help.

Q.   First, we must observe ourselves? We cannot do anything at all?

MR. O.   You can, and you cannot. You go by streets where you cannot turn, and then you come to cross-roads where you can turn. At this brief moment, theoretically speaking, one can change something. It is useful to see your life from this point of view, see long periods where there is no possibility of change, and then moments where there is a possibility of change. It is necessary to learn to find these moments. It is the same in the work, only in the work intervals are quicker.

Q.   What have we to do?

MR. O.   Think.

Q.   Is thinking enough?

MR. O.   You must begin with it.

Q.   You wish us to decide now?

MR. O.   No. We don't apply school methods, we only study them. We are not doing anything yet, not putting any conditions. I only wish you to understand the methods. Sooner or later you will come to a time when you can only receive new knowledge on conditions. Conditions are general for the whole group, or individual according to people's circumstances.

Q.   Will this interfere with our normal activities?

MR. O.   No. One may oneself start doing something that will interfere. But that would be one's free choice, not conditions, I had better give you examples. My work, for instance, began with the third line. Very soon after I began, conditions were put to me. My group was in Moscow. The condition put to me was to organize a group in Petersburg, or to come to Moscow. I could not come to live in Moscow, so I had to organize a group in Petersburg, without knowing practically anything. Then people began to come to Petersburg to give lectures there, and so I was able to study. I had a choice either to have nothing, or to come to Moscow, or to organize a group in Petersburg. You began with no conditions, but soon some conditions there will be, although not as big as mine was. This is an example of a kind of conditions in the third line.

In the second line, when groups were organized, a condition was put: when we meet we must tell our life—plain truth only.

After many attempts and efforts we realized that we could not, because no one knows his life. People invariably invented, only inventions were different. But in all cases it was unconscious lying. Only when we tried it did we realize the meaning of this condition. It seemed a very simple thing, but it showed how far we are from understanding. We think if we want to do something, we can. I will not put this condition to you.

If one decides to be sincere, one must remove artificial barriers. At the same time, it is very difficult even to decide to do that. We have many reluctances, for instance: 'I don't like these people'; 'I will not speak about myself in front of these people'. For twenty years I hear about <u>these</u> people.

Q. If one were sincere and went through all obstacles, a great obligation would rest on that person?

Mr. O. By the principles of the work nobody is expected to do what he cannot, but only what, in his position, is possible for him. I was in right position for organizing a group in Petersburg, otherwise this condition would not have been put to me.

Q. I was thinking more about letting down the system. You organize a group, and something happens. . . .

Mr. O. If circumstances make it impossible, there are almost always some circumstances created to help you to continue. Of course, there may be war, or revolution, like in Russia. At the same time, all who wanted to go away there had a chance given to them. . . .

Time is counted for everybody. After a certain time you are different for me, and I speak differently to you. Whether you satisfy this or not is another matter, but I expect different things from you after a certain time.

Q. Indulging in self-observation shows that it stops work.

Mr. O. Don't indulge. If you observe, it helps work. You can always observe without stopping energetic work. But if you begin to identify with it, it spoils work. But if you find it difficult to observe yourself doing energetic work, don't try. Begin with easier things. It is an expression of laziness to start with the most difficult. Then you justify yourself, saying that you cannot do it.

Q. If I find I cannot remember myself. . . .

Mr. O. You never can. You can observe the quantity of things you do without remembering yourself, and how useful it would be to remember yourself. The more you value it, the more you will try to get it.

LEARNING TO WORK AND A SHORT HISTORY OF THE WORK. WEDNESDAY. OCTOBER 9TH 1935

MR. O. I want to repeat something I said at some of the preceding lectures, for some of you have not heard it—if we work in the way we are working now it will need three hundred years to get any, even quite small, visible results. If we realize we have not got three hundred years, and if we want to get something, it is necessary to work with greater speed. What does it mean? It means that it is impossible to work theoretically. You remember about influences B and C. C is direct influence, by word of mouth. B influence can never become C influence, but C influence can easily become B. This means that you cannot reconstruct the system from books; you can only get fragments from books. C can easily be degraded. Work must be practical. Esoteric ideas that are not taken practically become mere philosophy, and this means simply intellectual gymnastics, leading nowhere.

What does it mean to work practically? It means to work not only on intellect, but also on emotions and on will. Work on intellect means to learn to think in a new way, creating new points of view, destroying illusions. Work on emotions means not expressing negative emotions, not identifying, not considering and, later on, also work on emotions themselves. Work on will; what does it mean? What is will in man No. 1, 2 and 3? It is resultant of desires. Will is the line of combined desires, and as our desires constantly change we have no permanent line. So ordinary will depends on desires, and desires can be very different; desire to do something and desire not to do something. Forms of manifestation of will in ordinary man are very definite. Man has no will, but only self-will and wilfulness.

We have to ask ourselves on what the will of man No. 7 could be based. It must be based on full consciousness, and this implies knowledge and understanding connected with objective consciousness, and a permanent 'I'. So three things are necessary: knowledge, consciousness and permanent 'I'. Only those people who have these three things can have a real will; that means will independent of all else and only based on consciousness, knowledge and a permanent 'I'.

Now ask yourselves on what is based self-will and wilfulness. It is very interesting that it it always based on opposition. Self-will is when, for instance, someone sees that a man does not know how to do a thing and says he will explain, and the man says, 'No, I myself will do it'. Self-will springs from opposition. Wilfulness is about the same, only more general. Wilfulness can be a kind of habit.

In order to study how to begin work on will, how to transform will, one has to give up one's will. This is a very dangerous expression if it is misunderstood. It is very important to understand rightly what to give up one's will means. The question is how to do it. First, one must try to connect and co-ordinate thoughts, words and actions with ideas, requirements and interests of the system. We have too many accidental thoughts which change the whole thing. If we want to be in the work we must verify all our thoughts, words and actions from the point of view of work. Some of them can harm the work. So if you want to work you are not free any more; you must lose the illusion of freedom.

The question is, have we freedom? Have we something to lose? The only freedom we have is to do harm to work and to people. By learning not to harm the work we learn not to harm ourselves, not to do irresponsible, unconnected actions. So we don't give up anything real.

In life one has no points of application of that; one does not know any work, so one cannot co-ordinate one's thoughts, words and actions. But when one begins to work, to a certain extent one already can.

Connect this idea with another idea—that time is counted. This means that requirements become different with time. At first, the only requirement is for people not to talk. After a certain time, understanding is demanded. There are two conditions then; not to believe anything and not to do anything unless one understands why and what one is doing.

After some time one comes to a position when nothing is independent of the work, when there are very few actions that are not connected with the work. It does not mean that one has to stop all activity, only one must not decide for oneself. One must not take the decision upon oneself, but one can ask somebody else's opinion. This does not refer to you at present. But time will come when responsibility will be taken from you. School gives the possibility not to be responsible. In that way you learn to keep a line, and this is how one creates will. If for a long time you work on a straight line, your will will go on a straight line afterwards. Will is created by repetition.

It is necessary to work on change of being. If you work on change of being as you do everything in ordinary life, life will be too short. It is possible to attain a durable change of being, such change as may possibly survive after death, only if we use the perfected methods of school-work. Otherwise our attempts are too scattered.

The first condition of such work is to know what to do and why.

Some people heard that, in connection with that, I gave a short history of the work.

Q. I don't understand how to give up will and, at the same time, not to do anything unless one understood.

MR. O. It is the same thing, exactly. It means, if you don't understand go and ask someone. If you don't understand whether it is right or wrong, ask. The first condition is that you must not do anything until you understand.

The change of these two principles was the cause why I parted with the original group.

I will give you a short history of the work. In the autumn of 1907 I met with some literature, books and people connected with very interesting ideas which were new to me. I remember one conversation in this connection. I said: 'If it were possible to accept as proven that consciousness can manifest itself apart from the physical body, many other things could be proved. Only it cannot be taken as proved.' I realized that clairvoyance, communication with the dead, and all such things are not proved. Some things may be true in it, some invented, but nothing proved.

I began to work on this line. I returned to old ideas that interested me ten years before, of higher dimensions and I took them not mathematically but psychologically. I began to read occult literature; I became very interested in Tarot, etc. Also, I made experiments and sometimes succeeded, but successful experiments could not be repeated, so they could not be taken as experiments in the right sense. I could not fix the results.

So I came to the conclusion that a school is necessary. It was at the time when the 'New Model' was finished that I came to the idea of the necessity of a school. So I went to India to find some Yogi schools. I stayed there till the beginning of the war. I found interesting things there, but not of the kind I wanted. I did not find a school as scientific as I wanted it, although I was convinced that they existed. The schools I found were more devotional schools, with the teacher and pupils grouped round this teacher, who believed everything he said and did what he told them to do. For this it was not necessary to go to India, for I could find schools of this kind in Russia. There were in Russia very good schools in some of the monasteries. But it was not my way. Also, I had peculiar suspicion of these devotional schools.

I returned to Russia with the idea that I had found something, but not what I wanted. I had an idea to go back to India after the war to continue looking for schools. That was the time when I thought that war will end soon. When I realized that war never ends, I abandoned the idea.

In Russia, I met in Moscow a small group, and very soon saw that it was a school. I began to work in it about 1915 and got many ideas there. The first principle of this school was to do nothing until you understood, and the result of every effort was measured by understanding. Understanding was the chief principle. One other principle was that one must not believe anything; everybody must verify everything, accept it or not accept but never act on faith. Another condition was that those conducting the school must keep people reasoning; not produce infatuation.

I worked there till 1918. There was a constant communication between Moscow and St. Petersburg, and then we all went to the Caucasus. In 1918 I parted with G. because something changed. He changed the first principles and demanded that people must believe, and must do what he tells them even if they don't understand. All people left him with the exception of four, of which three were new. Since then I came twice in contact with him and tried to help him, and it was only in the end of 1923 that I finally parted with him.

He was a Caucasian Greek, a very interesting man. He had travelled in Persia and Russian Central Asia, and had specially studied dervishes and sufis. Evidently he came into contact with a school that was not Eastern, and from this school he got his knowledge.

I speak about it partly in connection with questions people ask about Landau's book.

Some people say, how can I promise something if I don't know your final aim? I said, if you don't know the aim after two years, it is useless to continue. Aims were explained and should be quite clear. And the second—I don't want any promises. How can conditions and agreements be made with people <u>who are not</u>? They must begin to exist first. When something becomes permanent in them, and they begin to understand the work and its aims, then they can either go or continue. But there can be no promises. If people want to continue to study, they must accept certain conditions. This means they must make the study practical. Working on one side is not sufficient; one must work on all sides. If people do not take work seriously enough, it is a waste of time. You have a right to go away, and I have a right to stop lectures—so there are no obligations on either side. As a matter of fact, I want to write, and I cannot while I give my time to this. But this time is necessary, because it is the only way to establish a school. If I can say: 'If I die to-morrow, work will continue', it means a school is established. If it depends wholly on me, it means a school is not of sufficient strength.

And possibility of change of being is only with school-work and school discipline. For a certain period one must have that, and then one can work by oneself. School means people. People must have preparation. Things went wrong with G. because at first he was very strict in choosing people, but later he took people without any preparation.

Q. What are the conditions?

MR. O. There are no conditions, and there can be no conditions except one—try to understand what you are doing. It is better to do nothing than to do something without understanding.

Q. One cannot start on the second line until a school is started?

MR. O. It would be amateurish, and work on second line must be professional work. Also a school cannot exist on too small a scale. Only a certain number of people gives a sufficient variety of types. Particularly in England, and now, there is very little variety of types. For a successful group work, variety of types is necessary. Why is variety necessary? Otherwise there is no friction, no opposition; people would think they understood one another.

So at first I began with the idea of proving the existence of the miraculous. I found proofs, but came to the conclusion that a school is necessary. When I found a school, I came to the conclusion that one must change one's being. So you see, aim changes. First, I saw the necessity of proving certain facts; when

I proved them, this did not help. I found that a school is necessary; when I found it, I saw that one had to change being.

I also saw why I was suspicious in relation to devotional schools. For instance, Brunton found schools. He describes, very well, people, Yogis he met who could go into a trance etc. This is a very dangerous way. Bringing oneself into a trance means creation of imagination in higher emotional centre. And this is a blind alley. If you get there you cannot get out and cannot get any further. The idea is to control imagination. If, instead of that, by certain methods you transform it into imagination in higher emotional centre, you get bliss, happiness, but it is, after all, only sleep on a higher level. And there is no way out. Although I did not know the theory of it, I was suspicious about these emotional methods.

RULES

MR. O.   I want to speak about the principles and methods of the organization and work of schools—and particularly about rules—because without understanding them you will not be able to understand many other things about work.

Speaking generally, a school is a place where one can learn something. There can be schools of modern languages, schools of music, schools of medicine, etc., but the kind of school I mean is not only for learning but also for becoming different. Such a school must not only give knowledge but also help to change being; without that it would be just an ordinary philosophical school.

What makes a school? First of all it is understanding of the principles of school-work and second, discipline of a certain very definite kind connected with rules. When people come to lectures they are told about certain rules they must keep. These rules are conditions on which they are accepted and given knowledge. Keeping these rules or conditions is their first payment, and the first test.

One of the most important things in every kind of school is the idea of rules. If there are no rules, there is no school. Not even an imitation school can exist without rules. If it is an imitation school, there will be imitation rules, but there must be some kind of rules. One definition of a school is that a certain number of people accept certain rules and follow these rules, so rules are the first thing. It makes a very interesting subject of conversation between people if they meet together. I find that people do not think about the necessity for rules. People think about themselves as being connected with the work, but they don't understand the simplest rules. Rules are not for convenience, they are not for comfort—they are for inconvenience, for discomfort, and in that way they can help self-remembering.

You must understand that all rules are for self-remembering. First, they have a purpose in themselves; second, they are for self-remembering. There are no rules that are not for self-remembering, although in themselves they may have a different aim. If there are no rules, there is no work. If the importance of rules is not understood, the possibility of a school disappears.

Some people do not understand the very beginning of work; they do not think about work as work; they take it in the ordinary way. There is one thing which is necessary, obligatory, after a certain time, because one cannot work without it, and this is valuation. People want to work from one side, and from another side they want to take things in the same way as usual. If they want to work, then everything in reference to the work must be regarded differently, everything—and they think they can take things in the same way—that is the cause of it. What I find lacking is work, and understanding of work, and valuation of work. Valuation is lacking chiefly. Everything is taken for granted, and at the same time it is taken from an ordinary point of view, which changes nothing.

Much depends on personal attitude and personal work. An organization which is a school for one person is not a school for another.

Q.   If schools are real living things, why do they die?

MR. O.   What do you mean that schools are living things? It is vague and indefinite. But if we take it literally, it will make the reason why schools die quite clear. All living beings die sooner or later. If people die, schools must also die. It was explained in my lectures that schools need certain conditions. If these conditions are destroyed—the school is destroyed. If there was a school in Canton or Nankin now, it could be destroyed—it would cease to exist.

Q.   Ideas may remain.

MR. O.   Ideas cannot fly. They need human heads. And a

school does not consist of ideas. You always forget that school teaches how to improve our being.

Q.   Has communal life to do with organization of schools?

MR. O.   It depends what kind of communal life you mean. For instance, some time ago in Russia there existed the so-called Tolstoy colonies. Most of them had the same history. People decided to live together, bought some land and so on; then, after the first three days, they began to quarrel and it all came to nothing.

Q.   I meant a group of people who live in the same building.

MR. O.   It depends first of all on the condition by whom it is organized. If it is organized by themselves—it generally comes to nothing. But if it has been organized according to definite principles and with definite rules—in some cases it may be useful.

Q.   Is not to be able to go on with the system once one has started, worse than not to have started?

MR. O.   If you have really started nobody can stop you except yourself.

Q.   How can you reconcile this with what you said about there being no guarantee?

MR. O.   It depends on your work. How can I guarantee your work?

Q.   But facilities for work would remain—I mean, if a person does work?

MR. O.   Barring catastrophes. We live in insecure times.

About guarantee. What we can get depends on our own efforts and one must work at one's own risk. But after some time one begins to see: 'I got this that I did not have before', and 'I got that that I did not have before'. So, little by little, one can be more sure.

Q.   I suppose also you can give no guarantee as to whether people will suffer from some delusion as regards personal experience? One may take illusion for fact?

MR. O.   Yes, very easily; but if one remembers all that one is told one learns to discriminate, to be less under the power of illusion.

Q.   I saw the possibility of losing all that I had gained here and it frightened me. I wonder how to make this knowledge permanent in me.

MR. O.   It is a question of being—how much you acquire and how long you will be able to continue to work. It does not mean that work stops when war comes—it all depends on <u>you</u>. Nothing really changes. War has never stopped.

Q.   In order to work on being, is it necessary for us to occupy all our time during the day, not to have any spare time?

MR. O.   You begin with the impossible. Begin with the possible. Begin with one step, try to do a little, and results will show you. There is always a limit, you cannot do more than you can. If you try to do too much, you will do nothing. But little by little you will see that right thought, right attitudes are necessary. It needs time, because for so long people have been in the power of negative emotions, negative imagination and things like that. But little by little these will disappear. You cannot change everything at once.

Generally speaking, we know more about our knowledge than we know about our being. We know how little we know about ourselves; we know how, every moment, we make mistakes about everything; we know how we cannot foresee things, how we cannot understand people, how we cannot understand things; we know all that and it is all the result of our insufficient knowledge.

About our being we know, for instance, what the first sign of our being, the first idea of our being is—this plurality that we spoke about in the first lecture. We say 'I'—but this 'I' is different every moment. One moment I say 'I' and it is one 'I'; five minutes later I say 'I' and it is another 'I'. This is the state of our being. We are never one, and never the same. This is the beginning of the study of being, the study of plurality, the study of many 'I's in us, the study of useless functions, the study of negative emotions—this is all study of our being.

Q.   Does the study of our relations with other people help to understand being?

MR. O.   Certainly, yes. We understand, for instance, in relation to other people, our mechanical reactions. We decide to behave in a certain way to other people, and the next moment, or the next day, we behave in quite a different way.

Q.   Can we ever conceive of our being altogether as one thing?

MR. O.   No. We must always think about the next step—only one step. We can understand our being a little more collected than it is now: that we can understand. When we understand that, we can think of it a little more collected—but not completely, not finally.

Q. How does one develop one's being? Is it by attention, observing oneself and self-remembering?

MR. O. First, by knowing oneself; then by following all the practices advised, beginning with not expressing negative emotions, trying not to identify, struggling with imagination, trying to remember oneself. Try to remember what has been said. All that is the way for the development of being.

SHORT HISTORY OF THE WORK—LINES OF WORK
(N.D.)

MR. O. I have received many letters, and I cannot say that they show much understanding. The most important thing somehow escaped people. What I really said was that it is useless to go on if it is possible to say beforehand that one will not get anything. For one can get something only on certain conditions. The first condition is that one understands what one wants and how much one is prepared to pay for it. Because one has to pay for everything; everything one may get depends on a certain effort; nothing can be got for nothing. And in order to make this effort it is important to understand the conditions on which one can work. One must know what one is doing and why one is doing it, and what one can get by this effort. About material conditions we will speak later. Understanding is necessary above all. And first of all it is necessary to understand how to get understanding and what to understand.

I will give you a short history of the work. About twenty-eight years ago I met with a certain cycle of ideas which referred to the possibility of developing the latent powers in man. I remember one conversation on the subject. I said then: 'If it were possible to prove that man's consciousness (I would call it intelligence now) can work apart from the physical body, many things would be proved at once'. I began to read all the books I could find on these ideas; I returned to the ideas of dimensions which interested me before; I made experiments and got interesting results. Only I could not fix them; could not control these results. Finally, I became convinced that certain things exist but I could not command them; had no control over them. I became convinced that a school is necessary. So I went to the East to look for schools. I cannot say that I was entirely unsuccessful. I did find certain connections, but they were mostly devotional schools based on a very emotional attitude towards the teacher, and an acceptance of all one was told. I was not interested in such schools. But more reliable and psychologically sound schools I did not find.

When I returned to Russia I met with a small and very interesting school there. I liked the ideas of this school and little by little I discovered that these ideas were not an invention, but that they came from real school and were connected with real schools. The system shows that it came from higher mind, for it is based on ideas that cannot be found in ordinary science or philosophy. The original skeleton of the system obviously came from schools, and that means from higher mind.

I worked in this group till 1918, after which not only I, but also all the other people parted with this man. I will explain the reasons for this later. What I learned changed for me the idea of search for the miraculous. I understood that the cause of my comparative lack of success in my experiments and in my looking for a school was because these things cannot be studied by scientific methods. Scientific method presupposes an ordinary intellectual mind, and an ordinary intellectual mind cannot jump higher than itself. A higher mind is necessary. It is a question of change of being. On a certain level of being only certain things are possible. And one cannot change one's being for half an hour and then return to ordinary being. Also I understood why I did not like, or trust, devotional schools. In many ways it was cultivation of imagination. All these trance states, samadhi, etc., are imagination in higher emotional centre (or ordinary emotional centre). This leads to a blind alley from which it is impossible to pass to any higher experience.

So I realized that real work must be work on being, and that without work on being nothing can be done. But work on being requires understanding of aim, methods and the necessary conditions. There are two chief conditions in the work:

1. One must not believe anything, one must verify everything.

2. An even more important condition that refers to 'doing'—one must not do anything until one understands why and for what purpose one is doing it.

These two principles must be understood. It is true that one may realize that one does not know anything and does not know what to do, and one may ask for advice and may be told what to do. But that happens only in very favourable circumstances, and then, if one asks, one has to do it. If one asks and does not do it, one loses the possibility of asking another time.

The reason why I and the others parted with the original group was because although in the beginning these two principles that one can have no 'faith' and that one should not do anything until one understood, were very emphasized, later this man changed and demanded that people should believe him and do things without understanding.

Then it is necessary to understand about three lines. The first line is self-study and study of the system; the second—work with people, and the third—work for the school. You must understand that work on the second line does not depend on you. You cannot start work on the second line unless some special conditions are organized for you. You cannot organize work on the second line for youself. It cannot be a personal enterprise.

In relation to the third line it is very important to understand the general idea of why this work exists and how to help it. The idea is to establish a school, that is, work according to school rules and principles, first studying these school rules and principles and then applying them in practice. Many conditions are necessary for that. One condition—naturally, people are necessary. There are people who are prepared, who are capable of developing these ideas, but they do not know these ideas. So it is necessary to find them; find the right kind of people and give them these ideas. But for that one must oneself understand them.

The material question is certainly also necessary. Work needs money like any other work, any other enterprise. I will explain how this side is organized. Twenty years ago it was proved that one cannot establish a definite payment, because some people cannot pay; others can pay only very little. So it was decided that everyone pays as much as he can. No one was ever refused because he could not pay, but this was possible only because others paid. The principle is this: all who pay, pay for the past, but never in advance. So a sufficient time passes until they are allowed to pay. Also, those who pay cannot make any conditions or stipulations.

You remember about the staircase. The path does not begin on the level of life. Between ordinary life and the path there is a staircase, and the condition of going up this staircase is that if one wants to go up to the next step one must put someone else on his step. People often asked what this meant. This means work in connection with school—bringing people, finding means for the school, etc. You had now a year, at least those who came last September. You were able to come and study because it was all organized and financed by others who came before you. In this way they put you in their place.

The aim of the work is to establish a school. In it we may have many lines of investigation, scientific, psychological, etc. These lines will show themselves when people with a certain particular preparation will come and begin to be interested.

MISS S.   It is very difficult to believe nothing; always to test all statements.

MR. O.   What does it mean to believe? One can either take everything at once without verifying, or one can verify. I always explain which theories can be verified and which cannot, except by analogy. Some you can prove directly, some only by analogy, so at first they have to be taken as hypotheses. But in neither case must you believe.

It was very interesting that, although the direction was right in the cycle of ideas with which I met first the 'study of latent powers in man' was taken too far. All those things of which they spoke, all those powers, exist, but not for us. We may come to that level only on certain conditions.

MISS P.   What are those conditions?

MR. O.   Self-remembering. And that means also not identifying, not considering, no negative emotions, not being in the power of imagination, not being in the power of imaginary 'I'—many things.

MISS C.   Where do the Law of Three and Law of Seven come from?

MR. O.   They come from school. But you must not value ideas by their reputation but by their real value.

MISS C.   I was wondering if it was taken from the Bible.

MR. O.   It could not be got from the Bible. The Law of Seven helps to understand mechanicalness in life. Neither the idea of octaves nor the idea of triads could be invented. . . .

MR. C.   Concerning work on the second line—is it necessary to ask for an opportunity?

MR. O.   Everybody is given the opportunity, only it needs organized work.

MR. H.   Is any work on oneself possible without the second line?

MR. O.   You start on the first line. Then the second and third lines help the first. Each line helps the other lines.

Sometimes people themselves put things in such a way, or ask questions in such a way, that it becomes clear that there is no need for them to continue. For instance, one man asked whether he could also study other systems at the same time as this. So he has to go and wait till he has studied other systems and becomes satisfied or dissatisfied with them. By his question he has already made a choice. You must not mix things up. Although even charlatanic systems are useful to study if you know that they are charlatanic and if you are not identified.

Our work can, in short, be described like that: we will study systems, both recognized and hidden. We will make a certain choice and will study only those which have as their origin the idea of possibility of inner development of man. Only these systems are interesting. On others there is no use to spend our time, since they miss the most important thing. For only one thing is important—possibility of development, of change. If we remain as we are, there is no use to study. We are machines moved by circumstances. So our field of study is clearly delineated and sufficiently broad, but it has to be very exclusive. We cannot include everything in it.

Another person said that she does not need esoteric study or work on second and third line. She is only interested in psychological study. But psychology is not opposed to esotericism. And the first line is even more esoteric than the others. They all come from schools, and the second and third lines are only a help.

Last time I spoke about will. First it is necessary to understand what is will. We have no will: we only have self-will and wilfulness. Self-will is self-assertion. Wilfulness is going against something, against rules, etc. Both include a kind of opposition to something, and in that form they exist. Man has no original will than can exist without opposition and that is permanent. That is why it is necessary to subjugate it. This subjugation trains it so that afterwards it can follow a definite line. When will becomes strong enough, it is no longer necessary to limit it. So will cannot be left as it is. Now it runs in all directions. It has to be trained, and in order to train will one has to do many unpleasant things, such as, for instance, physical work. It was found by experience that physical work is very useful in school. Later, we tried to organize for people to live and work together. This gives an opportunity to study other people. In some schools there are some special physical exercises, but, in the absence of those, physical work takes their part. But all this refers to the second line; it must be organized work.

MR. D.   Were you referring, in speaking of the second line, to the fact that we cannot 'do'?

MR. O.   We cannot 'do' generally. But an individual person cannot organize work on the second line for himself; it must be arranged.

MR. H.   Training of will is going against desires. I find that when I enter an untidy room, I get angry. Should I work against the expression of this?

MR. O.   Yes, you must always work against the expression of negative emotions. But why do you get angry? Irritation is always a reaction to the mechanicalness of other people. But you can study the mechanicalness of yourself. All you can do in your case is to study the cause; find a right attitude; go against the expression of negative emotions.

Prepare questions for next time only in connection with what I said. We must first establish attitudes. I must see whether for each of you it is worth while going on, or whether it is better to wait.

MRS. W.   Shall we be told how we can help financially?

MR. O.   People subscribe in January generally, or at some other time. If you want to send money, Madame K. will give you the address. But you must not think it is a condition. Only later it becomes a condition. It is quite free. At the same time, if everybody will think that others will do it, sooner or later we would have to close.

MISS M.   What kind of physical work was suggested?

MR. O.   Nothing is suggested. I said that it must be organized.

MR. S.   Could one have an illustration (about physical work)? Candidly, I don't understand.

MR. O.   I don't know how to explain it. Any kind of physical work. I remember the first time in the Caucasus I had to carry all the luggage to the third story. It was very good physical work. The idea is this: when a certain number of people work together, in the house, in the garden, with animals, etc., it is not easy. Individually they can work, but working together is difficult. They are critical of one another; they get in one another's way; they take things from one another. It is very good help for self-remembering. But it is not work that one can organize by oneself. If one is interested in the idea one can get into the existing work. But only when one feels the necessity for it. You must not think it is some kind of magic help.

MR. H. What do you mean by work on the third line? Trying to interest other people?

MR. O. If you know the right people—good. In some cases you can try; in some cases it is better to ask me first. I don't know yet when we will have new lectures.

MR. L. May we speak about lectures then?

MR. O. Better ask me first whether there are to be new lectures in the near future. In some cases it is better not to speak to people before you ask me. There are certain rules connected with this. For instance, people who were in groups once cannot come again. So something must be found out about people first.

Q. You said we must not have faith, and New Testament speaks of faith.

MR. O. There is faith and faith. Faith in New Testament is a higher emotion, just like love—it is emotion in higher centres. New Testament is written in a strange way; the levels are mixed there for a certain purpose, because it is for school use. It is said—we must have faith. But how can we? In its full sense faith is a positive emotion. Imitation of it is only superstition or believing instead of verifying. In some cases it is simply laziness of mind.

Next time will be on Wednesday. You must understand that we continue only so long as it is useful. So you must ask questions. Later, I will divide people into small groups which will meet with older members and talk on special questions. Later, there may be reading, in about a month's time. Try to prepare questions in connection with what I said.

WHAT IS STUDY?

MR. O. What is study? From the ordinary point of view, to study means to study things as they are. For instance, a table is studied as it is. The idea of an improvement on a table does not enter into it.

In the system the idea of study is necessarily connected with the idea of improvement. We can use very little of our powers.

Study develops our powers. Man has the right to be self-conscious even such as he is without any change. Objective consciousness requires many different changes in him, but self-consciousness he can have now. In studying, one will see that man lives below the normal level. If one studies in the right way one changes. Change must be the aim.

In the beginning you will meet with many contradictions in man. Man is not always the same even in his ordinary state, he is always changing. By studying these changes he can learn about the possibility of further changes. Man is a machine, yet he is a bicycle that can become a motor car, and a motor car that can become an aeroplane. In such a machine there are bound to be contradictions; from one side it is so, and from another side it is different. Analogies cannot be complete because they cannot be continued indefinitely. Man is a machine because he is only a transmitting station; he cannot produce anything—any action from himself—without an external cause for it. But in his present state he is not even a rightly working machine.

In all this strange combination that is man the one thing that can be changed is consciousness. Actually, man can be more conscious. But first he must realize that he is a machine, so as to be able to tighten some screws, loosen others, and so on. He must study; that is where the possibility of change begins. When he realizes that he is a machine, and when he knows something about this machine, he will realize that the machine can work in different conditions of consciousness, and he will try to give it these better conditions of consciousness.

We are told that man has the possibility of living in four states of consciousness but that, as he is, he lives only in two. We also know that our functions are divided into four categories. So we study four categories of functions in two states of consciousness. At the same time, we realize that glimpses of self-consciousness happen, and that what prevents us from having more of these glimpses is the fact that we don't remember ourselves—that we are asleep.

The first thing necessary in a serious study of oneself is to understand about different states of consciousness and also the fact that consciousness has degrees. You must remember that you do not pass from one state of consciousness to another, but that they are added the one to the other. This means that if you are in the state of sleep, when you awake, the state of 'waking sleep' is added to the state of sleep; if you become self-conscious this is added to the state of 'waking sleep'; and when you acquire the state of objective consciousness, this is added to the state of self-consciousness. There is no sharp transition from one state to another state. Why not? Because each state consists of different layers. As in sleep, you can be more asleep or less asleep, so in the state in which we are now, you can be nearer to self-consciousness or further from it.

The second thing necessary in a serious study of oneself is to study functions by observing them, learning to divide them in the right way, learning to recognize each one separately. Each function has its own profession, its speciality. They must be studied separately and their difference clearly understood, remembering that they are controlled by the different centres. We have no means of seeing centres, but we can observe functions. By observing them you see that they are different; the more you observe, the more material you will have.

This division of functions is very important. Control of any of our faculties can only be obtained with the help of knowledge. Each function can be controlled only if we know the peculiarities and the speed of each of them.

Observation of functions must be connected with the study of states of consciousness and degrees of consciousness. It is necessary to understand that consciousness and functions are quite different things. To move, to think, to have sensations, to feel—these are functions; they can work quite independently from being conscious, they can work mechanically. To be conscious is something quite different. But if we are more conscious it immediately increases the sharpness of our functions.

You remember the illustration that was given of different machines working in varying degrees of light? Machines are such that they can work better with light than in the darkness; every moment when there is more light, machines work better. Consciousness is light and machines are functions. We cannot increase the light, we have no switch. We have no control over light, but we can have a certain control over the machines, at least over some of them.

Observing of functions is long work. It is necessary to find many examples of each. In studying, we begin to see that we cannot study everything on the same level, that we cannot observe ourselves impartially. Unavoidably we see that some functions are right and others undesirable from the point of view of our aim. And we must have an aim, otherwise no study can have any result. If we realize we are asleep, the aim is to awake; if we realize we are machines, the aim is to cease being machines. If we want to be more conscious, we must study what prevents us from remembering ourselves. So we have to introduce a certain valuation of functions from the point of view of whether they are useful or harmful for self-remembering.

Self-remembering is effort on functions. You begin to remember yourself with your mind, because we have a certain control over our mental processes and can form our thoughts in a certain way, and this formation of mental processes brings moments of consciousness. You cannot make efforts on consciousness directly, but you can make efforts on thoughts. If you continue to make these efforts, moments of consciousness will come more often and stay longer. Then, gradually, self-remembering ceases to be purely intellectual—it has an awakening power.

Q. Why should moments of consciousness be so rare?

MR. O. No fuel. If you have no electricity, or if you have a pocket torch, you may have a flash and then nothing—bad battery. Consciousness is light; light is the result of certain energy; if there is no energy there is no light.

Q. Would it be correct to say that the secret of all development in consciousness lies in the conservation and control of energy?

MR. O. No, not all the secret, though conservation and increase of energy is very important. But this in itself is not enough; one has to know how to control it. Energy is the mechanical side of consciousness.

Q. How can one learn to control energy better?

MR. O. We cannot begin with the idea of control. In order to control one small thing we must know the whole machine. First we must control ourselves from the point of view of consciousness; we must try to remember ourselves. Then, we have to stop unnecessary waste of energy. We waste energy in imagination, considering, lying, identifying, expressing negative emotions, idle talk. These are the chief leaks. So first of all we have to stop the leaks that waste energy; second, collect energy by self-remembering; then, adjust things. We cannot begin in any other way.

Q. Can energy be stored?

MR. O. Yes, energy can be stored when you are able to store it. But at present the question is not about storing but about not wasting. We would have enough energy for everything we want to do if we didn't waste it on unnecessary things. These were already spoken about—identification, negative emotions, many mechanical actions; but the worst of all is expressing negative emotions. If you can stop the expression of negative emotions, you will save energy so that you will never feel the lack of it.

We can only hope to become conscious beings if we use in the right way the energy that is now used in the wrong way. The machine can produce enough energy. But you can waste it on being angry or irritated or something like that, and then very little remains. The normal organism produces quite enough energy not only for all centres but also for storing. Production is all right, but spending is wrong.

Q. Can one by conscious effort create energy?

MR. O. What do you mean by that? Energy is created naturally by the three kinds of food. By self-remembering we can increase the production of higher matters. By struggle with negative emotions we can increase this still more. But we cannot create out of nothing. Even God himself cannot do that.

Q. When you spoke about adjusting things, did you mean trying to make centres work better? What will gude them to this better working?

MR. O. All work on yourself—self-study, self-knowledge, self-remembering. First we have to learn to know the machine and then we learn to control it. We have to readjust functions so that each does its own rightful work. Most of our activity consists of one centre doing the work of another centre; our incapacity to reach our normal level lies in our incapacity to make our centres work rightly. Many of the inexplicable things we observe are due to wrong work of centres.

Q. Does wrong work of centres mean interference one with another?

MR. O. There are two forms of wrong work of centres. Either they interfere, that is, one works instead of another, or one takes energy from another.

Sometimes centres have to work for each other. If, for some reason or other, one centre stops, the machine is so arranged that another centre can continue its work for a time—only, much worse, of course—in order to avoid interruptions. The original idea of such an arrangement is quite right, but in actual life it became the cause of mental and physical disturbances, because intellectual centre cannot work properly for moving or instinctive, and moving centre cannot work for intellectual. But in the state of identifying they like to do that. They like to do wrong work and not to do their own work. It had become a kind of bad habit, and by mixing functions they began to mix energies, trying to get more potent energies for which they are not adapted.

WORK ON ONESELF. FEBRUARY 3RD 1938

Q. Does work on oneself gather momentum after a time, or remain equally difficult? Like pushing a cart uphill.
Mr. O.   I think it becomes more difficult, because it is coming to more and more ramifications. You start on one line, then after some time on three lines, and each divides and divides and divides, and all the time requires attention and effort. There is no inertia in this action. That is a different triad.

On the other hand, one acquires more energy, becomes more conscious, and that makes it easier in a sense, but work by itself can never become easier.

STATES OF CONSCIOUSNESS AND PHYSICAL ALERTNESS. FEBRUARY 10TH 1938

Q. Are states of higher consciousness essentially accompanied by physical alertness? I know, for instance, that one cannot self-remember when physically asleep or anywhere near it.
Mr. O. In most cases, yes. One becomes more alert in all centres.
Q. Is inner awareness a matter of mind or emotion or both?
Mr. O. Of more even than that. Instinctive feeling and moving feeling.

In relation to the first question, about physical alertness, it is very difficult to make a general statement about that, because in some cases higher states of consciousness can produce trance states. That happens in two cases. First, when it is intentionally done like that, for the purpose of saving energy or something like that. Secondly, when wrong methods are used, wrong school. There are many schools which can produce higher states of consciousness only with a condition of physical half-paralysis, trance. Generally, this is wrong, because it cannot be done otherwise. Sometimes this can be quite right way when they can do it this way and in another way.

Sometimes to the casual observer it may look different from physical alertness.

WORK. JANUARY 13TH 1939

Q. What does MR. O. mean by 'work'?

MR. O. Work is a word of very large meaning. First, self-study is work. Coming to lectures is work. But 'work' in the system sense means work either for acquiring knowledge or for study of change of being. In any case you have to have some quite clear objective, and not only work for self-study and self-control or something like that. So in our sense 'work' includes acquiring knowledge and acquiring control of oneself.

Q. What formula would define most precisely the objective that all members of all groups have in common?

MR. O. I have already said that they want to know themselves, and they want to acquire control. The first idea is to know, and the second is to acquire control of oneself.

Q. Is it right to assume that all members have a common objective?

MR. O. In that sense, yes, otherwise they would not be in the same work. All the people who are connected with it have to work on certain definite lines, otherwise there is no meaning in it and it cannot go on. The direction must always be the same, so people who are not interested in this direction, and whose aims are not the same, go away. For those who stay, their aim must be the same.

Q. I think the general experience is that early contact with the system brings more destruction than construction.

MR. O. From my point of view, the idea of construction and destruction is wrong. Nothing is destroyed, but if we imagine that we have something that we do not have, then when we begin to work we may begin to see that we thought we had something but now find that we have not. This means it is an illusion, and we have to sacrifice it. We can have real things or illusions; that is how it is, and we lose nothing that we really possess; we only lose the idea that we possess something that we do not possess.

It often happens that many people become disappointed in the work because, from the very beginning, they begin to choose and take some things and not others, and so, after some time, they have not the system but their own selection from it, and this won't work. Other people want to understand only intellectually and do not want to make experiments on themselves and observe—they only want to think intellectually, but that is impossible, so you cannot take everything on the same level.

Q.   Shall we be told when we can start practical work?

Mr. O.   From the very first you have been doing some practical work. If you had done only theoretical work, that would mean you have done nothing. First, you must observe that you don't remember yourself and observe centres. This work is practical from the first.

The first condition of the work is that we must never forget our original aim—what we want to get. People come from different sides. Some want to know. They realize there is a certain knowledge and that maybe there are, somewhere, people who know, and they want to get this knowledge. Other people realize their weakness and understand that if they can get rid of weakness things will be different. So people come from different sides, and they must never forget the beginning. They can be reminded, but that won't help much if they don't remember themselves.

Q.   Is the development of a man with a very good intellect, bound to be quicker than that of another whose intellect is not so good?

Mr. O.   Sometimes yes, sometimes no; not so much can be done with intellect as by balance of centres and development of consciousness, because even in the ordinary state man 1, 2 and 3 can be more or less awake, more or less conscious, so to speak. Man with a very good intellect can be quite asleep, and then he may not start work, because he may be so sure and so identified with his own intellectual work that he will not start real work. So his intellect will stop him. That happens often.

Q.   Would you say suffering is to some extend essential for attaining change of being?

Mr. O.   Yes, certainly, but it depends how you understand suffering. We get nothing by pleasure; from that we can only get suffering. If we get enough suffering by pleasure, then it may be useful, but by pleasure we cannot get much. Every effort is suffering; every realization is suffering because there are many unpleasant realizations about ourselves and about everything like that, and there are many forms of suffering. And again some sufferings are unnecessary, and with some sufferings we must learn not to identify, so attitude towards suffering must be very complicated. But certainly suffering is necessary, and sometimes it happens that people cannot work because they are afraid of suffering. In most cases this is imaginary suffering.

INCREASING DESIRE TO WORK

Q. I want to know how to increase my desire to work.
MR. O. It is impossible to answer this question, because only you can know how to increase your valuation of the work. You must think; you must compare ordinary ideas with these ideas; you must try to find in what sense these ideas help you. It is impossible to give a general description. Everything we do in the work has this tendency to increase valuation. So try not to miss anything that is given, because all the ideas have this aim. Every principle will increase your desire to work; it cannot diminish it. But there is no special work for this, and there cannot be. It is necessary to realize that we are asleep, then this desire will come.
Q. I wonder if, as much as one desires other things in life, it takes away from one's desire to work?
MR. O. Not necessarily. There are many things we can have in life, and yet work. It is quite wrong to think they are always contradictory—though they may be contradictory. One may desire such things in life as make work impossible in one or another way. Suppose one desires things that will make one go to New Zealand, then one cannot have that and work in London. But if you want things in London, there is no reason why you should not continue to work. So one must learn to choose between desires. Certainly some things are impossible. It is formatory to divide things in life and things in the work and to put everything together, as you do. It is necessary to divide better, to see better.

DIRECTION OF THE WORK

MR. O. Speaking in general about work, about possibilities, about direction of the work, it was explained like this. First, one must realize one is asleep; second, one must awake. One awakes; one can die. When one dies, one can be born. That is the direction. It is useful to think about it, useful to understand what sleep means, what to awake means, what to die means and what it means to be born. And suppose we want to be born. We cannot be born until we die. We cannot die until we awake. We cannot awake until we realize we are asleep. So there are definite steps.

Q. What does 'to die' mean, in the sense of which you speak?

MR. O. 'To die' means to die, to disappear, not to be, not to exist. In several places in the New Testament it is written that until a grain dies it cannot be born. It is the same thing. It is useless to die in sleep; then one cannot be born. One must awake first. I said, <u>first</u>, realization of sleep; <u>second</u>, awakening. Other things come later.

THREE LINES OF WORK

Q. If three lines of work are necessary to work on oneself and conditions make it impossible, what can one do?

MR. O. Theoretically nothing, but practically one can begin with one line, and one generally does, and not always the right line. Then three lines come in gradually.

Q. But then the interval comes and we cannot continue.

MR. O. Why not? It will be more difficult, but intervals must not be taken as fate.

Q. If two people try to help each other, will that be second line?

MR. O. No. In the second line there is no initiative. But there must be a certain preparation. One must have understanding of the necessity of working with people. Most people think that it would be easier to work alone. When you begin to understand that that is physically impossible, that only because of these other people can you work yourself, that will be understanding, but it will not be second line. You must understand that the people you meet are as necessary to you as the system itself. Then you can do something. This will be a beginning.

Q. It seems to me I cannot do second line of work unless I am doing first line, and that third line must also contain first line.

MR. O. Please, please, please, please. About ten thousand times

I have said don't mix theoretical and practical matters. What do you mean by the second line of work?

Q. Work with other people.

Mr. O. Work means action. If you are in the same room with other people, this is not work. You don't know what second line of work is. Theoretically, work with other people is second line. It does not mean being in the same room with other people or doing the same work.

EFFORT. JANUARY 16TH 1940

Q. I have always thought that there is some virtue in doing a thing only because it is unpleasant and I don't want to do it.

Mr. O. No. There are many unpleasant things. You can make many efforts which are quite useless. This is a wrong point.

17. 1. 40

Q. How can I make better use of moments when I feel the miraculousness of the system?

Mr. O. Make more regular efforts, not occasional efforts.

Q. I cannot make even quite small efforts at will. How can I realize more fully that this is the case?

Mr. O. You can do nothing about it—you must begin with small efforts.

8
Will

. . . There are two things it is important to realize: we cannot 'do' and we live under the Law of Accident. In most cases people think they can 'do', they can get what they want and it is only accidental that they don't. About accident people think that it is very rare, that mostly it is cause and effect. This is quite wrong. It is necessary to learn to think in the right way. Then we will see that everything happens, and that we live under the Law of Accident.

People mix up octaves and crossings. The point of meeting of octaves is accidental. In relation to 'doing' it is difficult to realize that when people build a bridge, it is not 'doing'; it is only the result of all previous efforts. It is accidental.

Q.   But if they want to build it and it does get built?

MR. O.   It looks like it. You must think of the first bridge that Adam built and all the evolutions of bridge. At first it is accidental—a tree fell across a river, then man built something like that, and so on, and so on. People are not 'doing'. One thing comes from another.

Q.   But it is their doing when people try to become conscious?

MR. O.   Yes; then one sees that one cannot. In trying to become conscious all man's work is his own. In building a bridge he is using previous experience.

Q.   Is not inventing, 'doing'?

MR. O.   It is the result of what was prepared.

Q.   Isn't the added thing to former attempts the most important?

MR. O.   It is a small thing, associative, guessing. Even inventions are accidental.

Q.   You mean that bridge is one thing and effort another? When they come together, it is accidental?

MR. O.   No. I am trying to say that if there was no bridge

before and you built it, it would be 'doing'. Building a bridge is the agglomeration of accident, agglomeration of failures.

EFFORT

Q.   We are told we must use effort. What is meant by effort? In the ordinary way of thinking, effort is produced by will and followed by result (will-effort-achievement). How is one to reconcile that 'one has no will', 'one cannot do' with 'one must use effort', 'one must work on oneself'—in fact, apply energetic purposeful action? What comes before effort and what follows? Effort alone is just a word.

MR. O.   It is difficult to answer all at once. Our will is simply a resultant of desires. Will shows direction. In an ordinary man will follows a zigzag line, or goes in a circle. Will shows the direction of efforts. Effort is our money. We must pay with effort. According to the strength of effort and the time of effort (in the sense, whether it is the right time for the effort or not), we obtain results. Effort needs knowledge, the knowledge of moments when effort is useful. When the octave proceeds by itself, effort cannot help. It is necessary to learn by long practice how to produce and apply effort.

Q.   You talk about making efforts. It comes down to that the desire to make effort should arise occasionally, from time to time.

MR. O.   Not desire, but realization of the necessity.

Q.   What is the right time for making efforts?

MR. O.   The efforts we can do are efforts of self-observation and self-remembering. When people hear about efforts, they think about efforts of doing. That would be lost effort, or wrong effort. But effort of self-observation and self-remembering is right effort because it can give right results.

Q.   How can a man change, then?

MR. O.   He cannot change so long as he remains under the laws of mechanical life. The beginning of possibilities begins with the first step (in the diagram of 'Life, the Staircase and the Way').

Q.   What is man No. 4?

MR. O.   Man No. 4 has direction.

Q.   Is he a man who begins to work out of the laws?

MR. O.   All this means degrees. A man who lives in the outer circle is under the Law of Accident. Or, if a man has a strongly expressed essence or type, his life goes on under the laws of his type, or the laws of fate. But this is not an advantage. When a man begins to work towards consciousness, <u>this</u> creates in him a quantity of new triads (new actions). This means change, perhaps not perceptible, but still cosmically a change.

Only individual efforts can help man to pass from the outer circle into the exoteric circle. What refers to a man in the outer circle does not refer to a man who begins to work. He is under different laws, or rather, different laws begin to touch a man who begins to work.

Each circle is under different laws.

SELF-WILL. GIVING UP ONE'S WILL. OCTOBER 10TH 1935

MR. O. About the idea of giving up one's will: it is more an expression. Man 1, 2, 3 has no will, only self-will and wilfulness. Try to understand what it means. Wilful means when one wants or does something forbidden, because it is forbidden. Self-will is, for instance, when someone sees you are trying to do something you don't know how to do and wants to help you, but you say, 'No, I will do it myself'. These are the two types of will we have. They are based on opposition. Real will must depend on consciousness, knowledge and permanent 'I'. Such as we are, we have not got it. All we have is self-will and wilfulness. Our will is a resultant of desires. Desires may be very well hidden. For instance, a man may want to criticise someone, and calls it sincerity. But the desire to do so may be so strong that he must make a really big effort to stop it, and a man cannot make real efforts by himself.

In order to create will, man must try to co-ordinate his every action with ideas of the work; he must in every action ask himself: how will it look from the point of view of the work? Is it useful or harmful to me, or to the work? If he does not know, he can ask. If a man has been long in the work, there is practically not a single action that does not touch upon the work—there are no independent actions. In that way one is not free, in the sense that one cannot act foolishly and without discrimination. One must think before one acts. If one is not sure, one can ask. This is the only method by which will can be created.

And for that, school organization is necessary. Without school one can do nothing.

Q. What does giving up will mean?

MR. O. Giving up childishness, inefficiency, lying.

16. 10. 35

Q. Is it a law that if you give up self-will you always get the desired thing? It always happens with me: you want something, you feel a tremendous opposition from other people, you give up the desire and then you get the desired result.

MR. O. This is not self-will. You took certain things for granted. Indefinite things you made definite and definite things, indefinite. What is self-will? It does not mean everything you want. If I am hungry and want to eat, this is not self-will. Self-will is will of a particular kind—preferring to act by one-self; in our case—not taking into consideration the work and the principles of the work. We speak of principles of the work and self-will. We can do things in our own way or not. If my self-will is to swear and I give it up because it is against the principles of the work, where are the desired results you speak of?

Q. How can we work against self-will? Is it possible for us, as we are, to recognize the moments when we have real will?

MR. O. Not real will; we cannot have that. All we have is self-will and wilfulness, or small wills that change all the time. Real will is very far; it is based on permanent 'I', consciousness and individuality. We have not got it. And about how we can work against self-will—you can study the system. There are certain demands in the system; things you must not do or must do. For instance, you must not talk, because if you do you will only tell lies. You cannot speak about the system before you know and understand. In this way, from the very beginning, you meet with ideas of the work opposed to self-will. If you forget about the work, you don't work against self-will. The only way to struggle against self-will is to remember the work. It may be that at one moment the work does not enter at all, but at another moment it does enter, and then you can understand what it means to give up self-will. Ask yourself: is it right from the point of view of the work or not? This is struggle against self-will.

Q. Could you explain more about giving up self-will to will, and how it is possible to help start this?

MR. O.   This is rather a wrong expression—to give up will. In ordinary thinking it implies three things. First it implies that giving up will is a permanent thing. 'If we give up our will, what remains to us?' But people have no will to give up. In the best case will may exist only for a few minutes. So you can give up not all will but only a few minutes of it. And if somebody you give up your will to will agree to take it, he will take only about three minutes of it. Will is measured by time. You can give up only a moment of will.

The second thing is that people usually think it means doing something they don't want to do, but in most cases it is not doing that which one wants to do. This is very different.

The third thing is to avoid thinking in extremes; imagining the most difficult cases. Start with simple, ordinary cases. Giving up will means only remembering about the work, giving it up to demands, principles and rules of the work. This way you learn how to create will; this is the method of developing it. Giving up will is really developing will.

Q. I understand that the will to be given up is the self-will of temporary 'I's, and that the resistance to this self-will must come from the observing 'I'. Is the observing 'I' the embryo of permanent 'I'?

MR. O.   Observing 'I' is the embryo of permanent 'I', but it has no will. Its will is not opposed to self-will. What can be opposed to self-will? There are only two things opposed to one another: work and self-will. Self-will wants to talk; there is a rule against talk. A struggle results, and the result will be according to which of the two conquers.

Q. Isn't stopping the expression of negative emotions more or less the same thing as giving up wilfulness?

MR. O.   Why do you want to translate one thing into another? Wilfulness may have many forms without a definite connection with negative emotions.

17. 10. 35

Q. Does giving up self-will involve giving up your own judgment?

MR. O.   It depends in what. What does giving up will mean?

How can it be achieved? It is very important to remember what I say. You make three mistakes about it. First—you think it is a final action: you give up will and you have no more will. This is an illusion. We have no such will to give up. Our wills last for about three minutes. Will is measured by time. If once we give up three minutes of will, to-morrow another three minutes will grow. Giving up will is a continuous process, not one action. A single action means nothing.

The second point is remembering certain principles to which you give up will; for instance, remembering rules. For example, there is a rule not to talk about the system; the natural desire is to talk. If you stop yourself, it means you give up your will; you obey this rule. There are many other principles where, in order to follow them, you must give up your will.

Q. Does giving up one's will mean not to act without understanding?

Mr. O. You see, it is again about the same thing. We often think that giving up will means <u>doing</u> something. This happens very seldom. In most cases you are told not to do something. There is a great difference in this. For instance, you want to explain to someone what you think of him, and must not do it. It is a question of training. Will can be grown if man works on himself and makes his will obey the principles of the work. Things that do not concern the work cannot be connected with it. But the more you enter into the work, the more things begin to touch upon the work. But this needs time.

WILL

Usually, we have bad will. We very seldom have good will. You don't know how to think about this question. On one side you realize you are machines, but the next moment you want to act according to your own opinion. Then, at this moment you must be able to stop; you must be able not to do what you want. But this does not apply to moments when you have no intention of doing anything. It is when you find yourself going against rules, or principles, or against what you have been told that you must be able to stop. If often happens that people go on studying and miss these moments. They think they are working if nothing happens, and when such moments come, they miss them. Work cannot always be the same. At one moment passive study—

theories—are sufficient. At another moment it is necessary to oppose your movement, to stop.

WE CANNOT DO. JANUARY 11TH 1939

MR. O. It is important to remember that we can do nothing. If you remember that, you will remember many other things. Generally, there are three or four chief stumbling-blocks, and if one does not fall over one, one falls over another one of these. Doing is one of them. There are some fundamental principles which you must never forget. For instance, that you must look at yourself and not at other people; that people can do nothing by themselves, but, if it is possible to change, it is only with the help of the system, organization, and people's own work, study of the system. One must find things like that and remember them.

Q. How can one make sure of remembering them?

MR. O. Imagine starting to make plans to do something. It is only when you really try to do something differently from the way it happens that you realize it is absolutely impossible to do differently. Enormous effort is necessary to change even one small thing. Until you try you can never realize it. You can change nothing, except through the system. This is generally forgotten. Half of the questions are always about doing—how to change this, destroy that, avoid that and so on.

Q. Can you make it clearer about the importance of remembering that we cannot do?

MR. O. Everything happens. People can do nothing. From the time we are born to the time we die things happen, happen, happen, and we think we are doing. This is our ordinary normal state in life, and even the smallest possibility to do something comes only through the work, and first only in oneself, not externally. Even in oneself doing very often begins by not doing. Before you can do something that you cannot do, you <u>must not do</u> many things which you did before. You cannot awake just by wanting to awake, but you can prevent yourself, for instance, from sleeping too long or something like that.

Q. Does one sometimes have a choice between two possible happenings?

MR. O. In very small things. And even then, if you notice that things are going in a certain way and decide to change them, you will find how awfully uncomfortable it is to change things. And so you come back to the same things.

Q. When one really begins to understand that one cannot do, one will need a great deal of courage. Will that come from getting rid of false personality?

MR. O. One does not come to this understanding just like that. It comes after some time of work on oneself, so that when one comes to this realization one has many other realizations besides, chiefly that there are ways to change if one applies the right instrument at the right place and at the right time. One must have these instruments, and these again are only given by work. It is <u>very</u>, <u>very</u> important to come to this realization. Before this one will not do the right things. One will excuse oneself.

Q. I did not understand what you meant when you said that unless one had this realization one would excuse oneself.

MR. O. One does not want to give up this idea that one can do, and even if one realizes that things happen, one finds excuses. 'This is an accident, to-morrow it will be different.' That is why we cannot realize this idea. All our life we see how things happen but we still explain it as accident, as exceptions to the rule that we can do. Either we forget, or do not see, or do not pay enough attention. We always think that at every moment we can begin to do. This is our ordinary way of thinking about it. If you try to find in your life times when you tried to do something and failed, that will be an example, but you explained your failure as accident, exception. If things repeat themselves, you again think you will be able to do, and if you see it again, again failure will be just accident. It is very useful to go through your life from this point of view. You intended one thing, and something different happened. If you are sincere, you will see. If not, you will persuade yourself that what happened was exactly what you wanted.

Q. Is there no such thing as forcing a situation?

MR. O. It may look like that, but really it happened. If it could not happen that way, then it could not happen. When things happen in a certain way we are carried by the current, but we think we carry the current.

Q. If one feels for a moment that one is able to do, say, to put through a particular job in ordinary work, what is the explanation of that?

MR. O. If one is trained to do something, one learns to follow a certain kind of happenings or, if you like, to start a certain kind of happenings, and then these develop and one runs behind, although one thinks one is leading.

Q.   If one has the right attitude. . . .

MR. O.   No, attitude has nothing to do with it. Attitude may be right, understanding may be right, but you still find things happen in a certain way. Any ordinary things. It is very useful to try and remember cases where one tried to do differently and how one always came back to the same thing even if one made a slight deviation, enormous forces driving one back to the old ways.

Q.   When you say we cannot help the same things happening, did you mean until our being is changed?

MR. O.   I did not speak about work. I said it was necessary to understand that <u>by ourselves</u> we cannot do. When this is sufficiently understood you can think what it is possible to do: which conditions, what knowledge, what help are necessary. But first it is necessary to realize that in ordinary life, if you try to do something different, you will find that you cannot. When this is emotionally understood, then only is it possible to go further. So long as you are not quite sure, it is impossible to continue.

Q.   When one becomes aware of contradictory selves in one-self, one wants to do something drastic about it. Is there anything one can do?

MR. O.   In order to do something, it is necessary to know more in almost every case, particularly in this case of contradictions. For instance, I meet many times with this case: somebody says he knows what is wrong with him and wants to do something to stop it. I begin to talk to him and, after I have talked for some time, I realize that he thinks he wants to, but in reality does not want to as much as he says. If one really wants to, one will find a way, but sometimes some kind of special knowledge is necessary. One may know some kind of contradiction, want to stop it, and still it remains. It is sometimes necessary to know how.

DOING. JANUARY 17TH 1940

Q.   Is the full realization that one cannot do anything already a long step on the way to doing?

MR. O.   Sometimes the step is too long, because one can realize that one cannot do something one ought to do, and one realizes too late.

9
Laws under which man lives

MR. O.   Let us return to the question of justice. It is interesting for language. What is justice?

Q.   Something that is fair to two people.

MR. O.   Who would be fair? As conditional arrangement it can be understood. As a general thing, it is fantastic. You forget that organic life is based on murder. One thing eats another: cats and rats. What is justice among cats and rats? This is life. It is nothing very beautiful. So where is justice?

Q.   Why do people think that nature is beautiful if this is how it works?

MR. O.   What is beautiful? What you like.

Q.   How can God be love if He created nature like this?

MR. O.   For a certain purpose. Besides, what do you call nature? Earthquake is also nature. But for the moment we apply the term 'nature' to organic life. Evidently it was created like that because there was no other means. How can we ask why? It was made so. If we don't like it, we can study methods to run away. This is the only possibility. Only we must not try to imagine that it is very beautiful. We must not pretend that facts are different from what they are.

Q.   Are you going to put man on the same footing as the rest of organic life?

MR. O.   There is no difference, only other units are fully developed, and man is only half developed.

Q.   Man can be beyond the law of murder?

MR. O.   He has the possibility of escape.

Q.   What are ways of escape from murder?

MR. O.   Man is under 192 laws. He must escape from some of them.

Q.   You said that men are responsible for what they did, and animals not?

Mr. O. Men 1, 2 and 3 are less responsible; men No. 4, and so on, are more responsible; responsibility grows.

Q. What means responsibility?

Mr. O. First, an animal has nothing to lose, but man has. Second, man has to pay for every mistake he makes, if he has started to grow.

Q. That implies justice.

Mr. O. No, nobody would call it justice if you had to pay for your mistakes.

Q. Does not justice mean to get what we deserve?

Mr. O. Most people think it is getting what we want and not what we deserve. Justice must mean some co-ordination between actions and results of actions. This certainly does not exist, and cannot exist, under the Law of Accident. When we know the chief laws, we understand that we live in a very bad place, a really bad place. But, as we cannot be in any other, we must see what we can do here. Only, we must not imagine that things are better than they are.

Q. Things will remain as they are unless everyone is conscious?

Mr. O. Things will remain as they are, but one can escape. It needs much knowledge to know what can be escaped and what cannot. But the first lesson we must learn, the first thing that prevents us from escaping is that we don't even realize the necessity to know our position. Who knows it, is already in a better position.

PRISON

Q. You said before that if we can't get of prison in one lifetime, then one can't get out at all. What do you mean by prison?

Mr. O. Prison is prison. Same principles apply for all prisons. Too late to do anything after you are buried. From another point of view, if one did nothing in one life, double chance that one will do nothing in the next. Principle one can always do to-morrow what one didn't do to-day. Improvement of this prini-ciple is to do it day after to-morrow.

Q. To get out of prison—does that mean to escape some of the laws men live under?

Mr. O. One law only. And if you say 'Which?', I shall say, 'Formatory, formatory!'

LAWS

Q. Are there more or less than 48 laws governing our world—organic life?

MR. O. According to the diagram of the Ray of Creation 48 laws govern earth—gravity, things like that. Many, many laws under which earth lives—movement, physical laws, chemical laws. Organic life is governed by 96 laws.

Q. The same as moon?

MR. O. The same number but quite a different manifestation. Organic life is not similar to moon. Moon is a cosmic body, organic life is a film on the surface of the earth. The number of laws only shows the relation of a given unit, but not its being or consistency, so there is no similarity.

Q. Could you give an example of one law?

MR. O. Many of them you know. Take man: he lives under physical laws, biological laws, physiological laws peculiar to man, such as temperature, climate, etc. We know some of these laws, but there are many laws about which we know nothing at all. For instance, there are cosmic laws which don't belong to the three laws of earth itself—they are connected with some bigger sphere and govern certain things which, from our point of view, appear trivial and insignificant. For instance, there is a definite law that each class of living beings can only eat a certain kind of food (from a certain density to a certain density). Man can eat things from such and such a density to such and such a density, from such and such a quality to such and such a quality. And he cannot change this just as he cannot change the air he breathes or the temperature in which he can exist. There are many things like that—they are all laws under which man lives. But there are many things about it we cannot know; many things we don't know about the conditions in which we live.

Q. You said as we progressed we should eliminate some of the laws? You said man lives under 96 laws.

MR. O. I said organic life is under 96 laws. Man lives under many, many more laws. Some are biological, physical and so on; then, coming to quite simple laws—ignorance, for instance. We do not know ourselves—this is a law. If we begin to know ourselves, we get rid of a law. We cannot learn 'this is one law, this is another law, this is a third law'. For many of them we have no names. All people live under the law of identification. This is a law. Those who begin to remember themselves can get rid of the law of identification. In that way we can know these laws. It is necessary to know, to understand little by little, the nature of laws from which one can become free. Then it is necessary to try to get free from one law, then from another. This is the practical way to study them.

Q.   What are we to get rid of?

MR. O.   You can get rid of identifying, negative emotions, imagination. . . .

Q.   Aren't these habits?

MR. O.   Habits are smaller divisions. Laws govern us, control us, direct us. Habits are not laws.

Q.   You mean we must be subject to these laws on earth?

MR. O.   We cannot fall under them or not fall under them. They don't ask us—we are chained.

Q.   But can we get free?

MR. O.   We can—on conditions. Ways enter here—the four ways are ways of liberation from unnecessary laws. Without schools one cannot know from which laws one can get free, or find means of getting free from them. The idea is that we are under many mechanical laws. Eventually we can get rid of some of these laws by becoming subject to other laws. There is no other way. To get out of the power of one law, you must put yourself under another law. This is the general idea. You can be shown the way—but you must work yourselves.

Q.   Any personal attainment is the result of effort against fate?

MR. O.   Fate may be favourable or not. It is necessary to know what one's fate is. But it cannot liberate us. Ways enter here. The four ways are ways to liberate us from laws. But each way has its own characteristics. In the three traditional ways the first step is the most difficult. In the Fourth Way man remains in the same conditions, and he must change in these conditions. These conditions are the best for him, because they are the most difficult.

COMMENTARY TO FOOD DIAGRAM. JULY 4TH 1939.
(OLD VERSION)

MR. O.   It is important to understand that the Food Diagram or Diagram of Nutrition really consists of three different stages.

The first stage shows how things happen in ordinary normal man: the food octave goes all the way from <u>do</u> 768 to <u>si</u> 12;

there are three notes of the air octave and one note of the impressions octave.

The second stage shows what happens when a certain amount of self-remembering already takes place: <u>do</u> 48—impressions— is transformed into <u>re</u> 24, and <u>re</u> 24 transforms into <u>mi</u> 12. <u>Si</u> 12 (of the food octave) is already in the lower story. The air octave at <u>mi</u> 48 receives a shock from the impressions octave and becomes <u>fa</u> 24, which is then transformed into <u>sol</u> 12. <u>Sol</u> 12 is transformed into <u>la</u> 6 and even into <u>si</u> 3. But you must understand that the ordinary air which we inhale cannot contain much of these higher hydrogens. The chemical meaning and chemical formula is all known. The air is saturated with higher hydrogens which, in certain cases, are retained by the organism in the process of breathing. But you must understand that in any case the amount of these higher hydrogens is very small.

The third stage shows what happens when a second conscious shock is given at the second place. The first conscious shock is necessary at <u>do</u> 48. The second conscious shock is necessary when <u>mi</u> 12 of the impressions octave and <u>si</u> 12 of the food octave have stopped in their development and cannot go further by themselves. Although there are carbons which would help them to be transformed, they are very far away and cannot be reached, so another effort is necessary. The effort must begin from <u>mi</u> 12; so you must understand what <u>mi</u> 12 is psychologi- cally. We can call it our ordinary emotions, that is to say, all strong emotions that we may have. When our emotions reach a certain degree of intensity, there is <u>mi</u> 12 in them. But really only our unpleasant emotions reach <u>mi</u> 12; our ordinary pleasant emotions hardly ever reach <u>mi</u> 12, they remain 24. But our unpleasant emotions may reach <u>mi</u> 12; not that they actually are <u>mi</u> 12, but they are based on <u>mi</u> 12, they need <u>mi</u> 12 in order to be produced. So this second effort is work on negative emotions.

It is important to understand where conscious shocks are necessary, and if you understand this it helps you to understand many other difficulties in the Food Diagram.

You must understand too, that these three octaves are not of equal force. If you take the force of the food octave, it gives certain results, certain effects that can be measured; it can be understood. The air octave—although the matter taken from air plays a very important part—represents a very small quantity, while the impressions octave may have enormous meaning in relation to self-remembering, states of consciousness, emotions and so on. You can say that the relationship of the three different octaves is not equal, because one has more substance, another very little substance.

Q. Does the effort to control attention act as the first conscious shock and does it bring carbon 12 to <u>do</u> 48?

MR. O. No. It is not enough. There must be self-remembering; actually self-remembering connected with self-observation—two activities. This is what makes consciousness. I mean, one tries to become conscious; in that way one gives a shock. One tries to become more conscious of oneself and of one's surroundings— of everything. What does the word 'consciousness' mean? It means co-knowledge.

Q. Could we hear more about carbon 12? from what source does it come?

MR. O. The important thing is not the source. What is important is <u>how</u> to bring it. Where it comes from does not matter, because we can't see it, we can't find it, we don't know where this place is. Certainly, carbon 12 normally comes from emotional centre and hydrogen 12 is the matter with which emotional centre works; but it comes or is brought there <u>only by self-remembering and self-observation</u>. So the method is important, not the source.

Q. There seems to be no carbon 12 in a man's ordinary state.

MR. O. Very little—so little that there is just enough for life, but not enough for development.

Q. What is the potential source of positive emotion?

MR. O. <u>Mi</u> 12, combined with special effort, can produce positive emotion.

Q. What is the second conscious shock which changes the character of the factory?

MR. O. If you like, I can tell you what it is, but it will not help anything, because this is exactly what we cannot do. It is the transformation of negative emotions into positive emotions. It is possible only with long work of self-remembering, when you can be conscious for a sufficiently long time, and when higher emotional centre begins to work. So it is near to man No. 5. This is what brings us to the state of man No. 5. It is very far from the place we are in now.

Q. What is the connection between negative emotions and the Food Table.

MR. O. It is difficult to answer, because the two things belong to different lines of study. Negative emotions we study only psychologically, we don't need the Food Diagram to study them. Mi 12, in most cases, is negative emotion. It is very seldom that we feel any mi 12 that is not negative.

Q. Has something gone wrong with mi 12?

MR. O. No, it is not wrong in itself, but every moment it can become negative.

Q. Can we have a certain control of impressions?

MR. O. You can have control only with the help of self-remembering. The more you remember yourself, the more control you have. If you remember yourself sufficiently, you can stop certain impressions, you can just isolate yourself—they will come but they will not penetrate; and there are other impressions to which you can open yourself and they will come without any delay. It is all based on self-remembering.

Q. At first the effort of self-remembering seems to reduce impressions.

MR. O. They cannot be reduced, only increased, if it is self-remembering. If it is thinking about self-remembering, it may give the impression that it diminishes certain impressions.

Q. I do not understand how impressions can be food. I thought that would have something to do with consciousness.

MR. O. Taking in of impressions means that certain energy comes in with them. All energy that you receive is food.

Q. Can you tell us more about different kinds of impressions?

MR. O. You can know much more by observation than by asking questions, because you yourself know what attracts you more, what attracts you less, what repels you, and so on—and certainly there are many purely subjective things. One is attracted by one thing; another is repelled by the same thing. There are certain impressions that go to the intellectual centre, impressions that go to the emotional centre, impressions that go to the moving centre, and impressions that go to the instinctive centre. Some of them you like more, some of them you like less. This is all material for observation.

Q. Are all impressions received from external sources?

MR. O. From external, and from ourselves: from inside and from outside.

Q. Are some impressions good and others bad, or are they what you make them?

MR. O. There may be impressions that are bad in themselves; I do not know how impressions can be good in themselves.

Because, if one is asleep, how can one have good impressions? So even if impressions are good in themselves, in order to have benefit from them, it is necessary to be more awake—but bad impressions can come in sleep; nothing can stop them.

Q. I really meant impressions that are pleasant or unpleasant.

MR. O. No, maybe many pleasant impressions are quite bad. Try to visualize one thing. Impressions can be classified by hydrogens. You remember we said that each impression is food—it is a certain hydrogen, one or another or a third; we generally take 48 as a standard. Then there may be 24, 12 or even, very rarely, 6, but there are all hydrogens down to the lowest. Impressions can belong to the lowest hydrogens in the third scale—12,000 or something like that. And what does this mean? It means where the hydrogen comes from, from which level of the world. What does the Table of Hydrogens mean? We divide the Ray of Creation into three octaves and twelve layers, so to speak, and every hydrogen comes from one or another or a third layer. If we take hydrogen 96, we know exactly where it comes from. If we take hydrogen 12, we know it comes from a high place in the Ray of Creation. You can take impression 768 or any other impression and if you remember about the Table of Hydrogens, you will know where it comes from.

Q. We have been told to select impressions like food. How can one distinguish?

MR. O. Observe. Impressions are easier to analyse than food. People may persuade you that something is good food and sell it in a tin, and then you find you cannot eat it, but impressions—by observation, by comparing, sometimes by talk with other people you can understand which impressions belong to higher levels and which belong to lower levels. For instance, all negative impressions belong to low levels, so you cannot divide impressions themselves as 'pleasant' and 'unpleasant'. They are either positive or negative—not positive as we use the word in the sense of positive emotions, but positive as opposed to negative. But at the same time the chief thing is to be awake.

Q. Even if you can distinguish between one kind of impression and another, I do not see how you can accept or reject them.

MR. O. By being awake. If you are asleep you cannot. But when you are awake—not at once, maybe, it needs certain work—one time you are conquered by wrong impressions, another time you are conquered, then the third time you manage to isolate yourself; but before that it is necessary to know what kinds of wrong impressions affect you, and then you can find special methods for isolating yourself.

Q.   You mean that if you observe, you can avoid having those impressions which make you negative?

MR. O.   I did not speak about things that make _you_ negative, but about _negative_ impressions. You change the meaning. The question was: 'Are impressions by themselves all the same, or are they good and bad?' I explained that there are positive and negative impressions. I said nothing about making you negative. Anything can make you negative—the best possible thing in the world can make you negative. That depends on your state.

Q.   I don't understand what you mean about where impressions come from in the Table of Hydrogens?

MR. O.   From different levels of worlds. You must remember the Ray of Creation. What is the difference between different worlds? Take 3, 12, 24. World 3 is under the direct Will of the Absolute—there are only three laws. In World 6 mechanicalness enters—it already becomes more mechanical; in World 12, still more mechanical and so on. But 12 has an enormous advantage over 1536, so an impression that comes from 12 is one kind of impression, and an impression that comes from below the earth, say from the moon, is different. One is light matter, full of vibrations, another is full of slow, harmful vibrations.

Q.   But if impressions are, say, the same hydrogen as iron. . . .

MR. O.   But that has nothing to do with impressions. Try to understand. The question of matters by themselves is quite a different question. It does not enter here. Now we take the Table of Hydrogens from the point of view that each hydrogen shows the place where this hydrogen comes from. If you find that impressions are heavy, unpleasant—it is difficult to find right English adjective about impressions—by that very fact you can tell that this impression comes from some low part of the Ray of Creation. Things that make you angry, make you hate people and give you some taste of rudeness, coarseness, violence, all these impressions come from low worlds.

Q.   Could one stop having impressions if one wanted to?

MR. O.   No, certainly not. You cannot stop impressions altogether, but you can isolate yourself from a certain kind of impressions and attract to yourself another kind of impressions, that is, when you know them. You can attract desirable impressions and keep off from yourself undesirable impressions;

Q. So we are able to select impressions?

MR. O. Yes, to a certain extent, because we must already understand that certain impressions we must not admit. First of all you can avoid wrong impressions. People stand in the street looking for street accidents, and they talk about it until the next accident; these people collect wrong impressions. People who collect all kinds of scandal, people who see something wrong in everything—they collect wrong impressions. You have to think not about choosing the right impressions, but about isolating yourself from wrong impressions. Only by doing this will you have certain control. If you try to choose right impressions you only deceive yourself.

Q. Is it possible to know which are the impressions that are good for one and which are bad?

MR. O. What you want is a catalogue of impressions. It is impossible to do that. Later you will have to understand personally, for yourself and for people whom you know, which impressions are good and which are bad. After some time you have to begin the study of wrong impressions, because although you cannot bring desirable impressions to yourself, you can, even from the very beginning, isolate yourself from some kind of wrong impressions.

Q. Can we really control the impressions we receive?

MR. O. I have just said in which way you can control them. Again, you must understand that, in order to control impressions, you must already awake to a certain extent. If you are asleep you cannot control anything. In order to control quite simple obvious things you must awake and practise, because if you are accustomed to impressions of a certain kind which are wrong for you, it will take some time. One 'I' will know it is necessary to isolate yourself, and maybe ten other 'I's will like these impressions, because often some 'I's like quite wrong impressions.

Q. As we are now, are all impressions on the same level?

MR. O. Oh no. Impressions have an extraordinary range. In the Food Diagram we take H48 as a standard. They are indifferent impressions, so to speak—maybe of one kind, maybe of another; but by themselves they produce no effect. Yet at the same time they are food.

Q. Do we only have impressions 48?

MR. O. As an example, as a standard of impressions, impressions 48 are taken. Why? Because that represents the

great majority of impressions that we have. They reach us as
48, and in our ordinary state they don't go further, don't
develop, they produce no effect. Man wouldn't be able to live
in these conditions. But there are many impressions of 24—not
as many as of 48 but a certain quantity of them; and in very
rare cases there may even be impressions of 12, but let's say 24.
So man receives not only 48 but also 24. They don't enter in
this Food Diagram because they transform themselves. If they
come as 24, they may easily be transformed into 12 and maybe
further. But they come in very small quantity.

In ordinary man who does not learn to remember himself,
these ordinary impressions 48 are also transformed, but in quite
a different way. They are developed further, or helped to develop
further by reactions of a certain kind—for instance, by laughter.
Laughter plays a very important part connected with
impressions—again remember I said in ordinary man. With the
help of laughter many impressions 48 are transformed into 24.
But, as was said before, this is only because it is necessary for
life. You remember I said that the chemical factory works by
itself. It produces all kinds of very precious materials, but it
spends them all for its own existence. It has nothing in reserve
and nothing with which to develop itself. So if man wants to
change and become different, if he wants to awaken his hidden
possibilities, he cannot rely only on the mechanical means in
himself; he must look for conscious means. But man's organism
is such a wonderful invention that everything is taken into
consideration, everything has its own key, so to speak, so that
each function that looks just like a useless expression of something—like laughter—helps to transform certain impressions
which would simply be lost otherwise.

It can be said that for a man on the ordinary level who does
not try to understand what self-remembering means, or never
heard about self-remembering, or had no chance to remember
himself, laughter fulfils a certain definite function in the
organism. It replaces self-remembering in a very small,
insufficient way; in any case it helps impressions to pass further;
quite dull, uninteresting impressions become more vivid.

Q. Not all laughter, surely?

Mr. O. No. But this is its chief function. There are many
different kinds of laughter. There may be mechanical laughter
in the mechanical part of the mechanical part of emotional
centre—just giggling.

Q. Is it actually something that happens very quickly, if by chance impressions 48 come in and change?

MR. O. 48 enters constantly. As I have said, a certain amount of it changes mechanically; the greater amount remains unchanged. It can be changed by becoming conscious, or by trying to become conscious.

REALIZATION OF TRUTH. MARCH 21ST 1945

MR. O. You know it was said before we don't have positive emotions. This is called second conscious effort—if you know the way to make positive emotion.

First conscious effort is connected with self-remembering. Second conscious effort is connected with conscience. If one knows what it is, one must keep it. It is emotional understanding of truth. One gets it once; one must not lose. Wrong actions and talk make it very easy to lose.

Q. Is it the higher emotional centre?

MR. O. It is emotion. Try to get meaning.

Q. If one loses this conscience is possible to get it back again?

MR. O. Very difficult, and very dangerous to lose it. Much easier to live without it. One is relieved to lose it.

Q. Don't you think it is possible to twist it round to suit your convenience?

MR. O. Then it is not conscience.

Q. Is conscience acquired by degrees?

MR. O. Consciousness is acquired by degrees. Conscience is in us but it is asleep. You have to shake, shake. But if you lie to yourself or to others who are trying to show you, you lose it.

Q. How can one tell what is truth?

MR. O. Conscience knows.

Q. Then you have to follow your own direction or someone will tell you?

MR. O. Maybe you have to be told about it.

Q. Don't all people have conscience?

MR. O. Yes, but asleep. But if it awake, people must understand things; must understand things in the same way.

Q. Can we have conscience without consciousness?

MR. O. Conscience comes before.

Q. Does it come only after first conscious effort?

MR. O.   It is on the way to second conscious effort. Yes, one must do something on the first effort first.

Q.   If it's not the product of conscious effort how can one lose it?

MR. O.   One can lose everything. One can wake conscience and then fall asleep again on this particular point.

Q.   Doesn't it depend on one's standard of morality?

MR. O.   No, one thing may be moral in this country and immoral in another. Remember the word formatory. This means mechanical part of intellectual centre. It is not reliable.

Q.   Are people born with different degrees of conscience?

MR. O.   Some people have glimpses of conscience very early. But it is not reliable.

Q.   Does one feel the emotion of conscience as fear or remorse?

MR. O.   Truth—why use other words?

Q.   Is that what they call the still, small voice?

MR. O.   No! No! When you hear it, it is not a still voice at all.

Q.   In what way will one be different, with awakened conscience, from before?

MR. O.   One will not be so much in the power of buffers. Asleep one is completely in the power of buffers. Buffers are mechanical devices which prevent us from seeing truth. Destroy buffers and you begin to see truth. Maybe very unpleasant.

Q.   How does one begin to awaken conscience?

MR. O.   Not lying to oneself.

Q.   Then the realization of truth—does that destroy all buffers?

MR. O.   No, buffers must be destroyed before.

Q.   Does the emotional realization of truth vary with individuals? One has a different view from another.

MR. O.   That cannot be in conscience. It will be the same. One doesn't learn what is truth. One just sees it, if conscience begins to awake. But one must begin to remove real buffers.

Q.   Would awakening of conscience be accompanied by learning real aim?

MR. O.   How can one do it without? The method is not invented.

Q.   Is it a matter of sensitivity?

MR. O.   Maybe much sensitivity without buffers.

Q.   When you say conscience is emotional understanding of truth—truth is an abstraction.

MR. O.   No, no, fact, not abstraction.

Q. About a particular question of a particular moment?

MR. O. Yes, particular case, particular relation—always particular.

Q. If one feels conscience, can there be buffers at the same time?

MR. O. One or the other; not both at once.

Q. Can we know by ourselves that we are lying to ourselves?

MR. O. You always know. But that doesn't stop it.

Q. Why can't one stop lying to oneself? Is it laziness?

MR. O. Simply pleasant.

Q. What is a buffer? Is religious conviction a buffer?

MR. O. We never speak about religious things. No, it is some kind of self-guard that man creates himself to avoid truth.

Q. Doesn't buffer mean lack of understanding?

MR. O. No, one generally knows what one is guarding against.

Q. Means desire not to understand.

MR. O. Quite right. From time to time I gave examples. Long, long ago there was a man in Moscow who was always late. His buffer was that he was never late. He was so sure, that after he had created the buffer he could be late as often as he wished.

Q. Could we have a buffer like the one you're mentioning and still have conscience in other respects?

MR. O. No, no, either buffer or conscience.

Q. Does conscience destroy peace of mind?

MR. O. Some people think like that, particularly when they sit between two chairs.

Q. What do you mean by losing conscience again?

MR. O. Falling asleep in this particular sense.

Q. Could a machine develop the equivalent of buffers and be unable to develop conscience?

MR. O. Mechanical things develop mechanically. But opposite things can only be developed consciously.

Q. Is conscience mostly the realization that we are asleep?

MR. O. No, no, you must begin with consciousness. We cannot remember ourselves. We are not aware of ourselves. You then find many examples.

Q. Does conscience come into play only in relation to other people?

MR. O. Glimpses are possible. Long before we have control of consciousness we may have glimpses of conscience.

Q. If someone has conscience will he inevitably come to second conscious shock?

MR. O.   If one did quite good work on first conscious shock one may come to it.

Q.   Does he come to it by himself?

MR. O.   Nothing comes by itself, only falling.

Q.   When you speak of first conscious shock do you mean only successful effort?

MR. O.   Only successful. How long can we be aware of ourselves? One second is better than nothing. But you can't make much of it. You can't learn Chinese by learning one word a day.

Q.   Does the content of conscience change continually?

MR. O.   Direction, not content. One day you find one application, another day, another. Conscience bites you.

Q.   What is the nature of the truth our conscience recognizes?

MR. O.   Conscience realizes simple truths—in relation to people, what they say and do; not in relation to planets. Another thing in relation to Law of Three. Law of Three is difficult until one can realize difference in people's activities. This may be difficult for some time. Before we go further we must learn to distinguish difference in things which ordinarily we don't see.

Q.   There is a triad for building a house.

MR. O.   This is so formatory; forget all you heard. Necessary to think that there is difference between things which we cannot understand. There is a difference between actions—not motive, not reward; our mind does not distinguish. But when it is explained we can begin to see.

Q.   Does conscience see the difference between activities?

MR. O.   Not see—it can help.

Q.   The physical aspects of such activities are the same, so where do they differ?

MR. O.   If we see, we will see difference.

Q.   What stops us from seeing it?

MR. O.   Blindness.

Q.   Have we any possibility of ever seeing?

MR. O.   Oh yes. First we must learn with our mind—and then little by little we begin to see.

Q.   Do you mean to see the forces?

MR. O.   To see different activities. Before that, we can learn about it. But to see is difficult word—for if we become a little conscious we see many things we cannot see now. If we realize how many things we cannot see, we can learn much. We understand difference of matter—paper and wood, for example. But we cannot understand difference of action.

Q. Is it possible to follow different forces of a triad—for instance in building a house?

MR. O. No, learn these examples. First fact is that such as we are with ordinary mind, we don't see difference.

There are six activities possible for man—seventh only possible for Absolute. In all other worlds only six are possible:

$$
\begin{array}{ccc}
1\ 2\ 3 & 1\ 3\ 2 & 2\ 1\ 3 \\
3\ 1\ 2 & 3\ 2\ 1 & 2\ 3\ 1
\end{array}
$$

These are combinations of forces. Three forces have six possible combinations. Absolute is difficult to speak of in our language. So there are six activities, only we cannot connect them with forces. Well, first category—trying to remember yourself, esoteric work, also best forms of art, poetry, perhaps music. Second refers to highest intellectual, inventions, discoveries. Third refers to professional work—tailor, doctor, yes; fourth, simply physical work, sawing wood. Five, destruction. Six, crime. Only you don't know which triad is which, and you won't know for a long time. Only try to understand difference between building house—much effort, planning materials; and burning house—just one match. One needs effort; the other works by itself, no question of motive.

Q. I think you want us to find out connection between activity and awakening conscience?

MR. O. Trying, not awakening conscience! School-work, following school methods, same level as best poetry, best art.

Q. Does understanding of system ideas mean consciousness?

MR. O. Marching in this direction. No guarantee until you come there.

Q. Is the awakening of conscience an activity?

MR. O. It is in the same line. If one really does something.

11. 4. 45

Q. Whoever does this creative work—I mean people who come to school here who do creative work. . . .

MR. O. I cannot speak like that . . . of creative work. I only say there is one kind of activity which includes best art and poetry. It was asked if poets and painters are more conscious.

It was answered no, only they use this special activity. If an artist is conscious, then it is a question of objective art.

Q. Do you literally mean once conscience is awakened and falls asleep again it cannot then be awakened?

MR. O. It can in some cases. But very rarely. Not by itself—it means work.

Q. Are there degrees of conscience?

MR. O. Probably, same as consciousness. How long can you remember yourself? One minute, two minutes? Same with conscience.

Q. If one can only achieve a moment of conscience or consciousness, what happens when it is over? Do we slip back or is it lost?

MR. O. Needs constant work. It cannot exist by itself.

Q. You said if one lost it, it was impossible to recover it.

MR. O. I did not say 'impossible'. I said 'difficult'. But everything is difficult, with the exception of what happens. What happens is easy.

Q. Is crime a negative emotion which we act out. . . ?

MR. O. We cannot say it simply like that. Behind crime is always trace of negative emotion, memory of negative emotion, but you cannot say crime is negative emotion.

Q. Isn't crime against law itself?

MR. O. Well, my experience is not so big.

Q. It's not just sporadic action?

MR. O. It may be prepared action, it may be clever action; many things are possible.

It is all very necessary. Very soon you will see how useful it is. But it is difficult because it is quite a new idea.

Q. If the first activity deals with the highest form of art, where do we place lower form?

MR. O. Just nonsense; we don't count it.

Q. Some people spend their lives at it.

MR. O. If it is art, it is art—highest form, in any case sufficiently high.

Q. Then how do you describe this other activity—writers, musicians, etc.?

MR. O. Then it is just physical work, or professional work, I don't know. . . . It is very useful to distinguish between one activity and another. And one must remember that it is a new thing—your neighbours never thought of it.

Q. Of what value is the study of these activities?

MR. O. Well, this is one very important thing to know. When you understand activities, you will have answers to many of your questions.

Q. Would that make us better people?

MR. O. More clever.

Q. You said that when a man wrote a poem it might be physical work. I don't understand that.

MR. O. Quite. There are libraries full of such poems.

Q. Do you discourage activities that don't reach the highest plane?

MR. O. I don't encourage or discourage. Some I recognize as art, some I call nonsense.

Q. You described five activities but not crime.

MR. O. You must ask questions. Study all kinds of crime. See which you like more and which less. This is a very terrible thing. In ordinary thinking we don't even have beginning of understanding of the difference between activities. Some day when it begins to open to you, you will see it as a revelation.

Q. Are these activities related to different states of consciousness?

MR. O. No, we speak only of ordinary man, ordinary states of consciousness.

Q. Doesn't highest art take some degree of self-consciousness?

MR. O. Many good poets, many good painters—but they are ordinary. They can use the special triad, but it doesn't make them No. 5.

Q. Using right parts of centres—would that be clue to right activity?

MR. O. Right activity is what you want. If you want one thing and get another—wrong activity. Only this has nothing to do with consciousness. It is function like breathing, seeing. In some activities you can try to be conscious, in some you cannot.

Q. When carrying logs becomes a mechanical activity, where does self-remembering come in?

MR. O. Nobody forbids you to remember yourself carrying logs; some people even say it helps—the heavier the logs, the better the self-remembering. Some people who start trying to self-remember find it connected with hard physical work.

Q. Except for the particular activity we are engaged in, we can't have more than a superficial knowledge of the others, can we?

MR. O. I think we know more or less all. One refers to poetry.

This is the same activity as trying to remember oneself, though it is actually different.

Q. Are all six activities necessary for the existence of man?

MR. O. One can be missed.

Q. Which one?

MR. O. Crime.

Q. Could <u>man</u>, not <u>a</u> man, live without crime?

MR. O. They say so. I am not a specialist on that.

Q. Does an awakened conscience mean the self-conscious state?

MR. O. No, an awakened conscience means an awakened conscience, nothing more. Trying to be sincere and honest. You can say nothing more. Very interesting if you manage to get even short period of consciousness. You will see things you never saw before.

Q. Will we see things in ourselves or in others?

MR. O. With your ordinary eyes. In other people.

Q. It seems to me activity of first kind is impossible without awakening of conscience.

MR. O. That's for awakening. It has different colours—it can be music, it can be painting, it can be self-study. It is same triad.

Q. This type of seeing you just spoke about brings with it more negative emotions?

MR. O. Did you try it?

Q. Yes.

MR. O. No, you don't know what I speak of. For I speak of one definite thing. If several people come to it, we can speak. I speak of definite thing which it is possible to see. Some people speak of awakening; if they don't mention this, one knows it is imagination or simply lying.

Q. Could you cite one instance for us?

MR. O. Suppose I told you, and to-morrow you said you had it? It would be suspicious; I just wait.

18. 4. 45

Q. Is conscience the emotional awakening of consciousness?

MR. O. Conscience is a special emotion, and usually it is asleep. It has to be shaken a long time before it awakens.

Q. Is conscience our own personal recognition of good and evil—not related to law?

MR. O.   Not in general. In a particular case, conscience is special emotion by which we can see what is right and what is wrong.

Q.   Is there any connection between awakened conscience and activities?

MR. O.   No, no, quite different. Six activities are open to everybody, conscience or no conscience. Only some things can be combined and others cannot be combined.

Q.   Could someone be active in the first activity and not have awakened conscience?   .

MR. O.   Oh yes. There are many great poets who have [not] heard of conscience.

Q.   What one thing is specially important for us to do in order to awaken conscience?

MR. O.   We spoke about many things. Useful to think what self-remembering is and why we cannot remember. You cannot live on one thing. There are many things that help the awakening of conscience. Study of buffers, for example.

Q.   Do we delude ourselves about awakened conscience when we do nothing about it?

MR. O.   Quite right. Necessary to shake it a little.

Q.   It was conscience that had no connection with any one of six activities?

MR. O.   Only one—crime—is necessary. How can you be a criminal without conscience?

Q.   How do we even begin to study buffers? I never have understood.

MR. O.   Try to understand first what buffers are.

Q.   We have to stop lying to ourselves first?

MR. O.   Very useful. Begin with that, and in a comparatively short time you will come to it.

Q.   Could we think of buffers as contradictions in ourselves?

MR. O.   No, contradictions are the result of buffers.

Q.   What do you mean that it is necessary to have conscience in order to commit crimes?

MR. O.   Some criminals say so. No pleasure in crime if your conscience is not awake. Well, try something else—about activities; one man can write poetry, another cannot write even bad poetry. It is capacity to use triad.

Q.   Why are we able to use the right triad sometimes and not others?

MR. O. I never saw a man who could write poetry on Thursday.

Q. You think we could write poetry on Thursday with effort?

MR. O. No, effort or no effort. It is a Russian expression—'On Thursday after rain'.

Q. I want to ask about activity of destruction.

MR. O. Well, sometimes it is very pleasant, sometimes it is unpleasant. Generally it is easier than making soup, for instance. Making soup needs work, planning. Throwing it out needs none.

Q. Does the ability to use right triads depend on right use of centres?

MR. O. I don't know. I only know one person can use triad at a certain moment, others cannot. It is very useful to think of this, otherwise one can put it down to conscience or something.

Q. Is the purpose of this work to help us arrive at fully awakened conscience?

MR. O. It cannot be put specifically like that. On the way to having consciousness you must awake conscience. Otherwise you will stumble on something. You can describe it as awakening consciousness.

Q. Is the right use of triads connected with the right use of centres?

MR. O. You mean use of six triads? Almost everyone can use some of them. Some are more difficult. They need special capacity. Very useful to compare them and try to understand difference.

Q. Is a buffer a form of lying to oneself?

MR. O. How can a buffer exist without that? Neither man himself nor others realize that it is lying.

Q. How does a buffer start to grow in one?

MR. O. A child can fall and that can create buffer; he may say 'I never fall'.

10
Centres in man

Q.   Can one kind of energy be changed into another kind?
MR. O.   It changes by itself when it is necessary. Every centre is adapted to work with a certain kind of energy, and it receives exactly what it needs, but all centres steal from each other, and a centre that needs a higher kind of energy has to work with a lower kind, or a centre suited for working with quiet energy uses explosive energy, and so everything is quite wrong. That is how the machine works. Imagine certain stoves—one has to work on oil, one on wood, and a third on benzene. Suppose the one adapted for wood is given benzene; only explosions can happen, nothing more; and also imagine a machine adapted for benzene, and see how it cannot work on wood or coal.
Q.   Are there different kinds of energy; that is to say, can we talk of emotional energy, intellectual energy, etc., as if they were different kinds of energy?
MR. O.   Not exactly like that, but we can speak about centres and we can speak about energies—one centre with one kind, another centre with another kind; and energies can be designated by the kind of hydrogen in which they are contained. Intellectual centre works with H48; moving and instinctive with H24, and so on.

We must distinguish four kinds of energy working through us: physical energy (for instance, moving this table), life energy (which makes the body absorb food, reconstruct tissues, and so on—this process of the transformation of cells goes on constantly); psychic, or mental energy, with which the centres work, and, most important of all—energy of consciousness.

For every kind of action, thought, or for being conscious, we must have corresponding energy. If we have not got it, we go down and work with lower energy—lead simply an animal and vegetable life. Then again we have thoughts, again we accumulate energy and can be conscious for a short time.

Even an enormous quantity of physical energy cannot produce a thought. For thought, a different, a stronger solution is necessary.

Before thinking of storing energy we must stop waste. We waste energy in imagination, considering, identifying, negative emotions, idle talk—these are the chief leaks. This is why it is necessary to stop identifying.

Psychic energy is the energy with which centres work. You call it mental or psychological energy.

All kinds of physical energy can be reduced to movement. Physical energy cannot be accumulated beyond a certain limit. Psychic energy cannot be limited.

The energy of consciousness is quicker, more explosive than the other kinds.

But, though conservation and increase of energy is very important, it is not the whole secret in the development of consciousness. It would not be enough, for one has to know how to control it. Energy is the mechanical side of consciousness.

Q. How can one learn to control energy better?

Mr. O. One cannot begin with the idea of control. In order to control one small thing we must know the whole machine. First we must control ourselves from the point of view of consciousness, must try to remember ourselves. Then stop unnecessary waste of energy—considering, lying, expression of negative emotions. So first of all we have to stop waste of energy; second, collect it by self-remembering; then, adjust things. We cannot begin in any other way.

Q. Is there always the same amount of energy in the big accumulator?

Mr. O. That depends on many things: work of the machine, food, waste or not waste of energy. The normal organism produces enough energy not only for all centres but also for storing. Production is all right, but spending may be wrong.

VOICE. OCTOBER 14TH 1937

Q. I notice that I have different voices with different emotions or different people. Why is this?

Mr. O. Who has ears to hear can hear many changes of voice. Every centre, every part of centre, every part of part of centre has a different voice. But few people have ears to hear them.

Who can hear them, for them it is easy to hear many things. For instance, if you speak the truth it is one voice; if you lie, it is another voice; if you base things on imagination, yet another. There can be no mistake.

Q. Do you mean intonation?

MR. O. Yes, and also the actual sound of the voice. If you train yourself to it, the emotional centre can hear the differences.

FOOD DIAGRAM. JANUARY 10TH 1938

Q. Is it known what carbon 12 in the triad of self-remembering is?

MR. O. Probably some energy of the emotional centre. There can be no mistake about that, because intensified observation brought about by self-remembering always has an emotional element. It may come by itself when suddenly you begin to see things differently—it becomes emotional. It means that in this particular place we are not emotional enough. By self-remembering we bring the emotional element to this place.

This is partly connected with laughter. If we receive impressions and cannot do anything with them, they don't go any further, we throw them out by laughter. What produces laughter is when some impression falls simultaneously on the positive and negative parts of centres. To get rid of this unpleasant impression (unpleasant because it is contradictory), it is thrown out. Laughter means throwing out contradictory impressions that cannot be harmonized. That is why there is no laughter in the higher centres.

Q. So laughter is an unnecessary thing?

MR. O. In our state it is necessary. In higher centres it is unnecessary, because there what is emotional is also intellectual and what is intellectual is also emotional. And there are no divisions in higher centres into positive and negative parts.

Q. There are forms of laughter that do not mean throwing out impressions?

MR. O. Yes, there are different forms of laughter.

Q. The other carbons 12, are they the same stuff? I mean at mi 48 and at sol 48.

MR. O. May be the same. I think there is a little difference in sol 48. At mi 48 the same carbon works that works at do 48. But in sol 48 it may be a little different, although it has an emotional element always. But in <u>sol</u> 48 it may be instinctive emotional. It is quite possible that <u>sol</u> works through carbon 12 from instinctive centre, which is always there. But it belongs to a very small octave; it comes from the air. This octave comes to <u>la</u> 6, but it is very thin.

Q.   Laughter seems to have a physiological effect.

Mr. O.   Yes, maybe an impression creates tension, and laughter produces relaxation.

HIGHER CENTRES AND SEEING. FEBRUARY 3RD 1938

Q.   Can you explain what you mean by seeing oneself?

Mr. O.   How can I? How can I explain what means seeing oneself in a mirror? Just the same.

Q.   Well, but one sees many selves.

Mr. O.   No. Certain combinations. The more one can see them separately the better.

Q.   You would never expect anything theatrical, would you? Like what you quoted about a man who drove home in a hansom cab and was enveloped in a cloud of fire?

Mr. O.   Subjectively, anything may happen. Some people do react in that way. It means really in our language a moment of connection with higher emotional centre, and some people in this connection react by many subjective visions. But it is not obligatory. It may be with visions, it may be without visions.

Q.   Are there any signs one might look for?

Mr. O.   Signs only in the sense of self-remembering, because it happens as a result of self-remembering for a certain period. How self-remembering comes, that is another thing. In this case it was described in this book. (Bucke's book, I think, wasn't it?) That is one case; there may be many other methods. Always one or another kind of self-remembering which produces these connections with higher emotional centre. First it creates subjective visions. One begins to see things in allegories and symbols, sometimes in a very interesting way. Then one begins to see things which it is impossible to describe. Things we cannot see with our ordinary eyes, with higher emotional centre we can see them. I do not mean 'astral', but things which look quite ordinary. You are astonished you could not see it before. Things which you see without this, but at the same time you do not see them.

Q. What sort of things?

MR. O. How can I explain? Many things. For instance—only that is in higher degrees—you can see what one thinks. We do not see it, but we can through higher emotional centre. This is not the beginning, this is a higher degree. In the beginning you see many things you do not see ordinarily.

Q. What truth is there in the thing about 'Uncoiling Linga Sharira'?

MR. O. Just terminology of different school which we do not use, so it means nothing for us. Words. In any case, I never found anything serious in all that and, though I did not know anything at that time about, for instance, higher centres, yet when I learnt about higher centres everything fitted. For example, I knew the difference between higher emotional and higher mental—before I knew of the existence of higher centres.

Higher emotional centre uses same forms, may give more knowledge on the same subjects we know now, or present them in the form of allegories. But in higher mental centre there are no forms. It is quite different thinking—quite different ideas.

Q. This subject-object relationship I can never get away from! I do not know anything else.

MR. O. But I assure you, just one step, one step from our ordinary state and all these values change. . . . You see, we base our intellectual construction on certain ideas, certain concepts, certain words, and if we make just one step from our ordinary state, all this changes. That is why it is so difficult to trust to words.

MECHANICALNESS. AUGUST 1ST 1939

Q. I don't understand what acting mechanically means, because one seems to spend half of one's life learning to do things mechanically, like writing. Has all this got to be undone?

MR. O. That is moving centre. I don't mean that. Some, like many instinctive things, are mechanical and should remain mechanical. They are not mechanical for themselves, but mechanical for the man. And it is just the same with moving centre. But mechanical thoughts, mechanical feelings—that is what has to be studied and what can be changed, should be changed. Mechanical thinking is not worth a penny. You can think about many things mechanically, but you will get nothing. You can use, in a mechanical way, only one small part of your intellectual centre, only the mechanical part, the formatory apparatus, and it is not worth spending time on.

Q. Is mechanicalness to be looked upon as a fact to be observed or an evil to be fought against?

MR. O. You see, you will never understand mechanicalness if you speak in this way, in relation to small things. But when you see, or you may find in your memory, how quite mechanically you can do the most abominable things, which later you will not understand how you could have done them, then you will see what mechanicalness is. All our life we do mechanically what we would never do consciously. That is what we must understand. And if we look through our life, year by year and month by month, we see things we would have never done consciously, or things we don't do, which if we were conscious, we would have liked to do. This is the way to observe mechanicalness.

ABOUT MECHANICALNESS. (TRANSLATED FROM A NOTE IN RUSSIAN)

We can understand what mechanicalness is and all the horror of mechanicalness only when we do something horrible and fully realize that it was mechanicalness in us that made us do it. If we try to cover it, to find excuses and explanations, we will never realize it. It is necessary to be very sincere with oneself to be able to see it. It may hurt awfully, but we must bear it and try to understand that only by confessing fully first to ourselves and then maybe to other people, if we are told to do so, we can avoid repeating it again and again. We can even change results by full and complete understanding and not trying to hide it. This is the only possible way. If we become afraid of it; if we become negative and resentful when we are told about it and asked to be sincere about it, there is no chance and no possibility for us to escape ever from the tentacles of mechanicalness.

We are its slaves, but we can break its force, by big suffering. If we try to avoid suffering; if we try to persuade ourselves that nothing really happened and that things can go just as they were going before, not only [shall] we never escape, but we will become more and more mechanical, and very soon we will come to such a state when there will be no possibility for us and no chance.

In life it is always like that. But in the work there is a chance.

Only sincerity and complete recognition of the fact and its inevitable results, can help us to find and to destroy buffers with the help of which we deceived ourselves. Buffers in this case are always connected with self-justification and self-excuse. Sometimes self-pity is added to those, sometimes resentment against other people, sometimes accusations and bad feeling. 'They made me do it', 'we did not intend to do it'. Or, (it is also an expression of buffer) we can say and repeat to ourselves that, after all, it is unimportant. People can do really awful things, having persuaded themselves that it is not important.

CENTRES USING WRONG ENERGY. AUGUST 8TH 1939

Q. Can we hear more about centres using wrong energy—mainly in connection with all the talking that goes on inside me when I am doing a job? Is it connected with this?

MR. O. No, it is not connected with that, it cannot be taken in connection with your personal experiences—it must be taken on a bigger scale.

In this diagram higher emotional and higher mental centres are not connected with the lower centres: they work quite separately. But ordinary emotional centre sometimes reaches 12, sometimes 24—it depends. Unfortunately, it reaches 12 only in negative emotions, because, if it comes to 12 in emotions that are not negative, it comes to positive emotions and passes to higher emotional centre. 48 (intellectual centre) can work with the energy of sex centre; 24 (moving centre) can work with the energy 48; it is all mixed up, and first of all each centre tries to get for itself a wrong hydrogen—and that's how nothing comes right.

Q. What happens if intellectual centre works with H24?

MR. O. It becomes a little mad, invents impossible theories, fantastic theories, becomes very fanatical, keeps only one point of view on things and so on—like bolsheviks, fascists, or something like that. For instance, it makes a theory, a very formatory theory, and then it begins to knock people on the head if they don't accept this theory—this is what happens if it works with

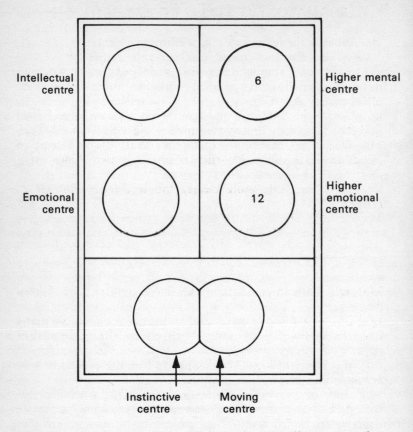

24. Normally it must work with 48. Then it will remain rather useless but more or less decent.

Q. Can intellectual centre formulate with 48?

Mr. O. Yes, certainly—again rather useless and long formations, using long words.

Q. So for thinking to use high hydrogens, it must be an entirely different apparatus altogether?

Mr. O. Certainly. Each apparatus is adapted for a certain hydrogen. One can work with 12, another with 24, a third with 48. Change them—and all work wrong.

FORMATORY CENTRE. JANUARY 16TH 1940

Q. What is the legitimate use of formatory centre?

MR. O. This is your business. If, generally, intellectual centre works normally, if other parts work, formatory centre works in its place quite all right; you must think only about wrong work of formatory centre.

Q. Could I have it explained again what it means when it was said that formatory centre can only see black and white?

MR. O. It was not said exactly like that. It compares two things as though in any particular line only two things exist; that is one of its peculiarities.

Q. How can I see more clearly the working of formatory centre?

MR. O. Remember examples from the past. This is an example of formatory thinking if you say, 'it was said'. Try to understand what was said.

Q. Is it characteristic of formatory thinking that one jumps to conclusions?

MR. O. Formatory thinking knows everything, or knows nothing.

Q. One of the things that helped me was that I found that I never really listen. I am always busy either getting an answer ready or finding another point of view. If I can make myself listen, I can think about what is said in a different way afterwards.

MR. O. That is a very good observation. It very often happens that we think that things are not explained to us, and really we don't listen. So just try to listen and observe yourself, how you listen.

17. 1. 40

Q. Are we using formatory apparatus when learning or reading something that requires a mental effort to understand?

MR. O. Yes, in normal conditions we use formatory centre in quite the right way, but you will remember I said that formatory centre is the very mechanical part of intellectual centre. And if emotional part and intellectual part are working rightly, the mechanical (formatory) part is in its right place. But if the emotional and intellectual parts are not working right, then formatory centre takes their place and begins wrong work. So in its own place it is quite right, like everything else.

MIRACLE. OCTOBER 4TH 1944

Q. What is normality?

MR. O. Normality is capacity for development. And you already must see what is included in that. One must learn to stop lying. We have very good definition of lying. In ordinary systems there is no definition of lying. So they can lie happily. If people speak of things they don't know as if they know—this is lying.

Q. Aren't there many instances when people think they know—they are mistaken, but are not aware of it?

MR. O. The result is the same. There is a sort of law of percentages. One can make some mistakes, but how many? I was recently studying some literature of the Society for Psychical Research. I knew about this in Petersburg. Lately I heard about the American Society. They are studying clairvoyance and thought-transference. But clairvoyance and thought-transference is function of man No. 5. Yet they think they can do it. So this is lying. They start from idea that if some things exist, they belong to everybody. This is the root of lying.

11. 10. 44

MR. O. I was trying to come to one question which nobody asked me here. But I asked in Petersburg. I asked, 'What is miracle?' I would not answer or I would say there are no miracles. But it was answered then. It is one level observing what happens on another level, under different laws. If one lives on earth under 48 laws, and observes what happens under 24 laws. I came to the conclusion that this question is often asked. For instance, last week we spoke of telepathy. This is miracle. People used this word too easily. I had chance to observe this and I know how difficult this is and how much it costs. People spoke to me about the American Society for Psychical Research. This is all quite fantastic. There was a Society for Psychical Research in London long ago. They studied dead bodies walking about, but also something about dreams which was interesting.

But now they think they talk about facts. This is lies! People ask me why I dismiss something like this. Some things are not worthy of investigation. Because these things have to be paid for in advance. People must pay and must be able to pay. And if people had paid as much as this would cost, they would not talk.

Q.   Dr. Rhine claims that it is not a matter of acquiring it—that it's inherent.

MR. O.   I say nonsense. It is not inherent. Thought-transference is only possible if one pays in advance. You cannot meet this in the street. In school you may have observations. But not in the street.

Q.   As I understand Dr. Rhine, he finds that some people have inherited this capacity from their parents and grandparents.

MR. O.   This is all imagination, because he never had one real case. If he had one real case he would not speak. I only quote this as a negative example. They must have some example. This has no value in any way. It must have some starting idea. First, I don't believe in heredity at all. It is quite wrong idea. First, one must pay. It may happen as result of <u>very</u> strong emotional experience—but not without it, not just like that. If you know this, you know that any attempt to avoid this point is useless. Because it is emotional, not intellectual. Clairvoyance must have its own reason. For man No. 5 it may be ordinary experience, but under laws of man No. 5.

Q.   Just what do you mean by a very strong emotional experience?

MR. O.   One has to have emotional states much higher than one can have in ordinary life. There are many experiments, but it is not my business to describe them. We talk of development.

Q.   Does strong emotion mean emotional part of emotional centre? Higher emotion?

MR. O.   No, ordinary emotion—not higher emotion—but much stronger than in ordinary life. Telepathy, clairvoyance, knowing future, that only comes from emotional state. Higher emotion is different. It is more or less permanent.

Q.   Is it extreme effort that gives people control over higher centres? I mean over powers on a different level?

MR. O.   No, higher centres are not from efforts, but from consciousness. When one is conscious for sufficient time, one comes to that. But I speak of experiments.

Q.   When you speak of strong emotions that bring on clairvoyance, do you mean he has to bring it on himself by some methods?

MR. O. I did not use these methods. I used other methods. One cannot do it by himself, I admit it. This way demands someone else. For example, clairvoyance. I spoke to many theosophists who were supposed to have experience of clairvoyance, but only one had the first experience which I knew must come in the beginning. That was Meade.

Q. But if a person is thrown into a sudden unexpected emotion, can there be telepathy transmitted during that period?

MR. O. You must turn it round. If he had a moment of telepathy, that means he must have had the emotion. But emotion does not necessarily produce telepathy.

Q. If a person sees someone one doesn't expect to see and who isn't really there, is it imagination or what?

MR. O. Either one has to go to a doctor or one went to a doctor too much.

Q. Can we not remember ourselves for a fraction of a second when we make the effort?

MR. O. No, seconds are not sufficient. What you can do now—you can remember you cannot remember yourself. At the same time, do other things that are told, like trying not to express negative emotions. Then you may find yourself able to remember yourself sometimes. But only when it becomes a certain length is it counted. If it becomes connected with certain emotions, then it works quicker.

Q. What does it mean when they become connected with stronger emotions?

MR. O. We know what strong emotional state is. If this is connected it may work hundreds of times faster.

Q. Is it an emotion that goes right along with self-remembering?

MR. O. It cannot be intellectual. One cannot just sit quietly and think what is under the table. One must be afraid first. Try to remember that if you do everything you are told and don't leave it, you will come to higher centres. This is aim. It is very important not to think you have it first, or this may become hysterical, neurotic. If you get it, you will know yourself.

Q. Are there conditions connected with the ability to perform miracles?

MR. O. Yes.

Q. Could you tell us?

MR. O. I don't know what miracles you want. Some twenty years ago in London, we spoke with one man how it could be calculated. The same night, in the house where I slept, there was a dark room in which I thought I had left a light. It was very cold, and I didn't want to get up. Then I began to calculate what efforts would be necessary, first to see if the light was on and then to turn it off. I came to conclusion that first.to see I would need all life energy I spend in twenty-four hours, so even if I did it I might die, while to turn it off I would need the energy the earth uses in turning on its axis in one day.

15. 11. 44

Q. According to the system, what is the meaning of the words 'Psychical Research'?
MR. O. If you ask me, I would say—first it is a question of school. Man cannot do anything by himself. If man starts with idea that school is necessary, then something may come. They speak of extra-sensory perception; it does not begin like this.
Q. Does it only come as a result of long work?
MR. O. That was put in Petersburg—'If one pays more and more and more, so much, can he get something?' That means sacrifice. But there must not be too much self-will, even about a sacrifice.
Q. Isn't self-will the illusion that we have—that we can control things on our own?
MR. O. Quite. It means illusion. And there is difference between control and illusion.

14. 3. 45

Q. Do the higher centres have accumulators?
MR. O. Probably, but we don't speak of them.
Q. Does self-remembering prevent leakage of energy from storage batteries?
MR. O. I think so, because very much energy is used by unconscious action.
Q. Has the lower centre then any relation to the big accumulator?
MR. O. They all have. Instinctive, yes. Direct connection is

also possible but it needs super-effort. This is dangerous. People can kill themselves—though usually they fall asleep. But in man No. 5, energy may just flow through these small accumulators.

Q.   We speak about stopping leakage of energy and accumulating energy. To what end?

MR. O.   Leaking is simply losing energy—if we lose attention we may give an enormous amount of energy when we need only an ounce. Negative emotions may suddenly explode and destroy all energy we have.

Q.   If we have enough energy for ordinary activities, when should I want to accumulate further energy?

MR. O.   For certain things you want to do, you don't have enough right energy. Many things you would like to do need very fine energy. You want positive emotion—for that you need in accumulator an amount of carbon 3. And also knowledge how to use them.

Q.   I observe I go from good to bad state with lightning speed. Is that because I don't remember myself?

MR. O.   No, it is because it is emotional centre—so quick change that you cannot follow it.

Q.   You spoke of everchanging 'I's; is that related?

MR. O.   Yes, if emotional feeling touches 'I's they may change so quickly you think there are millions.

Q.   Through intense pain I experienced a negative emotion on the verge of turning positive. Could that be?

MR. O.   It is possible, but it is simply luck. It doesn't mean it can happen again. It is very rare. But some people have it. It may be that in moment of intense pain, without knowing what you did, you made right effort and connected mi 12 with C3.

Q.   How does one make effort on mi 12?

MR. O.   One must learn for a long time before one can even think about it. I can say that it is very interesting but very bewildering; you have quite new experiences.

Q.   What sort of new experiences?

MR. O.   How can I describe them if there are no words for them? One must first come to them and not add anything from imagination.

11
Cosmology

LAW OF THREE

All the matter of the surrounding world, the food we eat, the water we drink, air we breathe, the stones of our houses, our own bodies—all this is permeated by all the matters existing in the universe. There is no need to study or analyse the sun in order to find solar matter; this matter is in ourselves, it is the result of the division of our atoms. In the same way we have in us matters of all other worlds. In this sense, man is indeed a miniature universe; it has all the matters which compose the universe, the same forces, the same laws act in him which govern the life of the universe. Therefore, by studying man we study the universe and vice versa.

But a full parallel between man and the universe can be drawn only if we take man in the full sense of the word, i.e. a man in whom the powers and possibilities inherent in him are developed. An under-developed man, a man who has not completed his evolution, cannot be taken as a complete picture of the world—he is an unfinished world.

As has been said earlier, laws are everywhere the same, on all planes. The same laws, manifesting in different worlds, i.e. in different conditions, produce different phenomena. The study of the relation of the laws to the planes on which they manifest themselves brings us to the study of relativity.

Thus, the Law of Three brings relativity into our definition of matter. From the point of view of the system, every matter may exist in four states, according to which force passes through the object in question. Thus, instead of one iron we have four irons, four coppers, and so on. These matters have different names. Father, mother, son: carbon, oxygen, nitrogen. The family is hydrogen. The beginning of a new family is the son.

If we place the three forces in a sequence, according to the order in which they unite, we will get the order 1, 2, 3; but the matters serving as conductors of these forces will, according to their density, stand in the order: carbon, nitrogen, oxygen. Therefore, the forces will stand in the order 1, 3, 2. But for future creation, for the formation of the next triad nitrogen must, as it were, return once more to the third place, in the order 1, 2, 3 and in this way become carbon of the next triad.

The Law of Three manifests equally in everything in the world. If we take the Ray of Creation, we must remember that the worlds are connected one with the other and affect one another according to the Law of Three. In other words, the first three worlds, taken together, produce that phenomenon which influences the following worlds, and so on. The Absolute is the conductor of the active force, the next world is the conductor of the passive force, the next, or World 6, is the conductor of neutralizing force. In other words, the Absolute is C, World 3 is O, World 6 is N. But World 6 (or nitrogen) stands, by its density, between World 1 and World 3. In other words, the force of the Absolute must first touch, as it were, World 6 and only then penetrate World 3. In order to understand this relationship, it will be helpful to try and find an analogy which would illustrate the relation of the Absolute to the following worlds. Everything in the world is alike: 'as above, so below'. The Microcosm reflects in itself the whole universe. It will help us to find this analogy if we remember that the Will of the Absolute reaches only World 3; further on it manifests itself in the form of mechanical laws.

If we take man as the Absolute and try to find the ultimate limits that can be reached by his will, inside himself, the most superficial knowledge of human physiology will give us an answer to this question. Man's will (taking this as a conditional concept) may govern the movements of the whole organism, of separate limbs, of some organs and of breathing. If a man concentrates his attention on the tip of his nose, he begins to feel it. By this concentration he may even provoke a slight sensation of irritation in some parts of his body, i.e. in some tissues. But he can in no way manifest his will in relation to some separate cell in his body. Cells are too small for this. My will can manifest itself only in relation to tissues; in relation to cells it can no longer manifest itself.

If we take man as analogous to the Absolute, tissues will correspond to World 3, and cells to World 6.

Let us now try to see how it can be that the forces, emerging from the Absolute in order to manifest themselves in World 3 must pass through World 6. The analogy shows us quite plainly the necessity of such a direction of the force. Man's will can influence a tissue, i.e. a fragment of tissue in certain parts of the body. But a tissue is composed of cells. In order to affect the tissue the will must first influence the cells composing the given fragment of tissue. The tissue is a different world in relation to cells, but at the same time tissues do not exist apart from cells for they are composed of cells.

World 3 is separate from World 6, at the same time it (i.e. All Worlds) is composed of worlds 6, i.e. worlds similar to our World 6—the Milky Way. In order to influence part of World 3 (All Worlds) the Absolute must first influence a certain number of worlds 6 (All Suns) of which World 3 is composed.

Thus, in the passage of forces, Worlds 1, 3, 6 stand, at first, in the order 1, 3, 6, then in the order 1, 6, 3. For a further passage of forces they must again resume the order 1, 3, 6. Nitrogen of the first triad becomes, in this case, carbon of the second triad, i.e. the Milky Way is the conductor of the active force in relation to the oxygen and nitrogen which follow.

What will be oxygen and what nitrogen in the second triad? In the order of the Ray of Creation oxygen will be World 12 or the sun, and nitrogen World 24, or planets. Since nitrogen stands between carbon and oxygen, the force coming from the carbon, i.e. from Milky Way, or from the stars, must first pass through planets in order to reach the sun. It may look strange at the first glance, but if we visualize the structure of the Solar System, we shall see quite clearly that it cannot be otherwise. No analogies are needed here. Imagine the sun surrounded by planets moving round it; in the distance, some groups of stars from which certain influences go forth towards the sun. But the sun does not stand in one place; we know that it also moves; planets, rotating round it, move with it in space, forming, each of them by its motion, a spiral round the central rod of the sun. This central rod of the sun is entirely enclosed in the spirals of planets which surround it, and no influence can reach the sun without first passing through the worlds of planets, i.e. penetrating through the rings of the spiral.

Further, nitrogen of the second triad, i.e. planets, becoming carbon of the third triad, must find corresponding oxygen and nitrogen. In our ray of creation, oxygen is earth. But there is no nitrogen in the astronomical ray of creation. Therefore, if planets had to pass their influence direct to earth, they could not have done it. Earth is incapable of receiving planetary influences. So, in order to make the passage of forces possible between the planets and the earth in the astronomical ray of creation, a special contraption, a special machine was created, which represents, as it were, the sensitive organ of the earth—organic life on earth.

Organic life on earth is nitrogen of the third triad. Forces coming from the planets fall first on the organic life; organic life receives them and then passes them on to earth. Organic life is a sensitive film covering the terrestrial globe, which catches planetary influences; otherwise they would be lost, reflected from the bare surface of the earth.

If we remember the extremely complicated organization of the ends of sensitive nerves in our own organism, for instance, the ends of taste and smell nerves, we shall not think it strange that man is defined as a sensitive nerve-ending of the earth.

Of course, a meadow covered with grass differs in many ways from man—it receives only some planetary influences, and very few of these. Man receives much more complex influences. But people differ greatly from one another in this respect. The majority of men are important only in the mass and only the mass receives one or another influence. Others are capable of receiving influences individually—influences which masses cannot receive, for they are sensitive only to coarse influences.

Organic life on earth, playing the rôle of nitrogen of the third triad, is by this very fact carbon of the fourth triad in our ray. In other words, it conducts the active force which meets with corresponding oxygen and nitrogen. Earth is oxygen, and moon is nitrogen through which the influences of organic life pass to earth.

Now, if we take the Ray of Creation divided into four triads and if we bear in mind that the sum of each triad is a definite hydrogen, we shall get four hydrogens or four densities of matter, or four matters of different density of which the universe consists. But before studying and examining the inter-relation of these four matters, we must study certain other fundamental laws which govern our life. After the Law of Three, the next fundamental law is the Law of Octaves.

Absolute	C
All Worlds	O
All Suns	N

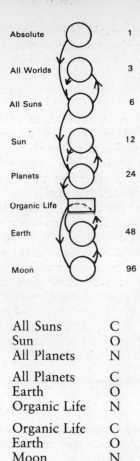

Absolute		1
All Worlds		3
All Suns		6
Sun		12
Planets		24
Organic Life		
Earth		48
Moon		96

All Suns   C
Sun   O
All Planets   N

All Planets   C
Earth   O
Organic Life   N

Organic Life   C
Earth   O
Moon   N

The Ray of Creation can be taken as a descending octave. After _re_ the octave has its _do_—it also is the Absolute. There are, as it were, two Absolutes: one begins the ray, the other ends it. One Absolute is All, the other is—Nothing. But there can be no two Absolutes, for, in its very nature, Absolute is one; therefore 'All' includes 'Nothing' or 'Nothing' includes 'All'. Our dualistically constructed mind cannot take in the identity of opposites. We divide everything, even the Absolute. In reality, what we call antitheses of opposites exist only in our conception, our subjective perception of the world. But, even when we understand this we are unable to express this under-

standing in words; our language has no words including simultaneously the thesis and the antithesis. But such words existed
in some ancient languages, for instance, in Sanskrit. Take, for
instance, the word 'sat' which means 'being' and 'non-being' at
the same time. For us these two concepts are opposed to one
another, our mind cannot grasp them as one idea, in the same
way as it cannot grasp the images of some Hindu gods,
combining complete opposites in themselves.

In the cosmic octave the first interval is filled by the Will of
the Absolute. Organic life is the special adaptation filling the
interval between planets and earth. It is created in the form of
a lateral or additional octave beginning in the sun. Now, if we
take the cosmic octave in the order of the passage of forces
according to the Law of Three, we obtain the first triad
consisting of Worlds 1, 3, 6, which, all together, give hydrogen
1. The second triad (6, 12, 24,) gives hydrogen 2. The third
triad gives hydrogen No. 3 and the fourth—hydrogen No. 4.
These four hydrogens can be taken as corresponding to the four
fundamental points of the universe. The first will correspond to
the Absolute, because the Absolute enters into it as the active
force; the second will correspond to the sun, the third to earth
and the fourth to moon.

Further we shall examine the passage of radiations between
these four points. We take the radiations between each two
points in the form of an octave. Thus we obtain three octaves:
Absolute-sun; sun-earth; earth-moon.

It should be noted that, although there are six intervals, only three of them require to be filled from without. The intervals between do-si are filled by the Will of the Absolute, by the influence of the mass of the sun on the radiations passing through it, and by the influence of the mass of the earth on the radiations passing through it.

RAY OF CREATION. JANUARY 17TH 1935

MR. O.   Several questions referring to the Ray of Creation can only be answered when the idea itself of the Ray of Creation becomes clear. There is nothing new in the Ray of Creation, nothing that you do not know—only facts are differently disposed. Certain facts, such as the fact that we live on the earth, that earth is one of the planets, that planets are part of the Solar System, and things like that are obvious, but, when we think about the world we live in we do not ordinarily put them in the same position. Yet, disposing is necessary for the solution of every ordinary problem—in ordinary arithmetic you have to dispose your material in a certain way, and the way of disposing this material includes a certain understanding of the way to solve this problem. It is called enunciation of the problem; so the Ray of Creation is also a kind of enunciation of the problem of how to define man's place in the world. This means not only man's exact place but also the relation of this place to as many landmarks as possible. So we find the place of man on the earth and establish this, then the place of the moon, and then the planets, the sun and so on. In this way we can understand one another when we speak about the world.

First of all the Ray of Creation is studied from the point of view of language, but many other ideas are also connected with the Ray of Creation.

There may be a certain difficulty only in understanding the idea of the Absolute. For instance, a question was asked why the Will of the Absolute does not manifest itself in our world. The Law of the Absolute is its Will. This kind of disposition of material shows that the Will of the Absolute, different from the mechanical laws of this world, cannot be manifested in this world because it would be necessary for it to destroy all the other worlds between. Try to think about it, it is very important. To a certain extent one can understand this idea by finding in

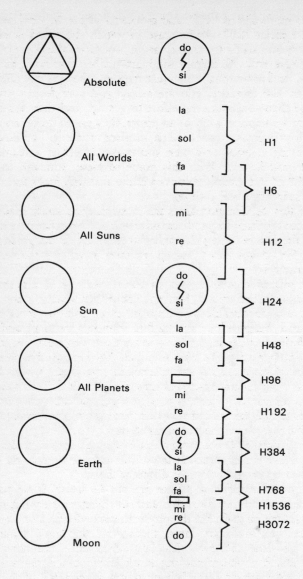

oneself moments of 'will', and moments of mechanical continuation. I mean 'will' in the sense in which the word is used in
ordinary life, ordinary conversation, not from the point of view
of creative will. At certain moments in life you have to make
efforts, and after that things just happen, they go on, one after
another. For instance, you are asleep and you do not want to
get up; then you make the effort to get up, and then for a long
time things happen without an effort, they go on quite naturally.
And then suppose you come to another moment: you have put
off writing a letter, and then you make an effort and take the
pen. If you look at from this point of view, you will see that
the Will of the Absolute cannot come through mechanicalness,
but it starts the ball rolling.

The Ray of Creation gives the possibility to study some very
important principles without which it is impossible to understand the world—the principle of relativity and the principle of
scale. But about this I will speak later when we have a little
more material.

The principle of scale is a simple thing. The idea is that we
can know much more than we ordinarily know if we study
things commensurable with us and having relation to us in one
way, and things which are further removed from us and have
no definite relation to our life—in another, a more abstract way,
on a smaller scale. In this way we can get all the necessary
amount of knowledge without learning too much; we can know
all that is necessary, and this knowledge will include very few
useless things. Only in this way you get the necessary amount
of knowledge, because if you learn everything indiscriminately,
you will not know the necessary things.

The principle of relativity enters when we begin to understand
that we live under different laws. We are not under one set of
laws but under quantities of different laws.

There was a question: 'What are the 48 laws?' If we take 48
laws, we must understand that each of them is a very big system
of laws. One of them are the physical laws which exist on earth,
another, say, biological laws, and so on. We know something
about physical and biological laws, but there are many laws
about which we know nothing at all. For instance, there are the
cosmic laws which don't belong to the three laws of the earth
itself—they are connected with some bigger sphere and govern
certain things which from our point of view appear trivial and
insignificant. For instance, there is a definite law that each class

of living beings can only eat a certain kind of food (from a certain density up to a certain density). Man can eat things such and such a density to such and such a density, from such and such a quality to such and such a quality, and he cannot change this, just as he cannot change the air he breathes or the temperature in which he can exist. There are many things like that—they are all laws under which man lives. But there are many things about it that we cannot know, many things that we do not know about the conditions in which we live.

The Ray of Creation is a help, an instrument or method for new thinking. We know about the division of man into seven categories—everything else should be divided in the same way. Ordinary thinking is divided into thinking No. 1, 2 and 3. Thinking No. 1 is chiefly imitative; thinking No. 2 is more emotional, based on likes and dislikes; thinking No. 3 is theoretical, logical thinking, which is quite good in its place, but when it is applied to things that are beyond its power it becomes quite wrong. This is all we know in ordinary life. From the Ray of Creation begins thinking No. 4, and this you must try to understand. The Ray of Creation is not another theory, like other theories you know; it is a certain rearrangement of the material you already know. And thinking No. 4 is such thinking which, little by little, disposes of all contradictions. In thinking No. 3, whatever line one takes, one immediately finds some other theory which will contradict that particular theory. In thinking No. 4, not at once, but gradually one comes to a certain understanding of the fact that it is possible to think without contradictions, to understand that contradictions are not really contradictions.

Ordinary thinking always has many contradictions. Every theory has another theory opposed to it. For instance, if we take the world, we either think that there is a kind of Divine Will that creates and keeps everything, or that things just happen by themselves. Another example is will versus mechanicalness, or predestination versus accident. When you study the Ray of Creation, you will see that it contains all these things. All these views are right in a sense and the Ray of Creation includes them all. There is a theory that the human mind we know cannot invent an absolute lie—it cannot invent anything that has no relation to truth. Everything human mind can invent will be a partial representation of truth. For instance, if a man tries to draw a new animal, he will have to take parts of known animals.

He cannot invent something that did not exist before, he has to use the material drawn from his actual observation of life. And he cannot invent a theory which is absolutely wrong. The Ray of Creation shows you how all contradictory theories about predestination or freedom, free choice, free will, if you like, divine will and mechanicalness and so on can be reconciled in one system, how, in their totality, these views, each of which shows one facet of the truth, do not contradict one another. In one place one thing is right, and another thing in another place is right, but each, if applied to the whole, is wrong. But later you will see that certain things cannot be applied to the whole because the whole is not one, it is so varied, has so many faces. The Ray of Creation shows that. Each view has its place, shows one facet of the whole, but it does not represent the whole and, in relation to the whole, it is wrong.

The Law of Three must be understood in a more complicated form than it appears at first. It is quite true that there are three forces. It must be understood that they do not differ from one another as activity and passivity differ in our ordinary idea of these terms. Active and passive are both active; a force cannot be passive, they are all active. But there is a certain difference in their activity at a certain moment and this difference makes the whole of the variety in the world. At the same time, each force, which is now active, next moment, in another triad, may become passive, or neutralizing, and this change of forces, one becoming another, makes up all the phenomena we observe. But even this is not sufficient. It is necessary to understand that there are definite combinations of forces. All the phenomena we observe, our own actions, the actions of other people, all that we observe can be divided into definite classes. These different kinds of happenings have nothing in common, they have different results, they need different effort, and so on. These divisions are very difficult because the classes are very big; at the same time, we do not see the third force, we only see the results.

We can distinguish, if we are told about it, two kinds of action. For instance, first, some kind of violent action, such as burning a house with one match. Another activity is building a house. The action with which the house is burned is not sufficient for building a house. The third kind is more difficult to see. Actions belonging to the first kind are violent actions or natural happenings. Almost all biological events belong to the first kind. So the first triad does not only mean violence, there are many ordinary things of life that belong to this category, such as birth, death and things like that. Most of human activity belongs to the second kind, although much of it belongs to the first kind. The second kind always means effort or sacrifice.

The first kind are either natural phenomena, or violence. When we say that things happen naturally, that means they happen by the first triad. There was a question once: 'If things happen naturally, if we arc naturally under 48 laws, should we try to change?' But all our conscious, intentional life is struggle against the natural. If we only want to follow what is natural we will never move from this dead spot where we are.

Perhaps somebody can find an example of the third kind. In the New Testament, and probably in other writings, you can perhaps find references to the third kind of triad. For instance: 'I will have mercy and not sacrifice'—that refers to the third kind, that would be an action by the third triad (but the word 'mercy' is not right—it has quite a different meaning).

Now we must try to understand the second big cosmic law—the Law of Seven. Triads refer to events; each separate event, whether big or small, means a certain meeting of three forces. But a succession of events proceeds according to the Law of Seven, the Law of Octaves. If we take the universe in quite an elementary way as consisting of vibrations, it will be noticed in observing these vibrations that they do not continue in the same way as they have started. Whether vibrations increase or decrease, there is a certain irregularity in their decrease or increase. If we take increasing vibrations, it was noticed that in a period between a certain number of vibrations and double that number, there are two places or moments when vibrations slow down, and then start again. Then it was found that this increase proceeds with a certain measured irregularity. This measured irregularity was calculated and was put into a certain formula. This formula, expressing a cosmic law, was later applied to music in the form of the major scale. But first the formula existed as a formula of a certain cosmic law.

In the study of events, if we speak of each event separately, we have to understand triads, to which triad each event belongs, and so on. If we speak about succession of events, we have to know descending and ascending octaves. Without knowing whether it is ascending or descending it is impossible to understand it, and this is what happens in ordinary thinking, because people study ascending octaves and take them for descending, and vice versa.

The Ray of Creation can also be explained as an octave, taking it as a succession of events. The first interval is filled by the Will of the Absolute. In order to fill the interval between planets and earth a special instrument, a special machine, was cosmically created. This machine is organic life on earth. Organic life plays a very important part in the Ray of Creation; it guarantees the transmission of energies and makes the growth of the Ray possible. The growing point of the Ray is the moon. The idea is that moon becomes like earth, and earth becomes like sun; then another moon will appear and so it will continue up to a certain point. But this is a little beyond us. Organic life is a sort of receiving apparatus for receiving planetary influences coming from the planets of the Solar System. At the same time, doing this work, serving as a means of communication between earth and planets, organic life feeds the moon. Everything that lives serves the purposes of the earth; everything that dies feeds the moon. This sounds strange at first, but when we understand the laws which govern organic life, laws on which it is based, we will understand that all organic life is based on a very hard law, the law that one class eats another class. It is a very cruel arrangement, but it makes organic life not only self-sufficient but enables it to feed the moon and serve for transmitting energies. In this way it serves the purpose of bigger worlds, planets, earth, and of the end of the Ray of Creation, moon. So organic life is useful for many purposes.

The question arises: how can we prove it? We can find certain proofs later by analogy, by studying man, because the idea is that man is built on the same principles as the Ray of Creation. There are many things which we cannot prove in the objective way, but perhaps we can find proofs by studying ourselves.

The Ray of Creation contradicts many accepted views, but it does not contradict anything really scientific. But our mind is full of quite unscientific speculations; one of these speculations is the nebular theory according to which the sun is regarded as the newest and the moon the oldest (if you take sun, earth, moon). It is generally supposed that the sun is the youngest and will cool and become like earth, and earth will cool and become like moon. But, from the point of view of the Ray of Creation, this is quite a wrong theory. According to the Ray of Creation, the sun is the oldest and the moon the newest. Moon is not fully born yet, it is only in the process of being born.

Q. Did you use the word 'effort' in connection with the second kind of triad?

MR. O. Yes, effort and sacrifice. In certain cases, as later you will see it in the human body, work proceeds without visible effort, because it is highly organized matter and machinery. But even there effort is necessary at certain moments.

Q. Could you give an example of people taking a descending octave for an ascending?

MR. O. Suppose we meet savages, wild people—we think they are primitive, and from these primitive people there begins to develop civilization and culture. But we don't realize that in most cases they are descendants of cultured people. Very often we take degeneration for evolution.

Q. Does ascending scale always mean improvement?

MR. O. Again it may, or it may not. The idea of mechanical evolutions is the worst kind of speculation; we never had any facts to support it; nobody ever saw a single small example of such an evolution. It would mean the formation of more complex units from less complex, by itself. It would be just the same as expecting a house to grow, by itself, from a heap of bricks.

Q. What is the interaction between the earth and the moon?

MR. O. The action of the moon in our life is purely mechanical. It would be simpler to understand if you take it that the moon acts by itself, by pure weight, on our life, and it receives higher energies, higher matters, which little by little make it alive. If we remember the four kinds of energies, mechanical, life, psychic and conscious, then it means that the moon acts by mechanical energy, simply by its weight, like an electro-magnet.

Q. Does the Law of Three work in successional events?

MR. O. Yes, all the time, but forces change their value; what was active becomes passive, and what was passive becomes neutralizing. In the beginning we take the ordinary definition of energy and matter. A certain kind of energy works in a certain kind of matter. Any kind of matter becomes slightly different when active force works through it; I mean different from the same matter conducting passive or neutralizing force. Take iron: when active force works through it, it is one kind of iron; when passive force works through it, iron is different. If the same iron is taken and no force works through it, it is a fourth kind of iron. All these four kinds of iron, four kinds of matter, have different names; they are called carbon, oxygen, nitrogen, or hydrogen, according to which force works through it. Any matter that has no relation to a triad can be called hydrogen; in other words, it is matter that has no relationship to anything else. But in a triad any matter can be called carbon, oxygen or nitrogen. Later I will show you a certain Table of Hydrogens where it will be possible, just by figures, to have very exact definitions of all matters in accordance with their functions in relation to man.

Q. If you take events instead of matter, can you say that they are of a different kind according to the force that works through them?

MR. O. Yes, certainly, according to which triad works, events will be quite different. It is interesting, you know, because we all know, for instance, how the same sentence, the same words, can have quite a different meaning according to who says it. If one person says it, it will have one meaning, but if another person says it, it will have a different meaning. Or even the same person can say it at different times and the meaning will be different.

All this only looks complicated, but soon you will see that it is very simple. There is no new information in all these things, or very little, but with the help of this language we will be able to speak of new things—without this language it is almost impossible, because our words are too vague, not definite enough.

GROWTH: RAY OF CREATION. JANUARY 10TH 1938

Q. In the Ray of Creation the word 'growth' seems to be used for the process when finer matters become denser. In man it is the other way round.

MR. O. Growth has many meanings. The Ray of Creation is on an enormous scale. Growth in it means expansion. You are quite right that in expansion finer matters become denser.

THE CONNECTION OF PLANETS AND EARTH.
FEBRUARY 9TH 1938

One of the faults of ordinary knowledge is that it takes things too separately. Things are more connected then we think. Everything is connected, you know. In the ordinary, what we call, scientific view, we take things very separately. For instance, take this question about the connection of planets and earth. In the past fifteen years there have been many new theories in science, particularly in geology, which are very interesting and exactly conform to the ideas of this system. Really, this direction in geology began a long time ago, but it was not expressed in any definite theory in books. But dissatisfaction with the current theories began more than forty years ago and it begins to give results now. Some books appeared which put geology on quite a different basis to what was thought forty years ago, and there is practically nothing in these new ideas which does not correspond exactly to this system. If you are interested, this will give you much material, for instance, about the meaning of organic life and all that is connected with it—the meaning of organic life in the development of the earth. Old science, nineteenth century science, took organic life as an accident on the earth, but modern geology proved quite definitely that it is the most important factor on the life of the earth. The surface of the earth, or life on the earth, would be quite different without organic life, so it is not an accident.

As a matter of fact, it is pointed out in modern geology that there is no proof that there ever was a time when there was no organic life on earth. It does not mean there never had been such a time, but as far as we can see there is no evidence.

If you are interested, better get some new books on that. I know of two books, translated from Russian into French (but a very bad translation). One is 'La Géochimie' by W. Vernadsky and the other 'La Biosphère' also by W. Vernadsky, but these are probably not the only books because these ideas always appear in bunches.

RAY OF CREATION. FEBRUARY 10TH 1938

Q. The Ray of Creation is a descending octave?
Mr. O. In the sense of expanding, differentiating.

Q. We cannot quite escape the conclusion that the Absolute is limited somewhere in space.

MR. O. It is space, although space begins only in World 6. Absolute and World 3 are beyond space or out of space. Space is limitation and that begins only in World 6.

Q. Do you remember saying that man's time is his life?

MR. O. His time. Earth's time is earth's life. For sun it is sun's life.

Q. What is space for man—life?

MR. O. Space is limitation of his possibilities on the earth. For all, it is only limitation in this case. Space and time are the same thing really. One way it looks like space, another way it looks like time.

Q. Then it is just subjective, really?

MR. O. There is objective limitation. One can have more time, one can have more space than one has.

Q. What is the average time for man?

MR. O. How long can a man live? That is his time.

Q. How is it connected mathematically with the time of earth and sun?

MR. O. About that we will speak later. It is connected. Did you hear about time in different cosmoses?

Q. About space and limitation. Isn't space infinite?

MR. O. No. On each level there is its own space. You see we are not accustomed to take these things practically. For instance, for the sun its space is the Solar System. It cannot get out of it. This is limitation.

COMMENTARIES TO THE RAY OF CREATION. JUNE 28TH 1938

MR. O. I spoke about the study of man and the study of the world in which man lives, first, in order to find the place of man in the universe and, second, to try and understand why man is what he is and why he cannot be different; why he is in such circumstances. We cannot find answers to all these questions by studying man separately from the universe; we have to study man parallel with the universe. In a certain sense, man is analogous to the universe. If we take the universe as a whole, the man in relation to it, then certain laws we understand better by studying man, and certain other laws we understand better by studying the universe. In relation to the study of the universe, you must first of all understand the method we use: we study the universe on the principle of scale in a very simple sense. For instance, your own house, where you live, you know on a scale proportionate to your body, but the town in which you live you do not know on the same scale—you know it on a much smaller scale; you know only such parts of it as you need to know, places where you have to go. Some parts you know well, others not so well, and there is probably no part which you know as well as your house. And you know England on a still smaller scale. The same principle is used in geography and astronomy. For instance, we study earth on one scale because we live on earth, but all other planets of the Solar System we take all together because we don't need to study them separately. In one or another way they affect our life, but these are only the planets of the Solar System we know. Planets of other systems we do not study at all; we just take suns with all that is included in those suns' influence. Later you will yourself find examples of this method as different from other methods. Ordinarily, people do not think about it, and they study the universe quite apart from the study of man. In this way they accumulate a certain amount of knowledge, but it is unrelated knowledge.

According to this method, different from the usual methods, we study man as part of organic life on earth. Organic life is a kind of sensitive film that covers the earth and serves a certain definite purpose. Generally, we can say that it serves the purpose of communication, because, without it, sun, planets and moon cannot communicate with earth sufficiently, and without the help of organic life many things would be lost. Organic life catches those vibrations coming from outside, and transfers them to earth. In that way men, animals, plants, each of them play their part.

We are here on earth. Organic life, of which we are a part, is under certain influences of all planets; we are also under certain influences of the sun; we are under certain influences of all suns and, maybe, under influences of all worlds. Of course, influences of all worlds on individual man are very small, but we know that influences come from the sun. We do not know much about influences of the moon, but it plays a very important part in organic life, and without understanding how everything is connected, and how organic life of man on the earth is connected with planets and the sun, we cannot understand the position of man and his present life as it is. For instance, it is impossible to understand one expression that is used in relation to man without understanding this diagram—the expression that man lives in a very bad place of the universe, and that many things which we regard as unfair, against which we fight, against which we try to fight, are really the result of this position of organic life on the earth. If we were on the moon, they would be still worse; there would be no possibility of development. On the earth there is a possibility of development—it means that we can develop certain parts in us.

Very little of planetary influences comes to us. Generally planetary influences are only felt by masses of people; so planetary influences are responsible for wars, revolutions and things like that; but individual man is very little under planetary influences, because the part which can be affected by planetary influences in man is undeveloped. This undeveloped part is essence.

To a certain extent man is also under the influence of the sun, and he can be under much higher influences if he develops higher centres and becomes connected with them. So development means passing from one kind of influences to another kind of influences. At present, we are more particularly under the influence of the moon. We can come under the influence of planets, sun and other influences, if we develop. We have to become more and more conscious to come under these influences.

Q. In what way are we under the influence of moon?

MR. O. Moon controls movements. If I move my arm—it is moon that does it, because it cannot happen without the influence of moon. Moon is like the weight on an old-fashioned clock—everything moves because of this weight.

Q. Why is it that planets affect man in the mass and not individual man?

MR. O. The part of man which can be affected by planetary influences is either very small and undeveloped, or mixed with personality too much. Personality reflects all these influences, and man is under the Law of Accident. If man lived in his essence he would live under planetary influences or, in other words, under the law of fate. Whether this would be to his advantage or not is another question; it may be better in one case and worse in another—generally better. But planetary rays cannot penetrate personality.

People in the mass are affected by planetary influences in

certain parts of themselves which are always there, so planetary influences can affect masses of humanity, but in normal cases they do not affect individual beings, or it happens very seldom.

Q. Have a crowd of people essence and personality?

MR. O. Every individual has, but a crowd is a little different. Most people in a crowd are No. 1, that is, living in instinctive and moving centre. And the chief motive powers of man No. 1 are imagination and imitation; and when they are under the power of imagination and imitation, they very easily accept mechanical influences; they begin to imitate one another, so it produces a big effect.

Q. Is our aim to develop ourselves so that individuals come under planetary influences?

MR. O. It will not be individual influence, it will be according to your type. But individual man will be different according to his essence.

Q. Could you tell us more about influences of the sun?

MR. O. But you can find it in books in the ordinary way. But conscious influence will come from another side, or the possibility of conscious influence.

Q. I don't understand what you mean by conscious influence of the sun.

MR. O. I cannot speak about it now: we will come to that later.

LAW OF SEVEN. JUNE 12TH 1945

MR. O. I have to explain my aim in <u>speaking about the Law of Seven.</u> We have to study intervals and in order to come to this, we have to study groups and group rules. I do not speak of schools because that is a big thing. But rules we must study. Many people who have been studying for many years do not understand rules. Only in using rules in work of groups, can shock be given and line be kept straight. There is no other way. But in school groups you can observe how the line is kept straight.

Q. Is there any order in which these rules—steps should be observed?

MR. O. This is not a rule. Rules are told from time to time and very necessary to discuss rules. Each person can say what he understands. Discussion of rules is a separate question. All wrong things occur because people live as if groups do not exist, rules do not exist. Rules are necessary for self-observation and especially for study of the Law of Seven.

Q. By study of rules do you mean observation of resistance to rules?

MR. O. No, no, that would be formatory. Take a certain rule and see when it is applied.

Q. Will you discuss rules here?

MR. O. If you want to discuss rules, find a moment when I speak about rules. Catch me.

Q. How do these rules originate?

MR. O. By necessity. I can even take rules I had to make myself. But there were many rules before any of us were born. But the rules I introduced were introduced because they were necessary. For example, one group went wrong. So I had to separate the rest and forbid speaking about that group. If they wished to talk about it, they could leave at once and go there.

Q. Last week I heard that shock was outside help.

MR. O. Yes, rule is sometimes outside help. One is in difficulty and remembers rule. This may be great help. One lady in England asked, 'Why must we have rules?'

Q. In seeking to achieve some degree of consciousness do we just think about it, or do we work on it?

MR. O. School. And group. This is the only possibility. If one works one may understand more.

Q. I don't understand what the descending octave is.

MR. O. First of all, Ray of Creation. Absolute, World 6, Milky Way, sun (meaning Solar System), planetary world, earth, moon. This is the descending octave. Then take hydrogens. How hydrogen 6 is created. Animal world, vegetable world, propagation. It is all descending octave. Quantity enlarges.

Q. I don't understand as applied to Law of Seven and vibrations.

MR. O. Well, we speak about descending octave. This is descending octave. Physical life—growing of animals, vegetables, fishes, growing, propagating. This is all descending.

Q. The ascending octave begins with us, does it?

MR. O. Ascending—only our own work creating consciousness in ourselves. This is only example we can know without much thought. And we can only do something on this line with the help of schools.

Q. Are animals the terminus of descending octave and man is the beginning of ascending octave?

MR. O. Yes, if he works. If he just sleeps, there is not much ascending octave. But if he begins to wake, yes, there is chance. [MR. O. put diagram of the Ray of Creation on the board.] The interval is filled with organic life. In organic life lives man No. 1, 2, 3, and to avoid useless questions, No. 4. Man No. 5 already belongs to different world. He is under laws of world fa and free from laws of world mi. If he continues to develop, man No. 6 belongs to world sol and No. 7 to world la.

Q. Do you mean that man is still himself but not subject to so many laws?

MR. O. I didn't say that, but you can put it like that.

Q. Does this have relationship to higher hydrogens?

MR. O. No, better not to mix it. Question about man. Some man can be 1, 2, 3, and become 4, then 5. As No. 5 he is supposed to live in inner world.

Q. What kind of laws can man escape?

MR. O. Some laws of his own stupidity.

Q. I could see he might escape Law of Accident, but I don't see any other.

MR. O. Well, some laws of accident he may escape. Very useful.

Q. What part of man would come under fa? He wouldn't change physically, therefore I say, what part of him?

MR. O. All man, I think, I don't think we can divide him in this case. Take man as unit. Well, you remember diagram of many 'I's. Maybe not so many, some not so insistent. You remember man No. 5 already had unity. His brain is not so divided. Not so many independent 'I's. Well, you got answer to your question. May be useful.

Q. During moments of attention, does man have greater unity—of 'I's?

MR. O. Maybe, but we cannot speak of that without knowing which scale. How long, how strong, and so on.

Q. Are rules in school made for growth of being?

MR. O. Yes. Sometimes they may be made in some other school. But they are all made to strengthen octaves.

Q. Do you suppose we are capable of recognizing man No. 5?

MR. O. Use imagination. This is good imagination. Imagine No. 5.

Q. Actually none of these laws operate in the ordinary way?

MR. O.   Laws operate everywhere.

Q.   We can only see them as we see them?

MR. O.   If we see them right, we might see them as No. 5 sees them. Some can see, others cannot. As some can write poetry, others cannot. Same kind of perception.

Q.   At this point, is there anything you could tell us that would help us with self-remembering?

MR. O.   Sorry, not this moment. Effort is necessary—and more effort. But before effort it is necessary to understand. Imagine man who remembers himself. I am not joking, it is very useful.

Q.   He wouldn't be an ordinary man if he remembers himself, would he?

MR. O.   Well, imagine him. We cannot judge by physical, only by physiological, results. Man aware of himself, of his actions, always aware.

Q.   Does that awareness mean the change of his own condition?

MR. O.   It must be, only we don't know which. In connection with Food Diagram, we can find something, only this is not proof.

Q.   Change wouldn't always necessarily be the same in No. 5? It would depend on what he started with?

MR. O.   Yes, only I think there must be changes on which we can rely—such as unity.

Q.   When you say try to imagine No. 5—each one of us would imagine a different one?

MR. O.   Yes, but supposing it coincides.

Q.   If we try to imagine what No. 5 is like, we would find certain coincidences of discovery? Physiologically?

MR. O.   We may, quite right.

Q.   Is man No. 5 always product of schools?

MR. O.   I see no other possibility. It is so difficult without the help of schools that I cannot imagine possibility without.

Q.   Seems to me we ought to know more about No. 4.

MR. O.   No. 4 is one who knows what he wants.

Q.   Last week I heard it said that Man No. 4 comes under the influence of World 24 consisting of vibrations. Does this mean that each world has entirely different vibrations?

MR. O.   All worlds consist of vibrations, first. And World 24 is for 5, not 4. You remember Ray of Creation.

Q.   Exactly what is meant by a vibration?

MR. O.   In this case, laws. World 1, one law; World 3, three laws, and so on.

Q. Does man No. 5 have personality?

MR. O. Ask him. How do I know? Why not? But he cannot have two personalities, or three.

Q. Last week you suggested we use our imagination. . .

MR. O. For a special purpose.

Q. . . . to ascertain what a man would be like who self-remembered.

MR. O. Well, did you find out?

Q. As near as I can find out, he wouldn't be guilty of negative emotions.

MR. O. Very pleasant.

Q. Secondly, he would have his imagination under control and it wouldn't become negative.

MR. O. Also very pleasant.

Q. It would develop a type of man unfitted for intercourse with man as he is now.

MR. O. Well, I am very sorry I can do nothing—that is your own conclusion.

Q. When are we going to get our shocks?

MR. O. When we need it, if we pray well.

Q. Isn't it necessary to develop will in order to fill in intervals?

MR. O. If you can, best of all certainly. But you can't wait until you develop will, you must take chances.

Q. In the kind of study we are doing here, is it possible to measure an octave?

MR. O. No, nobody can measure octaves. Only in music. Elsewhere you see results only when it is too late. But if you are under rules, you are warned at the right moment, turned at the right moment. This is what we can get.

Next time I want to speak about the Law of Three again. There are six activities. I want you to study them and see by what octaves they go. They cannot be compared even. What is right in one is wrong in another.

Q. If we try to use will-power in any activity, is it wrong?

MR. O. We haven't got it. Tell me how long you can remember yourself. How long you can stop thought without falling asleep and forgetting what you are doing?

Q. I meant will-power in other activities, like forcing ourselves to do things.

MR. O. Tell me how long and I will tell you how near you are to will-power.

Q. Is the descending octave ever used in school-work?

MR. O. We live by descending octave, we are born by descending octave. If we want to sow wheat or breed rabbits, we have to use descending octaves, growing, multiplying, diminishing. All life is populated by millions of descending octaves.

Q. Everything we do? Do all the small octaves, millions of descending octaves, do they enter into what we do every day?

MR. O. I didn't say we do, I said all nature does.

Q. In ordinary activities such as sewing?

MR. O. We don't do. We look and observe. We think we do but nature does it.

Q. Does each activity have its own small octave?

MR. O. Each has its own.

Q. You say the vibrations of descending octaves are manifestations of nature. Now the ascending octave. . . .

MR. O. Ascending is school-work. We don't know any other form. All the rest is descending in one form or another.

Q. How can we know when we begin to deviate from the straight line?

MR. O. We always know.

Q. We don't always know the exact moment.

MR. O. Sometimes we know the exact moment, sometimes we know in half-an-hour.

Q. Did you say observing rules can act as a shock?

MR. O. Not observing—using rules, remembering rules, following rules. In that way one brings action, results.

Q. Is there any reason why we always speak of three octaves?

MR. O. Three Octaves of Radiation or what? Three octaves in the human machine?

Q. It seems to me we always speak of three.

MR. O. It is made like that, why? Because it was more convenient.

Q. Does the overcoming of the expression of negative emotion give us any needed shock?

MR. O. If you do it well, it may. But that means well. Not do it once and then indulge.

Q. What are some of the ways by which we know we have gone off the straight line?

MR. O. I don't know. Have we any straight line? Well, in architecture you can see straight line you don't see in nature. Well, instruments are necessary for that.

Q. Is the most important thing for our development now to find out more about rules?

Mr. O. Always. Always from the very beginning it is useful. Only in this can you always find help.

Q. Must we always think of possible rules first and then ask about it?

Mr. O. No, no. I said when imagination can help, but not in relation to rules.

Q. But how can we find out what the rules are?

Mr. O. You must know at least one. Start from that and you can find another.

Q. Man No. 5 has control of the emotions.

Mr. O. Some at least. More than us, anyhow.

Q. Does this mean that negative emotions do not arise, man No. 5 is able to get rid of them?

Mr. O. They may arise, but he can control them. He can transform negative emotions into positive.

Q. Did I understand that the highest activity of man, i.e. school-work, is a conscious activity?

Mr. O. It is more conscious than hitting flies, anyhow. But it is not conscious. One must be careful with this word.

Q. Could I ask what effect the proper function of centres has upon the state of self-remembering?

Mr. O. It helps it.

Q. How does one approach to control of work of centres?

Mr. O. By trying to think right. It is easiest. We have a certain control of thought. So we can learn to think right.

Q. When man uses his centres correctly, do his activities change?

Mr. O. It is an important question. Later, but not now, it will be connected with types.

Q. I have been trying to see why it is difficult for me to understand the idea of descending octaves, and my thinking a symphony, solving a scientific problem, learning a language, building a house—all these I could see only as ascending octaves.

Mr. O. Why? All mechanical. Why should they be ascending?

Q. At the same time, I thought of crime and destruction as descending octaves.

Mr. O. Why? They may be ascending octaves. In any case, saying 'crime' and then calling it descending, is quite unjustified.

Q. Is this thinking wrong because of the level on which I see things?

Mr. O. On an ascending octave, something must ascend. If you don't know what, then it must be descending.

Q. Does result determine direction of an octave?

MR. O. Yes, if you see it right.

Q. If we deviate from our aim and fall away, but fresh impressions and new understanding stimulate new effort, what then is the position of the octave?

MR. O. They continue but in an unknown direction.

Q. What is the relation of our study here to the octave of evolution?

MR. O. Well, preparation if you like.

Q. Is it preparation for first step?

MR. O. Before first step.

Q. Are some octaves unfinished—ending at mi or si?

MR. O. The universe must be full of unfinished octaves. Like our lives, full of things begun and unfinished.

Q. When an octave changes direction at mi and si, does this mean a change of activity?

MR. O. One change may mean all changes.

Q. When an interval is reached in an octave, is it necessary for a different activity or triad to be applied in order to keep the octave from changing direction?

MR. O. Something must be applied—we don't know what. It needs a certain kind of shaking.

Q. Is 'good' always connected with ascending octave?

MR. O. Yes, it is connected with certain things. But I would not speak so definitely. Quite right, it is connected with development of consciousness. What happens cannot be called good. A good thing may happen—there is no law against it—but it is not reliable. Good must be created. It cannot come by accident. Evil can come by accident.

COSMOSES

MR. O. Try to remember what you have heard about cosmoses, because it is a very interesting division. It is different from the Ray of Creation. In the Ray of Creation we took the astronomical map of the world, where man does not exist. Here we begin with man. Man is part of organic life; organic life is on the earth; earth is one of the planets of the Solar System, and the rest is the same as in the Ray of Creation.

There are seven cosmoses in the world, from Absolute to man. They have Greek names: 'Protocosmos' (Absolute), 'Megalocosmos' which means great cosmos (World 3)—it is also called Hagiocosmos; 'Macrocosmos' (World 6); 'Deuterocosmos'—second cosmos (World 12); 'Meso-' (middle) cosmos (earth); 'Tritocosmos'—third cosmos (organic life), and 'Microcosmos' (man).

You find in books the expression 'Macrocosm' and 'Microcosm'. anything. It is a fragment of a much fuller teaching about cosmoses. Macrocosm and Microcosm are so far from each other that there is really no connection.

Try to remember what I said before about breath. Breath is a measure of time. Our breath is about three seconds. It is a cosmic measure; it cannot be extended or shortened. The same is true for twenty-four hours—part of the time we sleep, part of the time we walk about. This also is part of cosmic arrangements. In organic life individuals are more of less on the same scale, i.e. they are under the same law. And one interesting thing must be understood: day and night of man, sleeping and waking, twenty-four hours, is breath of organic life.

This is all the material that was given us in Petersburg, and from that we had to develop all the rest. First, we had to find the relation of breath to twenty-four hours, so we divided twenty-four hours by three seconds. This gave us 30,000, and we remembered that 30,000 was also the ratio of the speed of centres. Then we divided three seconds by 30,000 and this gave us 1/10,000th of a second, which, we saw, corresponded to the quickest eye impression. Then we multiplied twenty-four hours by 30,000 and got eighty-two years, which means the average length of human life. So we had four figures: 1/10,000th of a second, three seconds, twenty-four hours and eighty years. We spoke about it and heard from G. that it was quite right, that we had found the correct figures and the meaning of these figures, and that they are cosmic arrangements for all worlds. The relations of these figures are repeated in all worlds. Multiply them by 30,000 if you go to the right of the diagram; or divide them by 30,000 if you go to the left of man in the diagram. So, what is breath for us is impression for organic life; day and night for us is breath for organic life, and so on. So in organic life the quickest impression is three seconds; breath is twenty-four hours; sleeping and waking is eighty years. In earth impression is twenty-four hours, breath eighty years, day and night two and a half million years. Sun's impression is eighty years.

So, life of man corresponds to the quickest eye impression of the sun. So, if it can see us individually, and if we live for eighty years, for the sun it will be just an electric flash.

The relation between cosmoses is different from the relation between the units of the Ray of Creation. Every cosmos is three-dimensional for itself. At the same time, the relation of one cosmos to another is the relation of zero to infinity.

Every cosmos is alive and is built according to the same laws. Not only is each cosmos to a certain extent analogous to another, but also its time is based on the same law. Only it has its own time.

At the same time, cosmoses are not entirely analogous to one another. In order to understand all the laws which relate to cosmoses you have to take three cosmoses and study them side by side. Together they will give all the variations of laws. But one cosmos will not give you this by itself.

Q. Is infinity a definite term or a matter of comparison?

MR. O. I am using it just as it is understood in the ordinary way: as the limit of possible calculation. It means the relation of a unit of one number of dimensions to a unit of a bigger number of dimensions. It means one dimension added. So, although cosmoses are three-dimensional for themselves, one cosmos is, at the same time, four-dimensional for another cosmos. If you take man as three-dimensional, for man organic life will be four-dimensional, earth—five-dimensional, sun—six-dimensional, and, as there are only six dimensions, that means man does not exist in the Macrocosmos, but only exists in the Solar System. You remember how many times you have asked what 'immortality within the Solar System' meant? You see, it is because man does not exist outside the Solar System.

Q. Why do you say there are only six dimensions?

MR. O. Six dimensions means the realization of all possibilities. All is included in six dimensions.

Q. Is the speed of the time of organic life 30,000 quicker than that of time for man?

MR. O. That is material for thinking.

Q. Is there not a danger of confusing time with what happens in time? Are not these two really one and the same?

MR. O. No, it is different. Time is really based on immediate perception. The speed of perception for a unit with our perception is 1/10,000th of a second; for the sun it is eighty years. That shows the difference between man and the sun and gives you an idea of how man's time is different from the time of the sun.

Q. Does it mean that the whole lifetime of a man can be crowded into one flash of the sun's lifetime?

Mr. O. No, man's life is just man's life. It cannot be crowded into anything. But if sun is able to see man's life, it will be just one flash. But for man it will remain as it is.

Q. And man's time ends with his life?

Mr. O. It is measured by his life. Certainly, we cannot measure it outside his life. What you call man's time is time as observed by the intellectual centre. If we can be conscious relatively to moving and instinctive centres then we will be able to see the basis of time in organic life. Higher emotional centre is on the level of planets and higher mental centre is on the level of the sun.

Q. Is it possible to proceed to the left in the Diagram of Cosmoses?

Mr. O. Yes, it is. If we take even only two more, the next will correspond to what is called 'second microcosmos' and this corresponds to what may be called 'big cell'. Its life is twenty-four hours.

The next will be 'third microcosmos', 'small cell'. What is important about this at present is that if the capacity of being conscious in instinctive centre means capacity to be conscious on the scale above us, it also means we can be conscious on the one below. If the capacity to grasp time is increased in one direction, it is also increased in the other. If this capacity extends still more in one direction, it will extend correspondingly in the other.

Q. Has earth got a consciousness?

Mr. O. Intelligence. About consciousness we do not know. Everything has intelligence, that is, every unit having a separate existence, separate function. Certainly each cosmos has its own intelligence.

Q. All the different kinds of time seem to come to the same in the end?

Mr. O. That means you are thinking in the wrong way. Try to think what all this implies. It already shows you that man does not exist in the Macrocosmos—and that means something. Try to find several other implications.

Q. When you say man does not exist, is it in the same sense that an atom does not exist?

MR. O. Man does not exist in any way after the sun. If the sixth dimension ends at the Solar System, there is no place. You remember, I once said that this table does not consist of atoms? It is connected with that.

Q. Does this mean that cells die in twenty-four hours?

MR. O. Some cells die in twenty-four hours and they are very important cells. About the actual life of cells very little is known. About small cells it is absolutely impossible to establish anything. Anything we know remains simply the result of the work of higher mind.

Q. I do not understand what intelligence means when you speak about it in this way.

MR. O. The combination of all capacities of knowing and adapting. I think that is sufficient to cover it. Knowledge and adaptation.

Q. How can we start to think about the sun and earth receiving impressions?

MR. O. You can think only from the point of view of figures and how different everything would look at this rate of perception. And this is too big a gap. Take organic life and man, and you will understand how everything we see, the ordinary phenomena like the movement of stars, the apparent movement of the sun, atmospheric phenomena like rain and snow, will change with the change of perception. Because all our observations of the world are based on a certain definite rate of perception and this never changes. Suppose it does change, say, to the rate of the instinctive centre, then the whole world changes and we see how everything we see now is really subjective.

If you look again at this diagram you see that we can work out these measures of time. Twenty-nine figures will be the life of Protocosmos. There are some very interesting analogies in this which we will see later.

There are many things you can say or think in connection with this table of times. It is not finished. There are many other details, but you must first understand the fundamental principles with which it starts and what it really means.

Q. What do you mean by intelligence?

MR. O. Intelligence of this table, for instance, is its capacity of adaptation. In very dry circumstances it will shrink a little, or may even fall to pieces. In very wet circumstances, it will expand a little. There are many things like that. Certainly, adaptation in inanimate objects is very small, but this is what we mean by Intelligence. Sometimes we can see very interesting manifestations of this, and there are many we cannot observe because either they are too quick or too slow for observation. Living matter has much more intelligence. Even a vegetable has much more. It can turn towards the sun, can absorb certain things and refuse other things. Dead matter like this table is at a level of H1536 and has very little adaptability. Wood in a living tree is much more intelligent, more adaptable.

This is how we can compare. We can go very slowly in these things and we cannot explain them by words. We have to look for facts.

Q. Will it help us to understand time to say it is a dimension of space?

Mr. O. No, that will not help. It will help when we find analogies in ourselves in relation to time in different cosmoses. This is why we spoke in relation to centres, i.e. different time in different centres. The relation between centres is similar in some ways to relations between different cosmoses. This is the way to study it. The philosophical way will not help. It may be very interesting, very useful, but not for practical purposes.

Q. Is a violent storm, lasting for twenty-four hours, something that cannot be perceived by the earth?

Mr. O. Or that it could have quite a different meaning, quite a different form for the earth.

Q. How can we think about the earth?

Mr. O. It is necessary to understand the earth not only as a round body, stationary, but also earth in movement. For instance, if our psychological present is three seconds, then the present for earth will be eighty years. During that time earth turns round the sun eighty times, and the sun moves in its own direction, so it will be a very complicated body, not just a ball, which produces all this movement. And then you must remember that moon moves round the earth, makes a kind of sheath in which the earth moves—quite a different shape. There was a question the other day about the influence of stars and I said the influence of stars must be very small. All planets are shut in by their satellites. Imagine the Solar System and take this condition of different time and you will see it is quite a different picture than stationary balls. It is all connected, all one body.

Q. Are these scales quite hypothetical?

Mr. O. No, they are supposed to come from higher mind,

which is supposed to know what is right. Only they are adapted to our mind. They cannot be full, complete. The principles are right, but there are big gaps between them. We must try to do something with these fragments and in this way we come to fuller understanding. If they were given in full, we would not be able to understand.

We spoke of cosmoses smaller than man. Second micro-cosmos, cell, has life of twenty-four hours. Third—small cell, has life of three seconds. Then there is a fourth microcosmos; we can call it molecule, and the fifth—electron. The existence of the molecule will be 1/10,000th of a second, and of the electron even smaller. So you can see that when people say they can know about these, it is simply scientific superstition. People think they can see them, but they cannot. They can see only traces; not bodies in movement, but repetition of movement. You see, this table of times shows very well the impossibility of Aristotle's principle that everything is the same. On different scales things are different. Aristotle's principle was formulated simply to combat the ordinary conception of miracle—trees that can walk, dogs that can speak and so on. Trees do not walk in our garden, therefore they cannot walk in any garden. That was Aristotle's idea. But if things have a different time they cannot be analogous. You cannot expect to see a molecule which exists for 1/10,000th of a second.

Q.   If the life of the electron is so short, it does not exist for man?

MR. O.   Yes, it exists, but only in its repetition, like light. We cannot see the electron, but what are rays of light? Recurrence of electrons. That is what is called quanta. You see, scientists find a phenomena and give a name to it, but they cannot explain it.

Q.   Can intelligence of matter be changed by art?

MR. O.   Maybe. We are speaking only about density from the cosmic point of view, and intelligence varying according to this density. It is quite possible that the intelligence of matter can be changed by art—as a piece of machine is more intelligent perhaps than just a piece of iron. But that does not change the principle. There are other things, you know. For instance, later you will see how, apart from density, intelligence is measured by for whom it can serve as food. Because all things in the world either eat something or are eaten by something, and that determines their place. Everything in the world, from metals to the Absolute, is food for something. The Absolute does not feed anything.

All study of cosmoses is study of the relation between this time and that of different cosmoses. You will see that it gives a very good foundation for thinking in a new way. You have to deal with such differences, numbers, quantities! You will have to learn how to manage it, how to deal with it. G. said, when we heard about cosmoses, that science and philosophy begin from cosmoses and are nothing without this idea. Try to understand that.

And certainly this table of time is very important addition to the sytem. Later you will see how this knowledge was reflected in different systems, old systems. Because there are traces of it.

You can use this table of times for thinking in a new way. If you remember this diagram and continue to small cosmoses, you will have an enormous range of quantities to think of. You must learn how to make them easier to visualize, easier to compare. If you think just of a number, consisting of twenty-seven figures, it really means nothing. But perhaps you will find some way to bring it nearer.

You see, there are two problems. If you take a clock, a system of different wheels, then so long as the big wheel turns, the small wheels must exist. The whole mechanism must exist at the same time. At the same time, the small wheels run out. Then comes the idea of repetition. They finish their life, and their life is repeated so long as the big wheel needs it. If the big wheel disappears, the small wheels disappear. So, when we come to small quantities of which we can see visible results, that means we are dealing with their repetition, not with their time. You must try to understand that. We cannot see electrons because they exist for too short a time. When we see light, we see fifth and sixth dimension—repeated life of electron. That is why we cannot say what light is.

In Indian philosophy it is said that 'Brahma breathes in and out the universe'. This coincides with this table, if we take Brahma as Protocosmos. This breath of Brahma corresponds to life of Macrocosmos—our galaxy. You can find many such fragments. For instance, 'Day and Night of Brahma', 'Age of Brahma', 'a day of light is a thousand years of the world', 'half a myriad of years is a single year of light', and so on.

TABLE OF TIME. MARCH 21ST 1938

Q.   If the shortest impression of earth is twenty-four hours and it revolves on its own axis, how does it see itself?

Mr. O.   That means the earth does not know it revolves. Maybe we all turn like that and don't notice because it is too quick. If we turned at the same speed as the earth we should never notice it.

Then perhaps we should see ourselves as round. The earth sees itself quite differently—not as we see it. It has two movements—one round the sun and the other with the sun together, so it may have some strange shape. It may look like a cow, for instance, or a bird—we don't know.

WE DO NOT KNOW HOW THE EARTH SEES ITSELF. APRIL 25TH 1938

Q.   Mr. O. said we didn't know what the earth was like. I think he added that its movement was in a spiral. I did not understand what he meant by 'what the earth looked like'. If the earth moves in a spiral does that mean that every cosmos moves in a spiral?

Mr. O.   This is a very simple thing really. First of all, what I said is we don't know how earth looks at itself. I said if we take, for instance, breath as present—three seconds for us—and we know how we can stay three seconds and look at ourselves in a mirror. We know how our body is formed, its size and so on, in relation to other things in the room. How earth would look on itself during eighty years—I said in eighty years earth turns eighty times round the sun. That means it takes a spiral round the sun—an elliptical spiral. At the same time it moves sideways with the sun. But if we take the spiral—very long in shape—and at the same time it moves sideways with the sun, that will give quite a different shape. We don't know all the movements of the sun, but in any case there are several more movements which will again change the body of the earth during eighty years. Certainly the earth will not see itself as we imagine it—a round body in space. It will see itself quite differently from that, but how, we don't know.

About the question of other cosmoses, there are different

cosmoses and that I cannot answer. They are different and in different positions.

STEP DIAGRAM. MARCH 24TH 1938

MR. O.   Well, I will begin to speak about the new diagram. I must explain some things before I give it to you.

Very often questions are asked referring to animals. I always say that man is not an animal. His is quite different. It is necessay to understand that all living beings, all animals on the earth, including man, are divided, from the system point of view, into three categories: three-storied, two-storied and one-storied. Man has three stories, animals two stories and more elementary animals, like the earthworm, have only one story. So all 'living beings' have three, two or one stories. These categories are different one from another and are under different laws.

Then you know the usual classification in the scientific sense, grouping living beings by families, species, by what they eat—carnivorous, herbivorous, omnivorous, etc.—or by the way they are born, whether alive or in the form of eggs and so on. There are many different divisions and all are really unsatisfactory because they mix many things and there is no one general principle for division. In the system there is one definite principle for classification. At first it looks too simple, and people are inclined to think it means that many different beings can belong to the same category according to this division. Really, however, it is very definite and very strict in spite of being simple.

> What they eat;
> What air they breathe;
> In what medium they live.

If you understand this right you will see that there are no two identical beings on earth. They are all different. There are not two different animals which eat the same thing, breathe the same air and live in the same medium. In order to see it, it is necessary to think well and find many examples.

I remember a conversation I had a little while ago with a doctor who came down to see me at Lyne. He was not in the system. We were looking round and went to look at the pigs. He told me how near the pig was to man—perhaps the nearest animal—because of his length of intestines and many other things, because it is omnivorous and so on. Really, he was terribly mistaken; the pig is very far from man. It eats quite different things. Man will die if he eats what a pig can eat. The pig can easily live on pure ptomaines for a long time. So you can see it is dangerous to accept purely scientific classifications.

Man is limited in what he can eat to hydrogen 768. All other animals can eat something different from that or cannot eat all of that. Even animals as alike as a donkey and a horse are really quite different. They cannot live on exactly the same diet. The horse will probably die on the donkey's diet and the donkey will get too fat on the horse's diet.

Q. I do not understand what you mean by 'what air he breathes'.

MR. O. Just that. Take, for instance, the bee. The bee's food is higher than ours, but the bee can live in the hive where man could not live. He could not live in that air.

Q. Most birds can eat the same things, can't they? A lot of different birds eat worms.

MR. O. They eat different worms.

Q. What do you mean by 'medium'?

MR. O. Man lives in the same air he breathes. A maggot, for instance, may live in a flower, in what he eats. That is his medium, our medium is air. Fish lives in water, but breathes the same air as we do.

I must warn you that this diagram must be taken quite separately from all other diagrams. It is not parallel to any other and the expressions used cannot be explained by words connected with other diagrams. It is quite a different scale and is quite different. If you try to translate it into other language, you will get nothing from it.

ENNEAGRAM

We have seen the external side of the geometrical structure of the symbol. Its form is determined by the expression of the Law of Seven on which the octave is based. It is symmetrical as regards the tone do, i.e. in a certain sense the tone do may be regarded as neutralizing. When we talked about the application of the Law of Octaves to the structure of chemical elements, each substance, obtained in an orderly way, was symbolically named a hydrogen of different grades of density and other qualities, determining it as matter. According to the Law of Three, it was constructed from active, passive and neutralizing matters correspondingly named carbon, oxygen and nitrogen, i.e. the resulting structure is as follows:

$$C \atop O \quad N \left. \right\} H$$

In the same sense as the tone <u>do</u>, being the result, does at the same time neutralize the octave, hydrogen was also then mentioned as simultaneously resulting and neutralizing, i.e. as it were akin to nitrogen. The matter of hydrogen is a synthesis, the result of the interaction of three substances: active carbon, passive oxygen, connected together by the neutralizing nitrogen, i.e. it is built according to the law of triune unity.

In the same way the tone <u>do</u>, the apex marked by figure 9, in its completion is built according to the same law—the triangle 9–3–6 uniting these three points into one whole, points which did not enter into the period (let us so call the complex geometrical figure inside the symbol), unites into one the Law of Three and the Law of Seven. Only the three above-mentioned numbers do not enter into the period. Two of them correspond in the rules of the scale, the third is, as it were, superfluous and, at the same time, replaces the fundamental tone which did not enter into the period. But, if you remember that everything or phenomenon capable, according to the law of relativity, to interact with a phenomenon similar to it ('of equal rights' with it) sounds as the tone <u>do</u> in a corresponding octave, maybe you will see in this the symbol of the fact that <u>do</u> can get out of its circle and enter into an orderly relationship with another circle, i.e. in another cycle play the rôle which is played in the phenomenon under consideration by the shocks filling the gaps of the octave. This is why here also, carrying this possibility within itself, it is connected by the symbol of three-in-one with those places in the octave where shocks from extraneous principles occurs, where the octave is permeable for the purpose of connection with what lies outside it. The Law of Three emerges from the Law of Seven; the triangle outlines itself through the period and these two figures, in their combination, give the inner structure of the octave and its tones, its atomistic structure, as it were. . . [Explanation about the place of intervals.]

The laws of symmetry are little studied in the West, but even you must probably know what is called symmetrical asymmetry, i.e. an orderly symmetry of apparent lack of symmetry. And the symbol we examine is the picture of the most perfect synthesis of the Law of Octaves, since the symmetrical has to form and contains in itself the symmetry we have just mentioned. More than that, by referring, apparently, the gap into a wrong place, if above all those who are able to read the symbol, what shock—where and what— will be required to transfer si into do, and this explains the circumstance already mentioned in the lecture on the mechanics of the structure of the world, namely, that the passage of la—si has, from the point of view of the difference of the number of vibrations of tones, a greater length than all the other passages in the octave. In the same way the indications of the symbol as regards the shock needed in the gap mi—fa are almost definite, but of this I cannot speak now in detail. All I can say is to remind you about the rôle of these shocks in the processes taking place in man and in the universe. When we examined the application of the Law of Octaves to the cosmos, even if we take only the step on earth, it is expressed thus:

re
do
si
la
sol   Sun
fa
---
mi
re
do   Earth
si
la

It was said then that the transition of do into si, the filling of the gap, takes place inside the organism of the sun. When we spoke of the Absolute, it was said definitely that this transition is an inner act of will. But the passage fa—mi happens mechanically, by means of a special machine allowing the fa that comes into it, without changing its tone, by a series of processes to acquire the properties of sol standing above it, and together with this capacity of an independent transition (a store of inner energy, as it were) for transformation into the next tone (mi, in the given instance). The same thing happens in all processes. If we examine the processes of nutrition and of the work of the human organism, we shall find there the same gaps and shocks. Three kinds of food are taken in by man. Each food is the beginning of a new octave.

In order to find out the properties of the gap, we have examined in full the first octave of food of the lower story. When in its process of transformations it reaches the stage corresponding to the note mi (third), it draws near the gap which it cannot pass unaided. The second do coming to its aid, (air coming in through breathing,) passes into re and, combining with the third mi, makes it pass into fa. The food we eat, food and drink, is introduced into our organism, in an overwhelming majority of cases, in quantities far greater than required. It cannot be totally assimilated, i.e. the chemical process through which the body manufactures the substance necessary for existence, requires a strict correspondence of component parts. As illustration, let us take some example from chemistry. Common salt is a combination, under certain conditions, of the metal sodium with the gas chlorine. If we take 23 pounds of sodium and 35.5 pounds of chlorine, we shall get exactly 58.5 pounds of common salt. But if, instead of 23 pounds of sodium, with the same amount of chlorine, we take 30 pounds, the 7 pounds of sodium would not enter into the combination. In the same way, if with 23 pounds of sodium we take 40 pounds of chlorine, 4.5 pounds of it would remain free. In either case we shall obtain 58.5 pounds of common salt. In other words, sodium and chlorine combine in permanent relation of weights, proportionate to figures 23:35.5. All chemical elements have this quality of permanent proportions and all atomic weights have been worked out in accordance with this property. In the same way, in order to manufacture in the organism a substance with characteristic properties, it is necessary to introduce the original matter in strictly definite correspondence to the other matter with which it enters into interaction. This refers both to the qualitative and the quantitative aspect of the phenomenon. The food, entering human organism, is transferred from the matter transformed in the stage 3rd mi into the substance of the stage of 3rd fa by means of chemical combination with the do of the air. This means that the process of breathing enters into interaction with the process of assimilation and digestion of food. The final matter of this process will be a matter of the stage of 3rd si, which requires a new shock to pass to the completed <u>do</u>. As the diagram we examine shows that three octaves take part in the process, the influence of those is reflected in the final result, determining its quality. In other words, in the gradual transition of one stage into another, everywhere there are definite determinators. The matter of the stage of <u>3rd si</u> must be used to obtain a previously known result, which determines the quality and quantity of the given substance that is required. This is why breathing exercises, without the knowledge of all the laws, will give no desired result. But, even supposing that a man knows how to regulate the component parts of the process, two determinators, food and breathing; still it is not sufficient. In this case it is necessary to know and be able to regulate the third determinator—the food of the upper story—the first octave, what we have here called conditionally 'impressions'. Only with a full and harmonious correspondence of all the three kinds of food, by intensifying or weakening the different parts of the process, is the required result obtained. This is why all breathing exercises not strictly co-ordinated with other processes, connected with them, may inflict irreparable harm on the man. The shock—coming from without, with the materiality of air at mechanical process of breathing, and filling the gap <u>mi–fa</u>—is similar to the shock which fills this interval in any other octave. And the process itself of the development of the octave inside the human body, the transformation of the <u>3rd do</u> of food through a series of stages into <u>do</u> of the next octave, is similar to the same processes in other places. When we built the first cosmic octave of our already existing Ray of Creation, passing through sun and earth, the separate tones of this octave were distributed as show in the diagram.

Absolute	do
	si
All Suns	la
Sun	sol
All Planets	fa
Earth	mi
Organic Life	re
Organic Life	re
Moon	do

Then this original octave, according to the Law of Three in

one, fell into three sub-ordinated octaves and the same ray constructed it somewhat differently:

Absolute	do
	si
	la
	sol
	fa
All Suns	---
	mi
	re
	do
Sun	si
	la
	sol
	fa
All Planets	---
	mi
	re

In this way the cosmos, by the three stories of its structure became similar to the same three-storied structure of man. Where in the cosmic octaves of the second order lies the place of the gap fa–mi under the influence of all the influences meeting together at this place, there takes place a process similar to the full process of transition of food in the human organism—the transformations of do of one octave into do of the next octave. Therefore in these places are marked 'machines' similar to the human body which are present there. In the most schematic way the process of passage of fa–mi may be represented thus:

Earth	do
	si
	la
	sol
	fa
Organic Life	---
	mi
	re
Moon	do

the cosmic fa enters this machine similar to the food of the lower story and begins its cycle of transformations. Consequently, at first, it sounds in the machine as do, the 3rd do. The matter entering into the middle story, similar to air in breathing, is the matter of the note <u>sol</u> of the cosmic octave, helping the tone <u>mi</u> <u>3rd</u> inside the octave to pass into the tone <u>fa</u>, filling the gap between them, and sounding as <u>do</u>. In due place, the, as it were, doubled cycle is joined by the cycle of the matter of the tone of cosmic <u>la</u>, entering the upper story of the machine as the <u>1st</u> <u>do</u>. In the final count of the process, <u>fa</u>, entering the machine as the <u>3rd do</u> transforms into the <u>3rd do</u> of the octave above and goes out of the machine as a tone which is capable of passing into the next tone. I said earlier that fa, with<u>out</u> changing its tone, acquires the properties of <u>sol</u> as well as its capacity of passing into the next tone, i.e. <u>mi</u>, in the given instance. I wished to say by this the following: as we see, the food of the machine is represented by the cosmic tones <u>la, sol, fa.</u> In their consecutive order, according to the Law of Three, <u>la</u> will be active, <u>sol</u> neutralizing and <u>fa</u>—the passive principle. The active principle, entering into interaction with the passive (linking with it by means of the neutralizing principle) produces a certain result. It was pointed out before that if the number determining the properties of the active principle is 'n', the same number for the passive principle is '4n', and for the result '2n', i.e. symbolically it is represented thus:

$$2n$$

$$+n \qquad\qquad 4n-$$

Let us replace these quantities by the tones feeding the machine. We shall obtain the following symbol:

$$=sol$$

$$+la \qquad\qquad fa-$$

This shows at the same time, that matter <u>fa</u>, mixing with matter <u>la</u> produces as a result matter <u>sol</u>. And, since this process takes place in the octave developing, as it were, inside the tone <u>fa</u>, similarly to what was said in this connection about the tone <u>do</u> when we examined the symbol, so we can say that <u>fa</u>, without changing its tone, acquires the properties of <u>sol</u>. We appear to have digressed from our original purpose of studying the symbol. In actual fact, for those who can hear, we came nearer to understanding it. Like a perfect synthesis, it contains in itself all the elements of knowledge and of the law it expressed, and from this symbol can be deduced and fully elaborated all we have been talking about just now. All I have said to-day is less than a small fraction of what can be said about this question. Later we shall return to it. I do not think at all that I have explained something to you, and I did not even have this object in view. My object was to give the taste of that un. . . .

EXTRACT. WEDNESDAY. MAY 4TH 1938

MR. O. There are some good questions but not enough; you could ask more. The enneagram, even in this elementary form (although I gave more in this group first time that I spoke than we had in Petersburg)—when we heard about enneagram we heard very little, and all the rest we had to find ourselves, for instance, I gave three octaves and we had only one octave, just circle, lines and one octave, nothing more—you had more and you could ask more questions.

At first we begin with this explanation—what is enneagram? Enneagram is symbol: what is symbol? Can you explain it, can you formulate what you understand as symbol? We all use the word symbol, but can we formulate what is symbol?

MR. W. Is it a hieroglyph of an object, something that shows it in a nutshell?

MR. O. Yes, but this is not sufficient. I don't like definitions. I just ask, can anybody remember how symbol generally is defined, because this is not right definition even if you remember it. You see, first meaning of symbol came in very interesting way. In old Greece symbol was called very special thing— suppose man went away to the war, or travelled, or something like that, for long time, and they had to communicate with him somehow, so from time to time they sent a messenger—when he went away he took what is called symbol—flat plate which was broken in two, and messenger who went from time to time took one half, and if it coincided with the other part it meant that the messenger came from home, so symbol means coincidence—then it got many other meanings, but in this system it is used as simple drawing which has to coincide with big ideas, not full expression but only showing their connection, for instance, Law of Three is expressed in triangle, and square is symbol of four elements, which in old chemistry are called fire, water, air, earth, and which we call C.O.N.H. and there are

others called pentagram, hexagram. So it is symbol, not diagram
like ordinary [ ]; it is symbol including many diagrams. This is
how it must be understood.

EVOLUTION

You told me that at your group there arose the question of
evolution and that you do not know how to reconcile the idea
of evolution as it exists in modern thought with the ideas of our
system or the Special Doctrine.

First of all I must tell you that the idea of evolution in that
sense is neither contradicted nor affirmed by Special Doctrine,
and there is no obligatory acceptance or denial of Doctrine.
What is not accepted by Special Doctrine is evolution in the
ordinary sense, i.e. the evolution of species by mechanical
processes in relation to man. The word 'evolution' is used in
Special Doctrine in relation to man in the meaning of conscious
voluntary and intentional development of an individual man on
definite lines and in a definite direction, during the period of his
earthly life.

But in order to understand certain other theories of Special
Doctrine referring to the universe, cosmic processes and organic
life, it is useful to have a right view of the ideas of evolution.
This is why I introduce in the first chapter of my book, 'A New
Model of the Universe', certain views on evolution which helped
me to understand and appreciate the ideas of Special Doctrine.

The idea of evolution penetrates now into every line of
scientific thought. Cosmogony, astro-physics, geology,
biological sciences, palaeontology, social sciences, economic
sciences, anthropology and the history of culture, the history of
religion, the history of art, philology, psychology, they all try
to arrange themselves along the lines of evolution and each of
them takes the basic principles of evolution for granted. The
chief of these principles is the development of richer and more
complicated forms from simpler and elementary forms in all
the kingdoms of nature, produced by inevitable and immutable
universal laws. Evolution is generally accepted. Evolution is
taught in schools. No new theory is considered acceptable unless
it is explained from the point of view of evolution or explains
evolution. And at the same time, however strange it may seem,
evolution is only a hypothesis and, unfortunately, a hypothesis

that has existed too long. It appeared first in a scientific form in the Kant-Laplace theory—later it was made by Darwin a basis of his deductions and soon after was generalized and introduced into all possible branches of knowledge or speculation by Herbert Spencer. The chief impetus to the development of the idea of evolution was given by its application to biological sciences by Darwin and to general thought by Spencer. Both were geniuses and the idea of evolution as the work of genius would be one of the most beautiful memorials of human thought if it was refuted soon after its appearance, because really it is a mistake of a genius. But unfortunately geniuses are invariably succeeded by very common and insignificant men who try to attach themselves to their names and follow their steps without understanding where these steps actually lead. As a hypothesis 'evolution' shows the necessity of a generalizing system. As a theory it had to be refuted very soon because not a single proof of its smallest assertion was ever found. It sounds almost strange to say this, so strongly and deeply has evolution entered into our ordinary thinking. But the truth remains that in not a single line of scientific research there exist proofs of evolution. Each separate line of thought or knowledge which connects itself with evolution bases its assertions on other lines. Neither has proofs in itself and for itself. If a philosophical, that is, purely metaphysical idea of evolution did not exist, the Kant-Laplace theory would be impossible; if there was no metaphysical idea of evolution and Kant-Laplace theory, Darwin's theory would be very weak; if there were no metaphysics, no Kant-Laplace theory and no Darwin (or Wallace), Herbert Spencer and his contemporaries would not be able to create the general idea of evolution. And at present if every line of science or thought which is based on evolution, or accepts evolution, would stand for a moment alone and try to look for proofs of evolution in itself it would see none. Each one separately fails to find proofs of evolution. All together they affirm the truth of evolution, and evolution is generally accepted. According to that, the idea of evolution can be expressed by a very strange formula: a succession of minuses which added one to another give plus. It reminds me of a story I once read about an Irish woman who was selling apples, and who said that although she had a certain loss on every apple, she sold so many that on the whole she must have a profit.

Speaking quite seriously I want to point out that if there was some truth in evolution, definite proofs of it would have been found, and first of all in biological sciences. It follows from the theory of evolution that species change and that simpler and more elementary forms produce richer and more complicated forms. Nothing similar to this was ever observed since the birth of evolution. But the fact of the absence of such an observation is constantly obscured by the appearance of new and again new theories. When asked directly biologists answer that the change of species cannot be a matter of observation because for mammalia the period necessary for the change of one species into another would equal approximately thirty thousand years, that is, a large astronomic cycle. But ordinary readers or students do not see the catch in this answer. It may be true in relation to mammalia if the general assertions of the evolutionists are right, but it cannot be true at the same time in relation to <u>all</u> classes of living beings, simpler plants, certain insects and micro-organisms, that is, it cannot be true in relation to beings multiplying with much greater rapidity than mammalia. And the period necessary for the transition of one species to another must be shortened in proportion to the increase of rapidity of multiplying. Some plants, insects with their rapidity of breeding should have given definite examples of the change of species during the time that has passed after Darwin. And in the last decades micro-biology would have given absolute proof of evolutionary theories if there were any truth in them. I will give only one example of micro-biological observations which would necessarily show any evolutionary change in the given species, if such change occurred. About thirty years ago a certain experiment was started by Professor Metalnikoff in Russia with the aim of establishing the length of the existence of a genus of certain micro-organisms. At that time when the experiment was started two views existed in biology. According to the first view one-cell organisms multiplying in favourable conditions were practically immortal. According to the second view one-cell organisms multiplying by division could have only a certain definite number of generations or divisions after which they inevitably died out as a genus. The experiments were started in the beginning of the century in Moscow. During the revolution the bacteria that continued to multiply were transferred to the Crimea and from there to Paris and they still continue to multiply. From the point of view of Professor Metalnikoff the experiment proves the immortality of the cell. But what is particularly interesting for us, it proves the inexistence of evolution, for to a cell multiplying with extraordinary rapidity in hours, or in certain cases in minutes, thirty years represent a cycle of time comparable to our geological periods, i.e. to millions and millions of years. During this period nothing has happened, and we may take it from this that nothing will happen.

12
False personality

FALSE PERSONALITY

In answer to a question about methods for self-remembering Mr. O. replied:
  If you remembered all that has been said you would remember yourself at the end of ten weeks. For instance, take the study of false personality; this is one of the quickest methods. The more you understand false personality, the more you will remember yourself. What prevents self-remembering is first of all false personality. False personality cannot and does not wish to remember itself, and it does not wish to let any other personality remember. It just tries to stop self-remembering, takes some form of sleep and calls it self-remembering. Then it is quite happy.

Q. Is the study of false personality not analysing oneself?

Mr. O. Yes, to a certain extent.

Q. I thought you said that was a bad thing.

Mr. O. That was in the first lecture, I said the time for analysis would come when we knew the laws. We are studying these laws, so certainly we have to analyse more and more now. You see, rules for observation and thinking in the first lecture are one thing. With the passing of time they certainly change and modify. What one cannot do in the first month one already must do in the second month. Both difficulties and possibilities increase all the time.

Q. What about the idea of not being able to 'do'?

Mr. O. One is never doing. Things happen. But when I decide to work on self-remembering, then I am doing already. But it will not help if I ask why. I already know. Analysis must be used carefully, when it is necessary; not for everything. Sometimes it only wastes time.

Q. Is all false personality false?

Mr. O. False personality is something special. <u>You</u> are opposed to it. False personality must be made to disappear, or at any rate it must not enter into this work. It is the same for everybody; everybody must begin with that. First of all you must know your false personality, and you must not trust it in any way—its ideas, its words, its actions. You cannot destroy it, but you can make it passive for some time and then, little by little, you can make it weaker.

Q.   You said one must not trust anything connected with false personality, but it seems to be all there is.

MR. O.   It cannot be. There is one thing—you—and there are imaginary 'I's. You is what really is, and you must learn to distinguish it. It may be very small, very elementary, but you can find something definite, permanent, sufficiently solid in yourself.

Q.   Has everybody got to have false personality?

MR. O.   No obligation, but I never met anybody without it.

Q.   Would you say false personality is more inclined to leave you as you grow older?

MR. O.   No. If you do nothing against it, it grows. It cannot diminish by itself. By itself it only grows—tastes may change and so on—but it grows. This is the only development that happens in mechanical life—nothing else.

Q.   Is false personality directly connected with mechanicalness?

MR. O.   False personality is the most mechanical part of us—so mechanical that there is no hope for it. It must disappear, but it does not want to disappear.

Q.   How can we start to understand false personality?

MR. O.   You must know what it is—place it, so to speak—this is the first step. You must realize that all identification, all considering, all lies, all lies to oneself, all weakness, all contradictions, seen and unseen, all these are false personality.

Q.   Is considering always a guide to false personality?

MR. O.   Considering is considering. Certainly it is one of the functions of false personality, but you must not try to explain one word by another word.

Q.   Sometimes I observe myself considering or identifying, and find I do so because of a picture I have of myself. This picture has many aspects. Can I in this way come to know false personality and, by observing it, weaken it?

MR. O.   Very good, yes. It is the only way, but only if you do not get tired of it, because, in the beginning, many people start eagerly, but soon get tired and begin to use 'I' indiscriminately without asking themselves 'Which "I"?' 'Which part of "I"?' Our Chief enemy is the word 'I', because we have really no right to use it in ordinary conditions. Much later, after long work, we can begin to think of one of the groups of 'I's (like what has been called deputy steward) which develop from magnetic centre as 'I'. But in ordinary conditions, when you say: 'I don't like', you must ask yourself 'Which of my "I"s does not like?' This way you constantly remind yourself about this plurality in us. If you forget one time, it will be easier to forget the next time. There are many good beginnings in the work, then <u>this</u> is forgotten and people start to slide down, and in the end all that happens is that they become more mechanical than before.

Q. Does one's capacity for work increase just so much as one is able to weaken false personality?

MR. O. Everything one can get, one can get only at the expense of false personality. Later, when it is destroyed, one can get many things at the expense of other things, but for a long time one has to live, so to speak, off false personality.

Q. Are all forms of self-will necessarily contrary to one's work?

MR. O. All forms of self-will belong to false personality, so sooner or later you have to sacrifice them.

Q. Is it possible for false personality to be interested in, or attracted by, system ideas?

MR. O. Yes, very much. Only then you will have the system in the light of false personality, and it will be quite a different system.

Q. If it is possible for this to be, what happens to this interest in the process of weakening false personality?

MR. O. But this interest only strengthens false personality and weakens the system for you. The moment false personality takes the system to itself, it adds one word here and another word there. You cannot imagine in what an extraordinary form some of the ideas come back to me. One word omitted from some formulation makes a quite different idea, and false personality is fully justified and can do what it likes and so on. This is where the danger lies.

Q. I ask these questions because I sometimes doubt the genuineness of my interest in the work—I may be lying to myself.

MR. O. But only you can answer that; and there again only if you do not forget the fundamental principles and say 'I' about something when it is only one 'I'. You must get to know other 'I's and remember about them. If you forget this you forget everything. So long as you remember this you may remember everything. Forgetting about this is the great danger. Then one slight change in something is sufficient to make everything wrong.

Q.　Can the system create false personality in one?

MR. O.　Certainly the system cannot create it. System means all that is said in the sense in which it is said. If one corrects it consciously or unconsciously, then it cannot be called system. Then it will be pseudo-system, falsification of system. So your question is wrong. The system can be compared (if you remember that conversation) to objective art. Objective art differs from ordinary art in this way: a work of art created objectively, with all knowledge of methods, triads, octaves, will always produce the same effect, whereas in ordinary art the results are accidental, one day one thing, another day another. As with objective art, so with the system, but only so long as it remains correct. The moment it becomes incorrect or something is forgotten or falls out it will give wrong results at once.

Q.　Is false personality the main barrier to being aware?

MR. O.　First of all, yes, though there are many mechanical habits as well. Sometimes even, mechanical habits of centres can be a barrier, because mechanical habits in one centre will bring mechanicalness in another centre.

But false personality always says 'I', always considers itself permanent 'I' and ascribes to itself many capacities—self-consciousness, will and so on—and if it is not checked, certainly it is an obstacle to everything.

Q.　But false personality exists, doesn't it, as a dream?

MR. O.　It does not really exist but we imagine it exists. It exists by its manifestations, but not as part of ourselves. Do not try to define it, or you will lose your way in words, and it is necessary to deal with facts. Negative emotions exist, but at the same time they do not exist. There is no real centre for them. This is one of the misfortunes of our state—we are full of non-existent things.

Q.　In struggling against false personality one sometimes thinks one recognizes it, but wants to know what to do next.

MR. O.　Always do something false personality does not like, and you will very soon find what it does not like. If you continue it will get more and more irritated and show itself more and more clearly, so that soon there will be no question about it.

Q.　If you could eliminate false personality. . . .

MR. O.　You cannot eliminate anything. It is just the same as trying to cut your head off. But you can make false personality less insistent, less permanent. If, at a certain moment, you feel the danger of the manifestation of false personality and you find a way to stop it, this is what you have to begin with. The question of elimination does not enter at all—it is connected with quite different things. You must have control. But if people think that they can do something, and at the same time refuse to work on <u>this</u>, for some reason or other, then things become bad. And people can be enthusiastic about what they have to do until they know; and when they know what they have to do, they become very negative and try to avoid it or explain it in some other way. That is what you must understand—that false personality defends itself.

You must understand that you cannot even begin to work such as you are, on that level. You have to change one thing or another thing. But this is different for different people. You can find what to change only as a result of your own observations. Sometimes it becomes quite clear, and only then the fight begins, because false personality begins to defend itself.

You must know false personality first. All that we speak about refers to the first stage—understanding that we do not know false personality, that it is necessary to study to know it, that all the work we do is done at the expense of false personality, that all the work we can do on ourselves means diminishing the power of false personality, or that if we begin to try and work, leaving false personality without disturbing it, all the work will be nothing. There are many examples of how people try to deceive themselves, try to think they can work leaving false personality alone, and it comes to nothing.

You must understand that false personality is a combination of all lies, features and 'I's which can never be useful in any sense or in any way, either in life or in the work—like negative emotions.

Q. If one tries to watch negativeness, identification, and so on, is that the beginning of recognizing false personality?

MR. O. Yes, but one must be sincere with oneself. And sincerity again is not sufficient, because one must know how to be sincere.

Q. Is false personality entirely based on negative emotion?

MR. O. If it were entirely the same thing, why should we invent different words, and if they are different things, why do you put them together? In false personality there are many things besides negative emotions. For instance, in false personality there are always bad mental habits, wrong thinking. False personality—or parts of false personality—is always based on wrong thinking, so why should we mix it with negative emotions? Although to a certain extent you are right; if you take negative emotions away from false personality, it collapses—it cannot exist without them.

Q.   So all negative emotions spring from false personality?

MR. O.   Yes, certainly. How could it be otherwise? It is, so to speak, a special organ for negative emotions, for displaying negative emotions, enjoying negative emotions, producing negative emotions. You remember, I said there is no real centre for negative emotions. False personality acts as a centre for negative emotions.

RÔLES. FEBRUARY 5TH 1936

Q.   I should think certain groups of 'I's are useful?

MR. O.   Some are useful, some artificial, and some pathological. For instance, I have not yet spoken about the idea of rôles. All people play rôles. Each person has about five or six rôles he plays in his life. He plays them unconsciously or, if he tries to play them consciously, he identifies with them very soon and continues to play them unconsciously. These rôles, together, make the imaginary 'I'.

CHIEF FEATURE. JANUARY 11TH 1938

MR. O.   There was a question about chief feature. I want to explain this term better because I think it is sometimes not used in the right sense. As I said before, it is necessary to think about false personality, and in some cases you can see definitely a kind of chief feature coming into everything, like the axis round which everything turns. It can be shown, but the person will say: 'Absurd, anything but not that!' Or sometimes it is so obvious that it is impossible to deny it, but with the help of buffers one can forget it again. I have known people who gave a name to their chief feature several times and for some time remembered. Then I met them again and they had forgotten or when they remembered they had one face, and when they had forgotten they had another face, and began to speak as though they had never spoken about it at all. You must come near to it yourself. When you feel it yourself, then you will know. If you are only told, you may always forget.

Q. Is it the same as chief fault?

MR. O.   Yes, it is the chief feature of false personality.

Q.   How can one get to know this chief feature?

MR. O.   By studying false personality. When you find many manifestations of this you may find a feature.

STATIC TRIAD. OCTOBER 1938

MR. O.   Let us try to speak about the relation of false personality to other parts. It is necessary to understand that in every man, at every moment, his development proceeds by what may be called a 'static triad'.

The first triangle shows the state of man in ordinary life. The second shows the state of man when he begins to develop.

There are long periods between the first and second triangle, and still longer if we take the next stage. There are many stages,

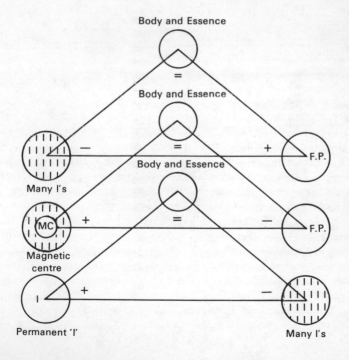

but this is the way of development in relation to false personality.

I have given three stages—it would be better to give four at least, or five or six, but even these three show the way. This diagram can be continued after permanent 'I'. Permanent 'I', again, has many different forms.

Many different stages can be shown, but again remember none of these states is permanent. Every state can be for half an hour and then another state may come, and then again a different state. But this is how development goes.

The triad is made by the body, the soul and the essence (at one point); by 'I', (that is myself: all feelings and sensations which do not form part of false personality) at the second point, and by false personality (imaginary picture of oneself) at the third point. In ordinary man false personality still calls itself 'I'. Then, after some time, if a man is capable of that, magnetic centre begins to grow in him. He may call it special interests, ideals, ideas, anything, but it means that when man begins to feel the magentic centre in him, he finds a separate part in himself, and from this part his growth begins. But this growth can take place only at the expense of his false personality. If magnetic centre is formed, he may meet a school, and when he begins to work, he must work against false personality. This does not mean that false personality disappears, it only means that it is not always there. It is almost always there in the beginning, but when magnetic centre begins to grow, it disappears, sometimes for half an hour, sometimes even for a day. Then it comes back and stays for a week. So all the work must be directed against false personality.

When false personality disappears for a short time, 'I' becomes stronger. Only it is not really 'I', it is many 'I's. The longer the periods when false personality disappears, the stronger 'I' (composed of many 'I's) becomes. Magnetic centre may be transformed into deputy steward, and when deputy steward acquires control of false personality, then it really transfers all the unnecessary things to the side of false personality, and only the necessary things remain on the side of 'I'. Then, at a still further stage, it may be that permanent 'I' will come on the 'I' side, with all that belongs to it. Then the many 'I's will be on the false personality side. But we cannot say much about that now. There will be permanent 'I' with all that belongs to it, but we do not know what belongs to it. Permanent 'I' has quite different functions, quite a different point of view.

This diagram represents a state, then a slightly different state, then again a different state. With the help of this diagram you can put on paper different states of man, beginning from the most elementary. In the most elementary state, false personality is active, 'I' is passive. Body, soul and essence always remain neutralizing. When, after many, many stages, permanent 'I' comes, then 'I' becomes active, many 'I's become passive and false personality disappears. Many different diagrams can be drawn between these two extremes and, further than that, there are several possibilities.

I called this triad a static triad because body, soul and essence always stay in the same place, as neutralizing force, and the other forces change only very slowly. So the whole triad is more or less in the same place all the time.

Q. Does this diagram imply that body and essence come in sometimes on the side of false personality, and sometimes on the other, according to which is uppermost?

MR. O. No. If body and essence are normal, they are impartial and do not take one side or the other. But if there is something wrong in them, they are on the side of false personality.

Q. Can other kind of work, besides struggle against false personality, be represented in the static triad?

MR. O. The static triad represents you, not work. It shows the state of your being, what you are at a given moment. One of the points, body and essence, is always the same, but the relation of the two other points changes.

All your actions depend on the kind of static triad. Certain kinds of action require a certain state of static triad. Other kinds of action require another state of static triad.

Q. In connection with this diagram, does false personality change from active force into passive force in the moment that one sees it?

MR. O. No, not at the moment one sees it. It cannot change into passive force without many efforts.

Q. I had the impression until now that false personality was the collection of all the many 'I's. This diagram has made things a little obscure for me.

MR. O. Amongst these many 'I's there are many positive 'I's which may be the beginning of another personality. False personality cannot develop—it is all wrong. That is why I say that all the work must be on false personality. If one fails in it, it is because one did not pay enough attention to false personality, did not study it and did not work against it.

Q.   Has false personality different 'I's?

MR. O.   It has many 'I's, only they are all imaginary.

Q.   What happens to magnetic centre when false personality goes?

MR. O.   Magnetic centre and false personality cannot be together. They are sun and moon from this point of view.

Q.   When permanent 'I' appears, does it mean that false personality does not appear at the same time?

MR. O.   That is so far away that we cannot speak about it. But false personality cannot appear even at the same time as magnetic centre. It will spoil it if it does. All work has to be on false personality. If you do any other work and leave this, it will be useless work and you will fail very soon.

Q.   Are all likes and dislikes false personality?

MR. O.   Most of them are. And even those which did not belong to it originally, which have real roots, all pass through false personality.

Q.   Does one have to know the whole of false personality in order to struggle against it? It seems to me you could only know little bits.

MR. O.   One must know it. It is like a special breed of dog. If you do not know it, you cannot speak about it. If you have seen it, you can speak about it. To see only bits, as you say, is quite enough. Every small part of it is the same colour. If you saw this dog once you will always know it. It barks in a special way, walks in a special way—everything about it is different.

This diagram shows that personal work or degeneration is going on in relation to different manifestations of false personality, but body, soul and essence remain the same all the time. After some time, they too will be affected, but they do not enter into the initial stages. Body will remain the same body. Essence will change later, but it does not enter into the beginning of the work. In this system, essence enters only as much as it is mixed with personality; we do not take it separately because we have no means for working on essence apart from personality.

Q.   Does the change of one static triad to another depend on change of being, i.e. a change dependent on the neutralizing force, or more especially on the vital principle of soul which changes after the second conscious shock?

MR. O. Yes, it is change of being, but change of being is generally applied to bigger, more serious changes, although every small change is also a change of being. When we speak about change of being, we speak about change from man No. 1, 2 and 3 to man No. 4, for instance. This is change of being. But, of course, this big jump consists of many small jumps. So you may call it change of being in this instance. Only, this is an auxiliary diagram: it helps to put on paper, to describe to yourself, all these stages which you pass through from ordinary mechanical existence to school-work. In this way you do not describe it in words—but give a complete picture of it. But who said that soul changes after the second conscious shock? This is all imagination. When I spoke about change, I never connected it with change of essence, or soul, or body. As far as we can say, the point body, soul, essence remains unchanged, provided they are normal. If they are ill—then it is a different thing, but that does not enter into our conversation: we take them as a permanent force. Change happens at two points in the triad.

Q. Is there a place in the static triad where a group of 'I's, unconnected with magnetic centre, are active and false personality is passive?

MR. O. What do you mean by active? When I said that certain groups of 'I's or personalities became active, I meant those that centre round magnetic centre. First magnetic centre itself, and then those 'I's that range themselves round magnetic centre are opposed to false personality. Then, at a certain moment, magnetic centre becomes active and false personality passive.

Magnetic centre is a combination of a certain group of likes. Magnetic centre does not lead you, for leading means progress—and you remain in one place—but when things come, then, with the help of magnetic centre, you are able to see which is which, or whether you like or dislike a thing; you can make a choice. Before one comes into the work, magnetic centre is a certain point which transforms into a certain group of interests. When we meet the work, it becomes interested in school-work, and then it disappears as magnetic centre, because magnetic centre is a weak thing. In this diagram I described the initial stages of the work, so I put in very few combinations. At the initial stage we can draw a triad with body, soul and essence, false personality and 'I's, supposing that these 'I's are already divided into certain groups. One of these groups is magnetic centre. There are other groups, maybe not attached, still not hostile to the magnetic centre, which can exist and eventually develop into something better. The groups of 'I's which are always hostile and always harmful are—false personality.

SEPARATION. JANUARY 16TH 1940

Q.   Could more be said about the question of separating? Is it a matter of separating 'I' from Mr. L., or of developing a special observing 'I' or guardian?

MR. O.   Guardian—I don't know. But you must know from which angle you want to separate. For instance, do you want to separate your personality that wants to work from that which does not know about the work? There are many divisions, so you must decide which division you want to separate. You can think about essence and personality—it is a theoretical question; you can think about different 'I's as opposed to one particular 'I'; or you can think about one personality as against all other personalities. I don't know which division you want, so you must decide first.

13
Payment

CONSCIOUS SHEEP. FEBRUARY 27TH 1936

Q. Is effort towards consciousness necessary for the Ray of Creation?
MR. O. Leave the Ray of Creation. Speak from your own interests. If you were more conscious, you would remain a conscious machine. The man from whom I heard this system told me that in some schools they could, by some special methods, make a sheep conscious. But it just remained a conscious sheep. I asked him what they did with this conscious sheep. He said, just ate it.

The idea of the conscious sheep is this: suppose a man is made conscious by someone else. He will become an instrument in the hands of others. One's own efforts are necessary because otherwise even if a man is made conscious, he will not be able to use it. It is in the very nature of things that consciousness and will cannot be given. One must buy everything, nothing is given free. The most difficult thing is to learn how to pay. One gets exactly as much as one pays for. But if this could be explained in a few words there would be no need to go to school. In the New Testament this is very strongly emphasized. Apparently, people who wrote the Gospels thought it a very important point—this idea of a good merchant.

Q. Can one acquire will by wanting something one has not got?
MR. O. Yes, by overcoming obstacles, otherwise one would be like the conscious sheep I spoke about.

LEARNING TO PAY

Q. You have told us we must understand the necessity for payment. Before any payment can be made I must understand the necessity for school and become interested in the organization. Then payment in the shape of service and money will follow with very little effort.

MR. O.   You are mixing two things—organization and payment. Payment is something quite different from giving any money or anything like that. Payment is a principle: giving service and money is a question of possibility. Unfortunately, there is only the one word, 'payment', so it has to be used in different senses. Money payment depends partly on understanding, partly on possibilities. The other payment is the more important matter and it must be understood that it is absolutely necessary. . . .

Q.   How can I find out what is payment for me?

MR. O.   I cannot speak in general. You must know. For instance, as regards myself, when I met this system I had no money but could organize things, bring money, arrange possibilities and things like that. But when I did that it was not payment, it was only helping the organization. Payment was when I remained in Russia after the revolution, when I knew it would be impossible to work and that sooner or later it would be necessary to leave. Instead of leaving Russia I stayed on for three years and did not know how I would get out. That was payment.

Q.   Is the understanding of rules a form of payment?

MR. O.   No, understanding is not payment, it is profit.

Q.   Is payment a right attitude?

MR. O.   No, this is not payment. This again is benefit. . . . Payment is a principle which must be understood from the first. Payment means effort, study, time, many things. But that is only the beginning, for payment must be useful for some purpose. Only, in this sense, payment has nothing to do with money.

Q.   Does payment involve giving up self-will?

MR. O.   I do not see why it is necessary to connect the two. You give up self-will for your own sake, not as payment.

Q.   By payment do you also mean sacrifice, such as sacrifice of certain forms of considering?

MR. O.   No, sacrifice of considering is not sacrifice. It is only pleasure.

Q.   Is there a right way of paying?

MR. O.   Certainly, one can pay in one or another way and everyone has to find that out for himself. . . . But nobody can get anything if he cannot pay for it. Things cannot be given, they can only be bought. If one has knowledge, one cannot give this to another person—again he must pay for it. Only then can we have this knowledge. This is a cosmic law. This idea is very strongly emphasized in the New Testament. Man must pay—he must buy things, he cannot get them for nothing.

Q. What exactly is meant by payment other than payment in money?

MR. O. This is what I am speaking about—you must find it yourself. Sometimes it is demanded of you, but sometimes you can see it for yourself. It always means a certain effort, certain doing, different from what you would do naturally, and it must be necessary or useful to the work. I gave you an example earlier. I saw the situation in Russia and I would never have remained when the revolution began because there were many difficulties and unpleasant things; and still because of the work I stayed in Russia in 1917, and I could not get out afterwards till 1920, so that was part of my payment. This is only an example—because it was necessary for the work, in some way it was necessary—you must not take it literally.

Q. I don't understand the difference between effort and payment.

MR. O. Efforts may be payment, but they must be useful.

Q. Isn't payment a question of feeling?

MR. O. It is necessary to understand work in general, the needs of the work, what is useful for the work, helpful for the work. When one understands all that, one will find ways of doing something useful, even if one has no money and things like that. Attitude depends on yourself and your understanding; opportunity depends on circumstances.

Q. Is there a connection between work on oneself and payment?

MR. O. If you don't work on yourself you won't be able to pay. This is the connection. Who will pay? False personality cannot pay.

Q. It would be easier to remember oneself if one could be clearer about certain things.

MR. O. We cannot remember ourselves if everything remains the same. If we really want to remember ourselves, we must try to change something. We cannot have old things and new things, there is no place for them, so we must make place for them. This is so even in regard to ordinary things. If one wants much, one must give much. If one wants little, one will give little. Measure it, then you will understand.

Q. I think perhaps one deludes oneself about wanting to change.

MR. O. Very often. This is a very good observation, because very often one persuades oneself that one wants to change but at the same time one wants to keep every small thing, so where is the change? Change is impossible if one wants to keep everything. To think about changing one must also think about what one would give up, what one will not want to keep.

Q. Is there something in ourselves that prevents us from wanting enough to change; if we desired enough, should we get the help?

MR. O. Yes, certainly, but I would not put it like that. You have all the help possible, it is your turn now to work, your turn to do something. Certainly, with different conditions, different preparation, and also different circumstances, things could be better arranged. But the question is not how much is given, but how much is taken, because, generally, only a little part is taken of what is given.

UNDERSTANDING. OCTOBER 25TH 1938

Q. You spoke about different payments for what one had, other than financial. Was one of them being willing to give up the whole of one's time to Lyne, if it were needed?

MR. O. In some cases it may be. Again, it cannot be put like that, as the same thing for everybody. It may be one thing or another thing. But I really spoke not about that. The chief point I spoke about was understanding. I mean understanding of the work, of the necessity of the work, of the general plan of the work. Interest in that—that is what I said was obligatory. One cannot, in oneself, understand methods and everything until one understands—I don't want to repeat 'plan', because that is more definite—but the direction of the work. And when one understands the direction, it will help in many smaller things that one wants to understand.

You see, one cannot avoid one's share in this part of the work, or if one avoids it for one reason or another, then one loses everything, or in any case, if one does not lose what one has acquired, one cannot acquire any more.

Q. Is there a way to increase one's understanding?

MR. O. Not one way, there are thousands of ways. All that .

we have spoken about from the first day is about ways to increase understanding. But chiefly one must struggle with obstacles, with things which prevent you from understanding. Only by removing these obstacles you begin to understand more. But obstacles, with the exception of the general description of identification and so on, are individual. You must find your own. You must find what is in your way. Generally, you will find it in one or another form of identification, but individually, for you personally, it may have a different taste. Another person's difficulties may look very simple to you, but your own difficulties look very difficult and you can do nothing—until you wish to. But it is not impossible. Nothing impossible is demanded of you. Only you must be persistent and act in a certain way, and remember what was said.

Q. It comes back to the question of how to understand more?

MR. O. I say first, about how you should study yourself, that you must understand your particular obstacle, what keeps you from understanding. When you find it, then you must struggle with it. It needs time. It cannot be found at once. In some cases it is very clear, you can see it almost at once. In some cases it is necessary to work before you can see it.

Q. Will group work help, for instance?

MR. O. When it is available, then you will see. But you must not put too many hopes in group work, because, although it is useful for showing many things, experimenting, testing and so on, in group work one is in an artificial atmosphere, artificial circumstances. The moment one comes out of group, one is in natural circumstances. So group work may show the way in some cases, but work must be in ordinary circumstances. What is the use if you are very good in group, and become a machine and identified the moment you walk out of the group? It will be quite useless.

Q. Has payment to do with some loss to oneself?

MR. O. Loss or effort. You may gain in that way but you may regard it as a loss.

GIVING UP. FEBRUARY 7TH 1940

Q. I find the idea that one must give up certain things entails a lot of negative emotion. I don't know what I have to give up.

MR. O. Don't worry. When it is necessary to give up something it becomes quite clear—you run ahead too fast. If you don't see what you have to give up, it means it is not yet the time to think about it. It begins in another way. This idea of the necessity to give up something comes only when you know what you have to give up, so intellectual thinking about it is quite useless. If you know what you have to give up, it never comes in the form of a puzzle. It is difficult enough even in an ordinary form, so there are no puzzles for you. As long as you can do something in the present conditions, it means that this question has not come to you really, it is not your problem; but maybe one day you will see some particular negative emotion and you will realize that if you want to keep this negative emotion, you cannot work—or it may be some kind of imagination, or something like that. It always begins in that way.

14
Thinking

Q. Is moon responsible for mechanicalness?

MR. O. All movements, whether mechanical or not, depend on the moon. Moon is like a weight on a clock. All movements of hands depend on the weight. If the hands become liberated from the weight—movement will necessarily stop.

Q. Efforts to work, to remember oneself, are efforts against that weight?

MR. O. It is incommensurable. . . . There are philosophical, theoretical and practical schools. And there is philosophical, theoretical and practical language. Even in this system we use three languages. We must not mix them. You put one part of your phrase in a philosophical language (about the moon) and another part in practical language (about self-remembering). These are two different scales. Different language means different scale. When we use philosophical language we speak on a small scale: Absolute, Ray of Creation, etc. When it is theoretical scale, we can calculate. Practical scale is when we speak of our own actions. It is important not to mix them. All cosmological ideas are spoken of in philosophical language.

Q. About languages: is the Food Table practical?

MR. O. Philosophical. We must know much more to make it theoretical. When we can give a name to everything and establish connections, then it will be theoretical. The study of centres is theoretical, or it may be philosophical—it depends how you take it. The same about self-remembering. It depends whether you really do make it practical. Some ideas must remain philosophical, some can become theoretical, and some—practical. But if we take them in a general. formatory way, they will all be philosophical. There is a purpose why certain ideas are spoken of in this or that language. In practical application it may change.

Q.   Must a philosophical idea become theoretical before it can become practical?

MR. O.   Certain ideas must remain philosophical. It is sufficient to divide them in order to know which can be taken only philosophically, which theoretically, and which must be practical.

THREE LANGUAGES. JUNE 14TH 1939

You must remember that I spoke not only about one language—when I said that the beginning of the study of this system was the study of a new language—but about three ways of thinking, or three languages if you like.

In our system—or in any system for that matter, whether recognized or not recognized—there are three different languages: philosophical, theoretical, practical. When I say 'that is theoretical' or 'this is philosophy' in answer to questions, it means the language is wrong. You cannot ask something in a philosophical way and expect a practical answer. An abstract question cannot have a concrete answer.

You must also remember that the difference in meaning between these words 'philosophical', 'theoretical' and 'practical' is quite contrary to the ordinary meaning. The philosophical is the easiest approach, the theoretical is more difficult, and the practical is the most difficult of all. There can be philosophical knowledge—very general ideas; there can be theoretical knowledge—when you calculate things. In philosophical language you speak not so much about things but about possibilities; in other words, you do not speak about facts. In theoretical, you begin to speak about facts—but very far away, not exactly here. And in practical language you speak about things on the same scale as yourself and everything around you. So it is really a difference of scale.

WHAT IS IMPORTANT AND WHAT IS NOT. FEBRUARY 27TH 1939

Q.   I find it difficult to know what is important and what is not. I see I am doing something because I am considering, and try to stop. Is it important to stop things in small ways as sort of practice for big things?

MR. O. Everything is important if you learn something from it, if it shows you something, explains something.

THINKING. JANUARY 16TH 1940

Q. When I come round each time to the different things to think about in the programme, I am not making any progress in thinking about them. I cannot do more than repeat what they are.

MR. O. Repeating will not help. You must try to think. You must try to find something new in that way that you have not seen before, or some new points of view or angles. Try to talk with other people about it, it is very useful to do that, not at that time, but in free time.

Q. My inability to think in a new way or to have any new thoughts over the same subjects has shown me really how very mechanical and formatory my mind is. In what way can I try?

MR. O. More self-remembering; that is the only thing; that is why for five minutes you must really struggle either to be aware of yourself or to put out all thoughts, and if you do it seriously, it will help.

Q. I have noticed that often thoughts of extraordinary lucidity and freshness flash into my mind. How can one try to get these flashes on the subject one wants?

MR. O. Remember yourself more—deeper—better. There is no other answer; and then try to think also from different viewpoints, or different scales. Try to connect one point, things that you thought before, or did before, or could not answer before. If you connect one point right, all the rest will become clearer.

Q. It is difficult to keep a line of thought compared with the ordinary things that happen in one's head—the material is so limited.

MR. O. No, material is very big—something else is limited. Either desire is limited, or effort is limited; something is limited but not material.

Q. I should like to know the cause of the resistance to keeping out thoughts—the strong thoughts that come creeping in.

MR. O. There are two causes—the cause of resistance is one thing and the cause of the thoughts that come interrupting is another. The second shows the ordinary way of thinking—we can never keep a line because accidental associations come in. Resistance is another thing; it is the result of a lack of skill, lack of knowing how to deal with it, lack of experience if you like—not intentional thinking, thinking on a certain line. But this capacity must be educated.

Q. Isn't it the pull of sleep, mechanicalness?

MR. O. Certainly.

Q. You said either to try to stop thoughts for five minutes, or try to be aware of oneself.

MR. O. It is the same thing—it gives the same result. For some people it is easier to do one thing, and for another person it may be easier to do it in another way. Certainly this stopping thoughts is a more mechanical effort, so sometimes it is easier. It does not matter, the result is the same if you do it well. Not result of each particular five minutes, but generally.

17. 1. 40

Q. How can I learn to think on a different level?

MR. O. You must look at the subjects for thinking and try to find some personal connection with one or two questions, some personal interest, then that will grow and develop. By personal I mean what you thought before, questions which came to you before by themselves, that you never could answer, or something like that. And when you find something that you can see more, that may push other things.

Q. When thinking on a given subject I feel that one can try to think about all one has heard about it and try to understand new aspects or new connections. Or one can try to prevent any thought, and sometimes one will feel something about the subject. Are both methods useful?

MR. O. You speak about 'doing', but really what you can get from this programme is: you can see and observe different ways of thinking, because one day you think in one way and another day you can think about the same thing in another way. You must observe this, not try to 'do'. You can '<u>do</u>' nothing.

JANUARY 25TH 1941. LYNE

Mr. O.   Well, if there are any questions, now is the time for them. Perhaps you can find some at the last moment.

Mr. V.   Have you any views as to how it will be possible for us to carry on?

Mr. O.   Certainly. So long as we keep this house some kind of work will go on. If this becomes impossible, then that will become impossible.

You see, that is chiefly why I am going. Here I can do nothing. There perhaps I can do something for the future, either for Lyne or start something new over there, arrange later when it will be possible for people to come there. That is how I see it.

Mr. P.   Is it the idea to start new groups over there?

Mr. O.   That I cannot say. It will depend how it will be possible—it may be possible to begin in one way, or in another way.

Some of the technical questions of organization of work here we can talk about to-morrow evening or maybe some other day (I still have three days). Now, if you have any general questions to ask, ask them.

Mrs. D.   You remember you said a little while back that you would hate to go, that it would mean collapse?

Mr. O.   Collapse of what?

Mrs. D.   I did not quite understand.

Mr. O.   Certainly I hate to go, but I can do nothing here; there I will be able to do something. That is all I can say.

Mrs. D.   I understood you meant collapse of the work here.

Mr. O.   It collapsed when the war began. I tried to go on with groups, started new groups, but nothing could be done outside, and this work cannot exist without growing. If it cannot grow it cannot go on. It is possible to keep for some time a certain number of people together, like in this house, for personal work. For that I gave the hint about stopping thoughts. It sounds little, but if you do it regularly two or three times a day you will see results. It is the best thing you can do at present. It is always, but now it is almost the only thing, almost the chief thing. If you do that you will see the way and will do many other things.

Mr. P.   What kind of other things?

Mr. O.   If you do it you will see. After some time. Months and months are necessary.

Mrs. R.   Do you mean if we learn. . .

MR. O.   No, you cannot learn, you can practise.

MRS. R.   ... then it will become clear what we ought to do?

MR. O.   No, no theories. It is a question of direct effort. There are no helps. All that you knew before, all that you learnt before. It is particularly necessary to avoid all theories about what may happen. Try it and then you will see.

MRS. D.   Can you explain why it is impossible to have meetings and why it cannot grow outside?

MR. O.   Because we cannot work at Colet Gardens. Many people went away; it is difficult to meet in the evening there; generally, communications are difficult; I cannot stay in London; one thing after another.

MR. L.   How can one prevent the strength one gets by stopping thoughts, becoming dangerous to one?

MR. O.   It never can be dangerous. Try, and you will see. You have some control, nothing more.

MR. L.   Cannot it be used dangerously?

MR. O.   How? First necessary to do it, then we will see what you acquire. You acquire only more self-control, more self-remembering. For whom can it be dangerous? In what sense?

MR. L.   Does not the idea of the devil enter into it and mislead you?

MR. O.   If you begin to remember yourself, the devil won't dare come near you. He is more afraid of it than of incense, as we used to say in Russia.

MR. A.   Is it going to be possible for us to remain in contact with you and get your instructions and so on?

MR. O.   As long as the Censor works we can communicate.

MR. A.   Yes, naturally while it is possible to write letters.

MRS. M.   Are there any special dangers as a group that we should guard against?

MR. O.   Dangers in what sense? The same things as always—identification, considering and so on. Dangers are always the same. There are no new dangers. External circumstances we cannot alter. Talking, negative imagination—these are the dangers. Useless talking, I mean, talking which is like dope—expression of negative emotions and so on.

At the same time you must understand that what is done at a time like this has much greater value than if it is done quietly. When things go more smoothly, then many things [happen] almost mechanically. At a time like this they need effort. Everything you do, everything you can do, all is counted, all will give results sooner or later. I hope it will not be so long as that, but it is the same sort of time, the same quality of time as when we were in the Caucasus—1917, 1918, 1919, all that time we just moved about to different places in the Caucasus, until we managed to escape to Constantinople, and everything done at that time gave much more results than things that could be done in a quiet time. But, as I already said, I hope it will not be so long.

Mrs. P.   Should we all try our best to get to America?

Mr. O.   I cannot say. I must get there first and then we can see.

Mrs. N.   How will we get shocks when they become necessary?

Mr. O.   Shocks are provided. At present you must pray to have less shocks! It is very important to keep together—the most important thing. If you manage to keep this house, then the future will be easier.

Mr. W.   Before you go, you will leave here some organization?

Mr. O.   It exists already. I only spoke about some technical details.

Mr. V.   I feel very much that this is the end of a certain period and that there may be later the beginning of another period, and there is a sort of intermediate stage which may be very difficult.

Mr. O.   Quite right. Only I do not quite agree with you that this is the end. The end was when war began.

Mr. W.   Is there any chief principle that we should remember to help us through that intermediate stage?

Mr. O.   Try to remember yourself and do not forget to stop thoughts, as often and as much as you can. In that way you will remember work, will remember everything else.

Mr. P.   That means stopping thoughts without anything special to think of after?

Mr. O.   No, no, nothing to think. Stop thinking. It is a great mistake to think that in order to stop thoughts you must think about something.

Mr. P.   And nothing to follow?

Mr. O.   No, just stop thinking.

Miss Y.   When you are more free from thoughts, do you then know more what you want?

Mr. O.   I cannot say about free. Two, three, four times a day for five minutes or so, try to stop thoughts. I never said anything about being free from thoughts. That is quite a different thing.

Miss C. Suppose there is a very small percentage of people trying to remember themselves or to stop thoughts or to do anything, what will happen?

Mr. O. I said to those who will do it and spoke about those who will do it.

Miss C. Won't the others disintegrate the whole thing?

Mr. O. I spoke about stopping thoughts, not about not stopping thoughts; about self-remembering, not about not self-remembering.

Mr. A. Will it be possible for us to get in touch at all with people who do not come regularly but do come sometimes?

Mr. O. Certainly. That depends on you and on them.

Mr. A. So people can come here if they want?

Mr. O. Certainly if they just come and talk about Mussolini or something, then it would be useless. If they come and work, that is another thing—in one way, or in another way or a third way.

Miss D. With whom should we get in contact?

Mr. O. People who want to work, if they do. It is they who must get in contact.

Mr. V. I feel one of the most important things now is to have a right attitude and right thinking about this situation here, and particularly in relation to you and Madame in America.

Mr. O. Me and Madame in America; what does it mean to have right attitude? It is a question of what will happen there. I spoke about your attitude to the work in general, and that depends on what you do now very much, on your personal work, self-remembering, not identifying, and also on the work of trying to keep this thing going.

Mr. S. Should we regard this idea of stopping thoughts as a sort of task while you are away?

Mr. O. No other words are needed. Stopping thoughts means stopping thoughts.

Miss Y. Is it equally valuable in different circumstances; stopping thoughts while working, while sitting still and so on?

Mr. O. That you can try. There are no instructions about that. It is individual. Try different ways and compare. You must understand the value is not in the result but in the effort. Certainly the more you understand why you are doing it, the more profit it will give.

Mr. P. I suppose really we are in the position now, or I am anyway, where I have up till now taken everything for granted.

You have given us everything. If we can manage to keep something going during this very difficult time, the result will be that everybody who does manage to keep going will learn to value and gain experience which will give right valuation in a way nothing else will?

MR. O. Quite right.

MR. P. It looks like a very big test.

MR. O. It is always test. Permanent examination. It is one thing, you know, just to take things that are given, talk about them, discuss them. But it is another thing to make efforts, create something.

MR. P. The difficulty is to have enough emotional feeling now to act as sufficient energy after all these months to make these efforts now.

MR. O. There are clear things—it is clearly seen what it is necessary to do now. In personal work try to remember yourself more; in external work, try to work with people and keep things going.

MRS. M. Can you explain what is the real value of stopping thoughts?

MR. O. Control. Thoughts go without control. By trying to stop them, you will create control. In that way you create self-remembering.

MR. L. In one of the early lectures you spoke of the knowledge of the system as symbolical to a broken coin, and of us as the guardians of this coin.

MR. O. No, then I spoke in quite a different way. It was an illustration of the word 'symbol'.

MR. L. Is this our responsibility?

MR. O. I only spoke what you can do for yourselves and in yourselves, not about keeping the ideas. But maybe that will help, if you like, if it reminds you about self-remembering in the right way, reminds you of everything in the right proportion, right form. If you feel there is something you do not remember well, try not to think about it. And in order not to think about it you must control your thinking, because you will want to think about it and it will keep on coming into your mind in a fragmentary form and spoil your thinking. In that way you can apply control.

MR. C. Is it useful to discuss amongst ourselves this trying to stop thoughts?

MR. O. I do not see what you can discuss about stopping

thoughts. Maybe it can be discussed in two years' time, if you work for two years on this particular line. Then perhaps you will have material for discussion. Now it will be just talk.

MR. V.   I meant not so much discuss results but as a reminder. A reminder to make the effort.

MR. O.   I do not see that discussion will help. Discussion will give satisfaction by itself and make you think, 'Now we can stop thoughts, we have already stopped. . . .'

MISS C.   Is it really possible to stop thoughts completely?

MR. O.   Try. Completely, not completely—I have just said, effort is important, not result.

MR. H.   The difficulty seems to be over this period that we shall have to compete against things running down.

MR. O.   Not necessarily running down. It is bad if it runs down because of our failure. That is one thing. If things are smashed by external things it does not matter. Something will remain. It can come on again later if circumstances become better, or in another place it can grow again.

MR. H.   So something must be kept going whether it runs down or not?

MR. O.   It cannot run down if you keep going. Those are two opposite things. We tried this ourselves. Particularly in 1918 and 1919 we were in very difficult position, many times, more difficult than can be described because there were many things impossible to remember, impossible to enumerate, but we managed to escape, so there is a chance to escape now. And we managed to start work again, so there is a chance to start work again.

MR. M.   There was a question earlier about communicating with you. . . .

MR. O.   It is always possible to write.

MR. R.   Are you going to leave us anything that has been written to read?

MR. O.   I was just thinking about it. If I finish something you shall have it. If I have time, and write over there, I will send you things from there. But do not rely too much upon it. It is the same difficulty of correction, translation, all complicated things, but after some time it will be possible to arrange. But you have enough material, you know.

You spoke, for instance, about people who come only occasionally. I heard the funniest possible conversations by people who had heard nothing at all from myself about the six activities, about triads, God knows what. That is dangerous. Dangerous for them. So you must try to explain, if they have not heard something, that it is better if they do not talk about it. In any case, nobody must talk about these things until I tell them to talk.

MRS. M. Last winter when we had small groups for reading here, it seemed to me it was of very great value, and I wondered if it would be possible to meet sometimes and have someone read to us.

MR. O. Yes, it is possible, but you know reading without commentary is sometimes very useless. I began to prepare something for reading, and Madam K. is translating a book about Mount Athos. There is nothing exceptional in this book—the man just describes his impressions—he does not know much but he is a good writer. When it is translated I think it will be useful to read and discuss it. Mount Athos is an interesting place. There are other books about it, but here is exactly the difficulty I mean. You read, but you do not know the author, and the chief thing is to understand his mentality, from which angle he sees things. For instance, I just read one book—I want to read it here and have your opinion, just on one short passage. You read this book, you trust this man in a sense, he gives a certain idea of what Mount Athos is, and then you meet with such funny, such strange things.

[Reading of excerpt from 'Monks of Athos' by Dawkins.]

So you get a picture of the mentality of this man. He did not realize anything about this monk. First, he did not realize that the monk probably did not want to make them tea; second, probably he had no tea; third, probably he had no place to leave his tea-pot or kettle or whatever it was. He was a monk without a permanent place, so he carried all his belongings with him wherever he went, and probably this thing was his most cherished possession. But this man did not understand that. So that is what I mean—you read such books and think the man understands something. So if you read, it is necessary to read very carefully.

MR. P. This man had no pupils when he gave lectures at Oxford!

MR. O. I do not wonder.

MR. N. Do you plan to come back before the end of the war?

MR. O. I can speak only up to to-day. The rest is only a

question of events, and you see what it means? Circumstances cannot be altered.

Then [to Madame K.] you can continue also Roussoff. Later, you can read it—it gives an interesting picture of life in Russia. You will see many things about which you had quite wrong ideas. The author was killed in 1917 by the bolsheviks, in company with a hundred and fifty other people.

Then, if I find something interesting to read I will send you something.

MRS. M. Will the printing of the psychological lectures be finished?

MR. O. Unfortunately, not yet—not even the correction of the type, but it still may be finished, approximately.

MISS Y. Does that mean we may get a copy?

MR. O. That we will see later.

MR. L. Are conditions in the East more favourable for work than in America?

MR. O. You see, I was in the East in 1914, and in America only in previous incarnations which I do not remember, so I cannot compare them!

You must understand it is not pleasant for me at all to go. It means abandoning (for the present, I mean, perhaps later on it can go on again) twenty years of work. But nothing can be done here. There, perhaps, I will do something. That we will see. If things become better here, then it will be important, and you will see why it was important to keep Lyne. If we have it we can start at once when I come back. If we manage to keep Colet Gardens it will be still better, but that will be very difficult to keep. If we let it on a short lease, then we may have it back again and be able to start groups at once, and all that. Perhaps it can be used in some way, Colet Gardens. I cannot think of anything, but circumstances change.

Certainly you may think, and it is quite useful to think about it, that we might have foreseen, might have gone to America before and started groups before the war began. That is all quite right in a sense, and some people tried to persuade me very strongly in 1937, 1938, to go to America at that time. But somehow I did not like it much, these people who went at that time, it was too much consideration of their own safety and at times like that you can be too clever, things may turn out differently. They could have turned differently practically at the last moment. War was inevitable, but it was impossible to say definitely when it would begin, and it could have begun differently. If it had begun differently, now it would be finished already. Last winter there was a possibility to turn things quite differently, so you cannot be too clever. I knew a man from Petersburg who was very clever, foresaw the possibility of revolution, took all his things and moved to Italy and died there!

MRS. N.   Is it possible to know how stopping thoughts helps to dispel this heavy energy of which we have too much?

MR. O.   You must stop thoughts first, and in two years' time you can ask what it means if you cannot see yourself.

At the same time I have already answered that—control. Now you have no control. If you do this for two years you will have more control, and then it will be possible to see how to use that control.

MRS. M.   I suppose stopping thoughts has extra value in times like these because one can lose a great deal of energy through thoughts that come from what we hear around us?

MR. O.   You lose energy by all actions, emotions, even movements, functions over which you have no control. If you begin to acquire control of one thing, you acquire control over another thing. That was always explained in the beginning of our work. There are many, many things to learn and to practise. You cannot do it all separately, but if you begin with the chief things that will change other things. So there is no need to do everything separately. This stopping thoughts is the easiest thing of all. It does not need any arrangements, any organization. In all conditions you can stop thoughts. If you make these efforts, it will change many other things. If you acquire control of thoughts, you acquire control of many other things.

MR. V.   Is there any special obstacle in ourselves that may prevent us from keeping Lyne going?

MR. O.   No, just laziness and lack of self-remembering, negative imagination. There are many things, hundreds and hundreds of things. Otherwise it would be simple.

MISS C.   How can people who do not live at Lyne keep in touch with Lyne?

MR. O.   Some can, some cannot, some do not realize it.

MISS C.   How is it possible?

MR. O.   We deal with facts. If they want to come, they can. It may be impossible because this is not a normal time. There may be many difficulties.

MRS. W.   For so long we have relied on your judgment and on Madame's judgment. . . .

MR. O.   You have to develop your judgment. Now is the chance.

RIGHT THINKING. NOVEMBER 22ND 1944

Q.   How can we awaken intellectual centre?

MR. O.   By right thinking.

Q.   Could we have a formula for that?

MR. O.   No, no formula. You have to do it. Formula is only for laziness.

Q.   I seem to observe that I don't use intellectual centre at all.

MR. O.   You use it too much. Maybe you don't notice it.

Q.   What is an emotion?

MR. O.   Different. Sometimes pleasure, sometimes not pleasure. I never interfere with people's pleasure. In London several people wanted me to go to Russia. I said Russia didn't exist since 1917. They said, 'Have you objection to my going?' I said, 'None. But you don't come back to groups.' It is all a question of right thinking.

Q.   Then you can say that the different centres think—not only the intellectual?

MR. O.   All centres think. You must learn to stop them all.

15
Observation

In speaking to small groups MR. O. said:

Try to think what it is that makes work so difficult, try to find what are the things that take so much of your attention. All these things have to be found.

I want you to understand that each person separately has a certain definite obstacle which stands in the way of their work, some definite point which prevents the possibility of right work. This obstacle you have to find. Each person has many difficulties—I mean difficulties in understanding—but one is bigger than the others. So it is necessary, for each of you separately, to find your own chief difficulty. When you find it, work against it may help you for a certain time and then perhaps you will have to find another difficulty and another and another. Until you find your difficulty of the present time you will not be able to work in the right way.

Of course, the first difficulty for everybody is the word 'I'. You say 'I' and do not think that it is just a little part of you that speaks. But behind and beyond this there must be something else and this is for you each to find personally. It may be a particular kind of negative emotion, a particular kind of identification or of imagination, or many other things.

Q. Could always putting off things be the big difficulty?
MR. O. Quite possibly—very good. But that is not exactly what I mean. This is a difficulty in doing and what I meant is a difficulty in understanding. You already understand this putting off, already think about it, so it is not the kind of difficulty I mean.

Try to think what makes things very difficult or takes much of your attention. All these things should be found.
Q. My difficulty is that I should give more time to the work,

but I am afraid of giving up something I enjoy. What can I do about it?

MR. O. Perhaps by agreeing to give up something. You cannot get anything without giving up something. But there are many imaginary things you can always give up. So you must give up imaginary things and keep for yourself real things. Again your misfortune is that you do not know what is imaginary and what is real.

When you meet together you can work on these lines. If you want to, you can talk about the theories—if you have forgotten something, you can ask other people, but more important than that is to try and find personal difficulties. I do not mean personal difficulties of an external kind, but inner personal difficulties—personal features, personal inclinations, personal disinclinations, attitudes, prejudices, activities which can stop your understanding and prevent you from working. These inner personal difficulties can be divided into three categories. For some people, the chief difficulty is in negative emotions—they just cannot stop being negative, generally in some particular direction. For other people, the chief difficulty is in imagination—they cannot stop imagining certain things which are quite wrong and distort their view of things. I do not mean imagination in the sense of daydreams; I mean imagination in the sense of some persistent wrong idea. The third category is formatory thinking. It is very useful to try and understand what formatory thinking means, to find some good examples of formatory thought and keep these examples in your mind. Then it will not be difficult to recognize and realize, always, when you see yourself thinking formatorily, and when you hear somebody else speaking formatorily. These are the chief kinds of difficulties which you have to find in yourselves. For one person, one thing is more permanent; for another, another, and for a third, a third—sometimes two together but better try to think which is the chief in you, formatory thinking, or negative emotion, or imagination.

Certainly, in addition to this, it may be that you did not listen well; maybe you do not know things you are supposed to know; perhaps you have not heard. I do not refer only to diagrams—I mean also on the psychological side. People can help each other; one can remember one thing better, another can remember something else.

SEEING ONESELF

Q. Does seeing oneself mean a combination of self-observation and self-remembering?

MR. O. No, just having a right picture of oneself.

Q. Is it possible to have a complete picture of oneself?

MR. O. Yes, certainly, this is the beginning. Before you get that you cannot begin any serious work, you can only study, but even that will be fractional.

Q. It is very difficult to make sure that one is telling the truth to oneself.

MR. O. Yes, that is why I said to see oneself, not to know. We have many pictures of ourselves; we must see them, one after another, and then compare them. But we cannot say at the first glance which is right.

Q. What is the means of verification that one is seeing oneself?

MR. O. Repeated experience.

Q. But cannot repeated experience also be wrong?

MR. O. Our capacity for deceiving ourselves is so great that we can deceive ourselves even in that.

Q. I wondered whether there was some way of checking?

MR. O. No, but when the emotional element enters— conscience—that will be verification.

Q. Do you mean when one suddenly wakes up and is ashamed?

MR. O. That is the emotional accompaniment. I speak only about seeing.

Q. Is it the same to see what you are not?

MR. O. One includes the other.

Q. Is it possible to stand seeing oneself without a big change?

MR. O. It is difficult to answer. People get accustomed to everything, even to seeing themselves.

Q. You said one does not begin to work until one sees oneself.

MR. O. Yes. One cannot speak to a person seriously until he begins to see himself, or at least realizes it is necessary to see himself and that he does not see himself.

Q. Sometimes I see myself as extremely confused and drawn in all directions, but I don't see how to get out of this confusion.

MR. O. This is one picture. Try to find another picture. This is what, in the first group in Petersburg, was called, to take photographs of oneself in preparation for seeing oneself.

Q. Does to see oneself mean some permanent realization? For

sometimes what I see at a given moment later on becomes something abstract and not emotional.

MR. O.   That means you cease to see yourself. Nothing is permanent in us.

Q.   Does to see yourself mean you see your faults and also see what to do about them?

MR. O.   Sometimes it may be like that. But you again try to find definitions and explanations, and I spoke not about definition and explanation but about actual practice—not how to define it, or how it can be translated into different words—actually to see. Suppose you speak about a certain picture, and never saw it but only heard about it; you can know all that is possible about this picture, but if you have not seen it, it is necessary first to see it and then verify all that you know.

LYING. JANUARY 16TH 1940

Q.   I never really understood that the centre of gravity of lying is talking about what you don't know.

MR. O.   There are many elements, but this is the only one which required particular mention in lectures, because it is not recognized at all and it is one of the most important—not intentional. Intentional lying is another thing, and there are mechanical forms of lying when certain things are accepted and people just repeat them without knowing details.

MR. O.   As I said before, try to use this time for observing life in general: the political situation, how people lie, how they do not understand the simplest things. Particularly now there is a certain thing which I call 'force of things'; it is difficult to describe, but the force of things at the present moment turns governments, and political people, and journalists in the right direction. But still they don't want to see things, and until people begin to see—the people who actually have control in their hands—until they begin to see things or their resistance, nothing will happen. It is just marking time and will not bring anything.

Q.   Can you help to show what would be the right way of looking at present things?

MR. O.   I spoke about it several times, but this is a wrong question because it is not important what I say. I talk about observing how people don't want to see things.

Q. Is this force of things entirely mechanical?

MR. O. It does not matter. Everything is mechanical. But there are different combinations of forces, and sometimes, when things become very absurd, the things themselves show the right solution and make people turn in the right direction. For instance, three months ago nobody wrote in the papers what they write to-day. The French papers realize the necessity to fight bolshevism, but they don't like to realize yet that bolshevism is the chief cause; and the second cause is the fault of the European governments which helped bolsheviks.

You remember I said in the psychological lectures that one of the divisions was the study of lying. Now you have a beautiful opportunity for the study of lying.

FEBRUARY 16TH 1940. (COLET GARDENS)

MRS. J. I find that doing the programme with regularity had helped me to go deeper into certain questions. For example, I have found that certain attitudes of mine, such as my dissatisfaction with my progress, are really negative emotions. I wondered if such attitudes are among the things MR. O. said we had to give up in order to awake.

MR. O. Certainly, you can't work with negative emotions. You must observe them and struggle against them. This is obvious.

MRS. W. In thinking after self-remembering, I know that I am thinking, and any noise that goes on outside instead of going straight through me remains outside and one can hear two or three noises quite clearly. Is this a slight variation in consciousness?

MR. O. No, just observations. You must have about a thousand of them before you can make conclusions.

MR. C. I have been trying to see what a moment of conscience would be, and I find I can only feel one emotion at a time. But I feel there must be many emotions in an emotional experience. How can I learn to separate them?

MR. O. This is useless. Try to see what means absence of conscience. It is just imagination to try to see what it will be. Try to be less asleep. Realize the difference between moments when you are more asleep and moments when you are less asleep.

MRS. C. Where does motive come from?

Mr. O.   Only from realization of mechanicalness.

Mrs. C.   Is a moment when I feel that I see emotionally the truth of something outside myself related to conscience?

Mr. O.   Definition is not important. If you feel more conscious, very good. Compare it with when you feel less conscious.

Mrs. A.   When thinking about right attitude towards negative emotion, it suddenly occurred to me that if one knew the whole truth about oneself and were able to act accordingly, that would be a change of consciousness. Would it?

Mr. O.   It would be a great thing. But it is very far.

Mrs. W.   Are all negative emotions in false personality or do they sometimes occur on physical grounds? I am especially thinking of depression.

Mr. O.   It doesn't matter. This is a formatory question.

Mrs. J.   I have sometimes found that as a result of effort one can remember oneself for a little time, not merely try to but really do it. Can one say that one's aim would be to have this state more often?

Mr. O.   Compare these moments with other moments. You will get a useful result.

Mrs. S.   A state of greater awareness seems often to just happen to me. But is it not likely to be the result of previous effort?

Mr. O.   It happens only as a result of effort. If you decide to work you can't just let things happen. If you try to stop thoughts, observe and so on, you will get results.

Mrs. J.   Is it not true that in a state of self-remembering, one's mind is clearer and one's movements better?

Mr. O.   Naturally, you are more awake.

Mrs. J.   Are we to judge that we are more awake by better functioning of the machine?

Mr. O.   No need to judge. Your business is to work.

Mrs. S.   Isn't it true that one must see what one wants even in the next small step before one can get any results? Just generalized efforts will produce no result, will they?

Mr. O.   Quite right. The more one is aware what one is doing, the better the result will be.

Mrs. J.   Is our aim not to be a machine or to control the machine?

Mr. O.   Our aim is to be awake and to control all functions.

Mrs. F.   It seems to me that the memory of negative emotions holds a great deal of energy in the body. How can one release this? If, for example, I remember a past negative emotion it seems charged with energy. Could it not be transformed into something more useful?

MR. O. Try, try, try. You can judge only by your own attempts.

MR. B. When we are thinking of bringing people into the work, do we just take it for granted that they are more or less prepared, or can we do anything about it?

MR. O. You can do nothing about it and you must not take it for granted. You must try and see whether they are prepared. You can do this by talking to them about a great many subjects. You do not need to use system language or to talk about system.

MR. B. What does preparation mean?

MR. O. You should have asked this question before the other.

MRS. A. What does MR. O. mean by friends of bolsheviks? Does he mean nations?

MR. O. No! No! I mean M. Heriot, M. Daladier, M. Blum, all who tried to arrange an alliance with bolsheviks. And the Labour people in the English Government, and Shaw, Wells, all those who went to Russia.

MISS H. Didn't MR. O. say that bolshevism has always existed implying a desire to force your ideas on people by violence?

MR. O. Yes, in different forms.

MISS S. If one makes a sudden discovery in a moment of emotion, is it wrong to talk about it, even if one thinks it will help the other person?

MR. O. It depends on the person and on the discovery.

MISS S. The goodness of an emotion seems to revolve on itself, so to speak, and to become its exact opposite. How can one stop this negativeness from developing?

MR. O. Negative emotion usually depends on negative attitude, sometimes on positive attitude. If one has positive attitude to the wrong things and negative attitude to the right things, all emotions will be wrong.

MISS S. I know, in certain cases, when I have got something from an emotional discovery, it is the feeling inside of wanting to appear clever which has made me speak about it. There are times when I am unable to stop this. I could replace this negativeness by the right attitude. How?

MR. O. Mechanicalness, not negativeness.

MISS S. By fate, I understand certain distinct happenings which direct one's life. Is that right?

MR. O. May be right, may be wrong. We can take as fate only unavoidable things.

MISS S. To what extent does man 1, 2 and 3, who is under the Law of Accident, come under the Law of Fate apart from birth and death?

MR. O. It depends on the relation between personality and essence. If personality is strong it makes a shell round essence, then there is very little fate. The planetary influences which control fate, type, essence, do not reach us when personality is very strong. But some people, quite without school, live more in essence; personality with them is very fated. These people are more under the Law of Fate than others. They depend more on certain influences on which other people depend less. I will not say what these influences are, for this only leads to imagination. You must find out for yourselves. For them there is nothing of fate except birth and death.

MISS S. Can man 1, 2 and 3 know his fate?

MR. O. This is very difficult. What do you mean by fate? If I say 'Yes', it may be true; if I say 'No', it may be true.

MISS S. By going over one's life can one know one's fate?

MR. O. I have already answered this. It depends on whether personality or essence is stronger. When personality is strong there is nothing to call fate except birth and death and certain attractions and repulsions.

MISS S. Knowing one's fate, how can one act along a line to avoid accident?

MR. O. I don't know what you mean by knowing fate. It has nothing to do with avoiding accident. One avoids 'accidents' in our special sense by creating causes and increasing effects. This is coming to will. It is not will but it is coming to it. It sounds very strange at first but only a certain number of things can happen in an hour or a day. So if one creates more causes there is less room for accident to happen.

MR. M. I know better and worse states in myself, but they always appear as emotional or physical or both; I do not seem to see any variation in consciousness. yet I have often been told that we do experience considerable variation within the second state of consciousness.

MR. O. You must make more observations. The same emotion and thought may be in different states of consciousness. They will be different in different states of consciousness.

MR. M. I find it difficult to be really sincere about the

programme. Sometimes I am able to do it properly and then it may give a result, but mostly there is a tendency to scramble through it.

MR. O.   You must do what you can. You cannot deceive yourself about stopping thoughts.

MR. M.   In trying to think about conscience, I cannot fully understand why it is that we cannot feel our different emotions at the same time. I give myself the theoretical answer that it is because we have so many 'I's. But this does not seem enough. How can I understand it better?

MR. O.   Understand that we cannot feel different emotions at the same time. No use to describe why. And this is a separate question from that of conscience.

MR. M.   How can one work towards conscience?

MR. O.   By trying to be sincere with oneself.

MISS D.   How can one keep in touch with the system when one is forced to live out of London owing to war conditions? There seems only first line of work to carry on; is this any use?

MR. O.   This does not enter into our programme. It is a matter of personal circumstances. There are no methods. One person can do one thing and another perhaps cannot.

MISS D.   Sometimes during an effort to remember myself things round me seem to become more vivid. At other times the effort seems to shut out impressions. Which state is nearest to self-remembering?

MR. O.   This is for you to decide. It is material for observation. When you feel attempts to remember yourself give no results, try stopping thoughts. In this you cannot fail. There are no conditions, unless one is very ill or perhaps other very unusual conditions in which one cannot stop thoughts.

MISS D.   In the programme we were given, I find great poverty of thought in trying to think of problems insoluble to our minds. Is there any way one can gain more content?

MR. O.   You have not given me enough material. First make more effort. And see that you think all the time about problems insoluble for our minds.

MRS. S.   Might not patriotism be an unconscious religious impulse?

MR. O.   I don't know. It may be simply a word.

MRS. S.   I have been trying to think about laziness and inertia, and although I know that it is a dense state of sleep which disappears with any shock, there seem so many aspects of it. Could MR. O. say something about it?

MR. O. You speak about words. There is no example here. I try not to think about words.

MRS. S. In trying to think differently the effort seems to produce a different sensation in one part of the head. Is it because I am trying to use a hitherto untapped energy, or just that I have been intellectually lazy except when stimulated?

MR. O. This is pure fantasy.

MRS. H. Is there any way, except through persistent efforts of stopping wandering thoughts? These exercises have made me see more clearly than before that this constitutes the greatest difficulty.

MR. O. Make these exercises. You will see results.

MRS. M. Is all our thinking formatory except when we are trying to self-remember?

MR. O. Self-remembering has nothing to do with it. Very much thinking is formatory. But when we think about serious things, either we don't think or our thinking is not formatory. Formatory thinking is always bad, but for some problems it is ridiculous. I have just had a perfect example in one of the letters I frequently get from America. In 'Tertium Organum' it is written that one does not need to have many books, that about ten books would be enough. And about ten, twenty times a year I get a letter asking me to give a list of these ten books.

MRS. M. When I try to stop thought, time appears to stop too. Would time change altogether for us if we were a little more awake?

MR. O. This is subjective. Time is different from subjective feelings about time.

MRS. M. I realize that to be reliable is something much deeper than my suggestion about burning the programme. But is there not a rule that we should keep no written notes?

MR. O. Certainly there is such a rule. No one keeps it, but there is a rule.

MRS. M. Is it helpful to try to face death?

MR. O. Until it comes, quite useless; it will only be imagination.

MRS. M. When an attitude at the back of a negative emotion is very old and habitual, possibly a feature, how can I attack it?

MR. O. Begin from the feature. Find the feature, talk about it, and so on.

MISS M. When I am ordinarily identified with life things and try to do the programme afterwards, I often feel quietened. But when I am identified with the ideas before I begin, I can neither stop thought nor think at all, and afterwards my identification seems worse. I cannot stop this. Is it better not to try the programme when I know this will happen beforehand.

MR. O. I don't know. It is for you to decide. If you feel you cannot think, try to remember yourself for five minutes or stop thought. This you can do. It will bring results. This does not mean that you will become man No. 7 or something, but you will see results.

MISS M. When I try to think of one of the ideas in the programme, I try to recollect what I have heard and then compare it with my own observations, but it seems to me that I am not thinking. How can I think?

MR. O. It is very good thinking, but there are other ways.

APRIL 5TH 1940. (COLET GARDENS)

MRS. C. I find that I have a deep-down feeling of discontent that there is something wrong with my circumstances and not with me. I know that it must be in myself because it is there under all circumstances. This emotion particularly interferes with self-remembering. I can't get at this emotion to overcome it but I want to very much.

MR. O. This is a very good observation. That is all. Everyone accuses circumstances. Then the circumstances change and they continue to accuse them.

MRS. L. When MR. O. speaks about making more causes, does he mean in ordinary life or only in system work?

MR. O. I don't know. I can't refer to things I said three weeks ago. This is not a general principle. It refers to a special conversation.

MRS. L. What do planetary influences feel like? For instance, I always feel in a much better state if it is a fine day, and wondered if this had anything to do with planetary influences.

MR. O. No.

MRS. B. I feel that I seem to be getting less control and more energy than I used to have, and I want to know if this is not dangerous. I have less vague negative emotion than I used to have but I lose my temper much more easily. It is so quick I can't catch it.

MR. O.   It is necessary to observe for a longer period. Things change very much from day to day.

MRS. B.   I want very much to be a useful member of a group and I feel that I strike a line only for myself. How can I be more useful to the group?

MR. O.   To all questions of that kind there is only one answer, remember yourself. The more you remember yourself, the more you can get on in any line you want.

MRS. P.   In trying to watch the different states I am in during the day, I have observed a particularly heavy physical state which comes after the night, for no apparent reason. In that state it is quite impossible to self-remember. Should I make physical efforts to overcome this?

MR. O.   I don't know which physical efforts can help. You must try. Causes may be very different. But if you refer to the programme there is one thing to be said, that if you cannot self-remember you can always stop thought. Unless you are actually ill this is always possible.

MRS. J.   I have found that saying to myself that I could not self-remember in certain physical states was a profound negative attitude. When I changed this attitude everything changed for me.

MR. O.   Quite possible.

MRS. H.   I want to ask about the relationship of one's work in the system to one's work in life. When I first came in contact with the system I felt I was attaching too much importance to my work in life; then, later, I felt that this was a lazy attitude. I want to understand the relationship between work in life and work in the system.

MR. O.   There are many kinds of work in life. One has one relationship and another has another. There can be no general answer.

MRS. S.   MR. O.   once said that subjective imagination may stop development. Can we see the real in ourselves or must we always have corroboration from someone else?

MR. O.   You must give examples of what you mean. Sometimes one can see, sometimes one cannot see.

MRS. C.   Does second line of work mean rather a different kind of work on oneself that first line of work?

MR. O.   Work on oneself remains the same. Second line of

work is the study of discipline. Without understanding school discipline one can't have inner discipline. There are people who seem as though they could do good work and who fail because of that. They don't have discipline.

MRS. A. I have noticed in trying to self-remember during the last fortnight that some of my reactions have changed, and this led me to wonder why our reactions are so difficult to catch and to order. It seems to me that many reactions come in all centres. Why, I don't know.

MR. O. There is no order and no discipline in these reactions. But it is important to know what you mean by self-remembering. Do you mean these exercises or do you mean self-remembering in connection with some actual thing which happens? One is preparation; the other is the actual thing.

MRS. A. Is the capacity to see planetary influences part of one's own make-up and nothing to do with one's particular attitude? Is it a part of one's being?

MR. O. It is a part of one's being. It must be understood why we spoke about planetary influences, why they were mentioned and in connection with what. The chief idea is that planetary influence may be very different. Our state attracts and repulses planetary influences. You speak of planetary influences as if you knew what they were. You cannot know that, you can know only your state. If you self-remember, you can attract good planetary influences; if you are mechanical you attract wrong planetary influences.

MRS. B. This has often been described as a way for individual man. Yet all that has been given to us in the way of knowledge is so objective and common to all. It seems impossible to get anything for oneself alone.

MR. O. It is difficult to see what you mean. What one gets one gets for oneself. One can't get anything for someone else. Ten people cannot decide together what they will get. People are very different. The same awakening has different effects in different people.

MISS M. Desire for activity again seems to be my stumbling-block. I make plans on how to spend my time during a period of forced inactivity, but I find that every few hours my whole body seems to be up in arms against it and even my work period seems to suffer. Is it good for me to struggle against this desire to be active at intervals or can I attain a more balanced state of mind through activity?

MR. O. It is impossible to say because you don't say what you mean by activity or in what way you wish to be active. It may be right and it may be wrong.

MRS. W. I do not understand accident in relation to recurrence. Is accident as unavoidable as fate?

MR. O. Explain what you mean by accident.

MRS. W. We have been told that while our birth is fate, marriage can be accident.

MR. O. It is always accident.

MRS. W. In a case like that where accident affects one's entire life, does it recur?

MR. O. Even that may happen. The same kind of accident may repeat. We speak only about theory, but theory may be better or worse, nearer or further to possible facts. In mechanical life even things which happen don't change things practically. Things are important only when a man begins to awake, through school or by himself. From this moment things become serious. So do you ask about mechanical recurrence or the beginning of awakening? Remember this principle in school-work. If people work little or badly they have more time. If they begin to work, then time is counted for them. They have less time. The same is true of recurrence.

MRS. S. This seems very theoretical but it is important to me. In your chapter on Eternal Recurrence you said that the rôles of Pilate and Judas would be enacted through eternity. Why could it not be remotely possible for a conscious man to reincarnate into the past and influence these rôles? Is it because the law of types is so fixed and also within the plan of life?

MR. O. This is so theoretical that it doesn't count. We must be practical. All these Judases and Pilates are too far away.

MRS. M. In answer to the question of why influence C should not be wasted, you said that influence C is conscious in its origin and in its results.

MR. O. Influence C can be wasted, everything can be wasted, only it should not be. Influence C is conscious in origin, not in result.

MRS. M. If influence C is received mechanically, i.e. as influence A or B, it ceases to be C.

MR. O. That is quite right. Then it is lost.

MRS. A. Has this type so great an ascendancy over man 1, 2 3, that he is ruled by it?

Mr. O. No, I explained many times. This is so only in comparatively rare cases. Most people live in personality.

Mrs. A. Can it be modified through work on essence?

Mr. O. What means work on essence? It means nothing.

Mrs. A. Is type planetary influence and made by it, or is it a kind of law which governs us?

Mr. O. You may say so. But as one is X and another is Y, you don't know which is which. Planetary influence, type, these are only words to us. They may be useful to teach us to separate.

Mrs. A. Are the 48 laws under which man 1, 2, 3 lives known by name and classified?

Mr. O. Earth is under 48 laws, not man. Man lives under many more laws and on a different scale. He also lives under 48 laws since he lives on the earth.

Mrs. A. What makes the three forces obedient to good and bad conditions alike?

Mr. O. I don't understand your question. Give an example of what you mean.

Mrs. A. The three forces operate in bad times like these and in good times.

Mr. O. When are good times? I think times are much the same. There is no particular difference between them. The three forces are in everything that happens on all scales and in all worlds. You speak as if time and circumstances were different from the three forces. They are the same. The cause of your being puzzled about this is wrong formulation.

Mrs. A. Does the Law of Seven stop and end their activities, or transform them by a shock into higher or denser matters? How are they used in the true evolution of inner man?

Mr. O. There are many different things here. We can observe the Law of Seven in life, and in historical events, in that nothing comes to a final result.

Mrs. P. How can we use the Law of Seven?

Mr. O. We can only use things in relation to ourselves, not for outside things. We can't begin from a definition of forces. We must understand ourselves. It is in one of the first lectures; man is a machine, but a machine that knows it is a machine is already something different.

Mrs. A. In trying to self-remember I am sometimes able to see the result of a change in reaction. What makes them so difficult to change? So ready to revert to type and their usual channels?

Mr. O. If you can calculate the amount of energy you give to ordinary things and how much to self-remembering you will understand.

MRS. H.   I have been trying to think about cosmoses and, in practice, I have found it very useful as a help against negative emotion. When I am worried or annoyed, the thought of our relative position compared with the cosmoses above and below seems to put the negative emotion into its right perspective and at once it seems a very trifling thing.

MR. O.   Can you say how this comes? It is a very interesting observation, but do you know what you are doing? You think about it. It is very important to know what you do to yourself by thinking about cosmoses. It is simply that you pass into another centre, no more. So, if you are in emotional centre, begin to think about things and you are in intellectual centre. It may be difficult. You may be so angry and displeased that you don't want to think. But if you make yourself think you will get results.

MRS. A.   Would that stop formatory thinking?

MR. O.   Formatory thinking does not enter. Formatory thinking changes nothing.

MRS. H.   What is not clear to me is this. If each cosmos is zero to infinity compared with the one below and the one above, how does this affect the unity of all creation? Each cosmos seems to be closed within itself. What relation can it have to the rest of creation?

MR. O.   It is a question of scale and of comparative size.

[Questions left over from the previous week were read.]

MRS. A.   Does MR. O. mean that had we got all we could from the system we should have changed? Where is the hall-mark to show we have not changed?

MR. O.   Many things can be said. If you could—it is very difficult—imagine what would happen to you if you were not connected with any kind of work, it would answer your question. If you could compare yourself with yourself as you would be. Or you can take people who have left the work. Certain things happen to them or don't happen to them and you can think that if they had stayed with the work it would have been different.

MRS. S.   Didn't MR. O. mean that if we don't work this time we shall not meet the school next time?

MR. O.   To what conversation does this refer? School of any kind, even very elementary kind, is not under the laws of recurrence. They are more free compared with things in life. Wars, revolutions, are like lamp-posts, conscious things are like the light from passing cars. If you go out you will always see the same lamp-posts but you are not likely to see the same cars.

MRS. M.   Is it that opportunity never comes twice?

MR. O.   The same opportunity, no, that would be a waste of time. When people meet with certain opportunities they become responsible for the energy spent on them. If they don't use it, it never recurs. Lamp-posts stay fixed, cars don't stay, they are not for standing still, they are for moving.

MRS. J.   Isn't it that next time it would be over our heads?

MR. O.   No, this is imagination.

MRS. C.   Does MR. O. mean that if recurrence comes to an end one passes out of existence?

MR. O.   Such possibility exists.

MRS. S.   Isn't it true that if one doesn't work, self-remembering also goes?

MR. O.   Naturally. This you can observe. All you can acquire needs effort.

MRS. N.   Hasn't there been something said about working back to the source of knowledge? If we don't work, then the school wouldn't be in a position to work back to the source.

MR. O.   This is on a quite different scale. It is so big that it can't be applied to individual life.

MRS. A.   Is the proportion determined as to what number of people are necessary in a school?

MR. O.   Schools are different. One may exist with a very small number of people, another needs more people, and so on. It varies according to time, conditions, people. That is why it depends on circumstances. In relation to this work we had a definite plan. We were very near to this plan. Then war came. Will we be able to exist under these circumstances even if they don't get worse? Our organization was made for one plan. Without the organization can we continue to exist?

MRS. A.   If one has been in contact with the work and hasn't worked, is one in a worse position than if one hadn't met it at all?

MR. O.   It depends what you mean by better or worse. If one has attained something then one is in a better position. If one has got nothing, then one is in a worse position.

MR. M.   It seems that this question of limit is a question of time. We don't live for ever.

Mr. O.   Mechanical man returns and returns. But if one begins
to awake then time is counted.

Miss R.   I have noticed that I get an increase in physical energy
by right thinking. How can I get an increase in emotional
energy?

Mr. O.   You cannot. No one can. You can increase consciousness and self-remembering. Thus you will increase all functions.
You cannot work for it directly. What is the effect of right
thinking? You waste less energy. You are in the right centre for
any given work. So there is less waste of energy. A very good
example is this thinking about cosmoses.

Miss R.   With regard to discipline: is self-imposed discipline
useful or must it be school discipline?

Mr. O.   Discipline is good if it is discipline. But if it is just
invention then there is no result. The most important aspect of
discipline is not expressing negative emotion and not indulging
in negative emotion. All mechanical tasks cannot give result,
but to catch yourself in a moment of negative emotion; this is
discipline. Or not indulging in negative emotion.

It is useful to think about the question that the same opportunities may not occur next time. You expect things to be the
same, but they may be different. It depends on other people.
Other people may begin earlier. For example, I began these
lectures in 1921, but next time I might begin them in 1900. You
will be prepared only for 1921 . . . this is just an example for
thinking about.

Mrs. A.   It is very difficult to think of preparing for meeting
the system earlier.

Mr. O.   You can prepare nothing, only remember yourself.
You will remember things better; the whole thing lies in negative
emotions. We enjoy them so much we have no interest in
anything else. If you remember yourself now, next time you may
remember. But if you don't self-remember now, next time you
can't remember. At the same time, this is different for different
people.

Mrs. A.   Is this the reason for the 'I have been here before'
feeling? The feeling that one has already some piece of knowledge that one could not possibly have heard.

Mr. O.   I want facts. It may be simply a compound picture of
different ideas. If you can really remember something of the
kind it means you can self-remember. If you can't self-remember,
it is imagination.

Mrs. S. Is accidental self-remembering of any use for this purpose?

Mr. O. Accidental self-remembering is a flash for a second. One can't rely on it.

Mrs. A. Is there any sign by which you can tell that we have not been here before?

Mr. O. No one can tell. First of all, I don't enter into the conversation. I only know that I have not been in this house before.

Miss H. Then we haven't either.

Mr. O. I don't know. But you will be much nearer to the truth if you begin with this as the first time. If we did something before, then it was only so much as made this possible. The relation of different lives is the same as the relation of days and years. If people do nothing in one life there is more chance that they will do nothing in the next life.

Mrs. B. There are happenings in one's life, both bad and good, that don't seem one's own fault. They seem related to surroundings. Say you go into an environment you could have avoided, events follow which seem out of relation to your ordinary life. One is powerless against them. One simply has to wait until they are over. They seem to be related to each other and not to the rest of one's life.

Mr. O. I am trying to understand your question. You see, different types of people have different lives. With most people unusual things don't happen. All things are of the same pattern in their lives. It may be true that things of unusual character are interrelated and that you can do nothing against them. They have to come out.

16
The Lord's Prayer

THE LORD'S PRAYER. MARCH 5TH 1937

The Lord's Prayer is divided into three times three, but we cannot call it three triads because we do not know their relation to one another and we cannot see the forces. We can only see that there are three parts. We must know how to think to find the meaning. It is necessary to study. If we understand and can find more then we will see more clearly: there is no question of guessing or hints. Take each point separately and see which principles can be applied. We can find a meaning in some, in others we cannot.

First <u>Our Father</u>—we must leave this to the end; it is the most difficult.

<u>Hallowed be Thy name</u>. We must think of the name of God. It has a special meaning in many relgious systems—Hebrew, Mohammedanism and certain Christian sects. We can study the literature on this subject. For instance, in Cabala the Tetragrammaton stands for the four elements. In the Greek and Latin versions the word used for 'hallowed' means 'let it become holy'.

<u>Thy Kingdom come</u>. It is necessary to think of 'Kingdom'—all it can mean. Meanings are given in the 'New Model'—and there may be more than these. Many things are connected with this. It is connected with the idea of miracle in the system. Miracle means manifestation of laws of higher plane or world in lower world.

<u>Thy Will be done</u>. Necessary to remember all we know about the will of the Absolute—how far the will of the Absolute can go and why it cannot go further—because will itself creates laws which make it impossible for it to go further.

Each word in Lord's Prayer contains much meaning. I am only trying to show you how to study it. Not by guessing. For instance, people ask questions about the most difficult verse:

<u>Forgive us our debts</u>. Many principles are connected with this. First of all 'forgiving': such as we are we forgive when we should

not and we do not forgive when we must. All identification, sentimentality. . . . Forgiving is a function of higher emotion and is connected with positive emotion. This is impossible for us.

Our debtors. If we had positive emotions we would be open to higher influences which would do something for us. This is the explanation of 'forgive us our debts'. It refers to the idea of changing the past which can only be understood with the idea of recurrence. If we change to-day, we change the future for next life, and if we change the future for next life, we change the past.

If we put these ideas together we see how impossible are ordinary meanings given to Lord's Prayer and how much is necessary for even a glimpse of the real meaning. It is not possible to understand by just keeping these words. I am only trying to show you several principles: positive emotions, influences, changing the past, recurrence.

Bread. Bread is food. It is necessary to remember all that we know about food. To which food does this refer? What can be food? Impressions, influences. . . higher kinds. . . for ordinary man B influences are already this 'supersubstantial' food: for man with magnetic centre formed, it is C influences.

Temptation. For us—all that is easy, mechanical; letting things go; when we are angry—to express anger, when we are irritated—to express irritation; the comfort of 'letting things go'.

Evil. Evil is easily explained. When one resists temptation one becomes proud, thinks one is awake, others are asleep; how much better one is, etc. . . .

Forgiveness. Positive emotions ('Love your enemies'). Result of positive emotions. If you forgive, it opens you to higher influences. Obstacles to higher influences—negative emotions.

If you try to love your enemies with ordinary emotions, you will make more enemies.

Higher influences can change the past—and in connection with recurrence.

These very big ideas are put in the form of a prayer. When you decipher this idea of prayer, prayer i.e. supplication disappears.

Q. What is the difference between forgiving and being forgiven?

MR. O. Subject and object. What do you mean? We cannot be forgiven. We did something and, according to the law of cause and effect, a certain result will be produced. We must

change the past by a very complicated process through higher
influences and positive emotions. The law of cause and effect
begins in World 6. We cannot change the law but we can become
free—escape from it. We can change the present, through the
present the future, and through the future the past. There is no
other way.

Q. 'Forgive us our debts' refers to the past?

MR. O. No. It means that we cannot be forgiven our debts.
We must pay them. By paying them we change the past, but
there are different ways of paying.

Q. I can see how 'as we forgive our debtors' must belong to
higher emotion.

MR. O. Only if we have positive emotions, not as we are.
There are several stages. This does not come at once.

Q. How is it possible for others to be our debtors?

MR. O. If we think they owe something to us they are our
debtors.

Q. What are the different ways of paying our debts?

MR. O. Mechanically or consciously. We pay them in any
case. By waiting for the results of causes and paying thus, or
changing the past and paying in another way.

Q. Can we only change the past by coming back here again?

MR. O. How otherwise? Thinking will not help. We must
change it now. Not only by coming back. To-day is the result
of some past. If we change to-day, we change the past. If we
change the future, we change the past. The future will be past
after some time.

Q. Regarding the phrase 'Thy will be done'. . . .

MR. O. Connect it with the idea of miracle, higher cosmos
and lower cosmos. This is not about us.

Q. Is changing the past struggling against the way things go?

MR. O. This is the beginning only. Positive emotions and
higher influences are necessary. We cannot change anything
without them.

Q. You said that nothing can change without positive
emotions?

MR. O. Positive emotions don't come by themselves. It is no
good sitting and waiting for higher emotions. It is necessary to
work. I have put some principles. It is necessary to see how we
can reach this.

REPETITION. JANUARY 23RD 1934

I have already spoken for a long time about the necessity for the education of the attention and about the necessity for remembering ourselves. And we don't get results because almost every person is unable to keep his attention exactly where he should keep it and exactly on what he should remember. He can keep attention on things on which he is accustomed to keep attention in life, but what is shown to him, shown maybe ten times, explained in the work, still escapes his attention, and he forgets that this is his work.

This is exactly what there was in this question (MISS D's). We don't realize how easily things which are connected with the work become just ordinary with us. This happens only because we lose attention or because attention disappears.

There have been many questions during this period relating to special methods. Are there any special methods by which it is possible to increase self-remembering or to increase attention?

There were many questions which were formulated similarly or which had the same aim, and I think we must now try certain exercises which may help, first, to remember ourselves and, second, to keep attention, to have more control over attention. As you must already know, this is almost the same thing, because one cannot exist without the other; in any case, self-remembering cannot exist without attention. My intention was to speak about these exercises later on; I thought I would speak about them when I published my book 'Fragments'. But as I am not sure now when I shall publish it, and as it is no use repeating the same questions and returning to the same things, I think that those who wish can try certain exercises. I don't think I shall be able to explain everything in one evening, so you will have to think about it and we will speak about it again; you will ask for details and then you will decide which one you will take and for what purpose, because different exercises can be done either in one way or in another way or with one or another aim.

The fundamental idea of all that you can do in the Fourth Way and in this kind of school where we are trying to work, is that the more conscious you are the greater will be the results of your work, so that the result of one or another effort is always modified and controlled by the consciousness of your aim, intentions and desires.

About the first method of exercises I have spoken many times; I have spoken of my experiments with that and some other forms of these exercises with reference to repetition. These exercises exist in the Eastern Church and in other forms they exist in Buddhist and Mohammedan schools. Some short prayer is usually taken and then repeated continuously; and this repeating is generally connected with breathing, listening to heart-beats and many other things, but this is sufficient. It is necessary to remember that it is definitely connected with breathing and that I do not advise it. And I think it impossible because it needs complete solitude, at least for a long time; one cannot do exercises connected with breathing when among people or during ordinary work; one must have several hours a day absolutely free and without any disturbance. I tried these exercises long before I met this system, and in the beginning, when I heard about this system, they helped me very much in appreciating self-remembering and even in the first tasks that we were given.

But this exercise, that is, repetition of a short prayer, needs breathing and fasting, otherwise it very soon becomes too easy; it slips over things without touching them. I mean that it awakes attention only in the very beginning. So I replaced the short prayer of seven words mentioned in the Philokalia by the Lord's Prayer. I heard about the use of the Lord's Prayer for the same purpose, for constant repetition, in Russian monasteries. It gave very interesting results in the sense of keeping the attention, and attention was much more awake when I did those exercises. But as it happened I was busy over some things; I travelled and I went to Russia; and then I met this system and I tried these exercises again. I varied it—I took the Lord's Prayer in Greek with school pronunciation, and when it had become almost automatic I began to try to speak this prayer with the modern Greek pronunciation; or I alternated them because when the school pronunciation became automatic it was difficult to remember to pronounce it differently. But in this way I kept attention; when attention disappeared the repetition just stopped, or it got mixed or went only in the way I had first tried it.

I tried several other things but will not speak of them here, but I want to say that an exercise of this kind, I mean repeating a long prayer, is used in many schools and, if it is used in connection with certain ideas of the human machine it may be connected with very interesting and important work. First of all it can be connected with the study of the parts of centres because you start in the intellectual part of intellectual centre, otherwise you cannot do it. When you take a new thing you have to keep attention, and when you keep attention you use the intellectual part of the intellectual centre. But if it begins to repeat by itself or even starts by itself and does not need any attention it means that it has passed into the moving part of the intellectual centre. Then later it can pass into moving centre and then into the instinctive centre; and then by interesting methods it is possible to make it pass into the emotional centre. This is the aim of these exercises, not for keeping the attention only but for the study of centres and parts of centres.

You may remember that in some conversation described in 'Fragments' I came to the conclusion that the whole thing was to awake emotional centre. Before that I had had some interesting experiences and had come to the conclusion that one can have such experiences only in a very emotional state, and I asked G. if there was any method by which emotional centre could be roused. What he answered and what this was I can say later. But it is quite true that at a certain stage of the work it is necessary to make the emotional centre work more intensively, and this is one of the aims of this prayer of the mind; I mean a short prayer used continuously with breathing and fasting because without breathing and fasting short prayer does not give any result. The prayer of the mind in the heart is described in the short book 'The Way of the Pilgrim'—in a fuller form it is described in the Philokalia, but I do not know of any literature describing the other method of repeating a longer piece which I have mentioned. I mean repeating a longer prayer and making it pass from one centre to another. I have never read any descriptions of this but I have heard such descriptions, and other things I can speak of from my own experience. Whoever wished to try this thing I would advise in the beginning not to think about moving centre, emotional centre or instinctive centre but to do it first of all for the purpose of keeping the attention, that is, not to let it slip into becoming automatic, because the longer you keep attention on it, the longer you keep it conscious, the easier it will be manipulated and guided afterwards.

This can be done, for instance, by taking different pronunciations, different languages or by counting. Suppose you take the Lord's Prayer in English. After a short time it begins to go so easily that you do not notice it; but this is not interesting, so it is better to take it in some other language, not exactly in a quite unknown language but in one which you know slightly. Then do not pronounce it without counting for a long time; count on the fingers or on a rosary or in some other way, or simply by memory, because by counting in this way it cannot escape attention. At the same time it may be interesting. If someone wants to try it, to let it go on automatically, but in this case no interesting results can be seen for at least two years. It may be that in some lucky cases results can be felt; when this automatic repeating will arouse attention by itself by touching such sides of a man, such inner associations of inner octaves that nothing else can touch. The idea of repetition in this form is to create a new function which in the beginning is conscious, and then in passing at a certain moment from one centre to another it becomes unconscious when it is in mechanical centres and conscious again when it is in higher parts of centres. And this higher function can pass through all centres and later it can become the means for passing into higher centres. But it is very dangerous to let imagination go on this because one can imagine anything. I have heard from people who have tried it that they have had such wonderful experiences that could not have happened for at least five years from the time they started; but they had them in two weeks. So it is necessary to be very careful in this.

I can point out the exact degree of this penetration. You can say that it has begun to pass into moving centre only when you can read an easy book and continue to repeat your prayer. But not for five minutes only—if you can follow the book it means that it has passed the first stage and that repetition is going on in the moving centre. The third stage is much further. You come to it when you are able to speak without it stopping repetition. With different people it happens differently. I mean that being able to follow a conversation can serve as an indication of progress because some people can follow conversation before they can read, but reading and speaking are definite signposts. The first means that repetition has begun to pass into moving centre, and the second means that it has begun to pass into instinctive centre. But this is very far—so I will not listen to anyone who tells me that he can speak and repeat.

17

Autobiographical fragment

I was born in Moscow in 1878. My first memories are connected with my maternal grandmother's house on Pimenovskaia Street. My grandfather died in 1882. He was a painter, chiefly a portrait painter, and in his young days a good pastelist. Later he became a church painter, which means that he had a studio and undertook contracts to paint pictures in churches or for churches. Church painting was a special industry and church painters almost a special caste.

My grandmother was a very clever woman. I never forgot the wonderful stories of old Moscow life which she told me and my sister.

My mother was also a painter and she had a very good taste in Russian and French literature.

My father, at the time I was born, was an officer in the survey. He was very fond of music and painting and was a good mathematician. He had a particular interest in the problems of the fourth dimension to which he gave much of his spare time. All his writings were lost. He also died when I was quite young.

The house on Pimenovskaia Street had several unusual features. It was in many ways a very old-fashioned house and, in other ways very much ahead of its time. And in both cases it was my grandmother's influence. The family did not belong to any particular class and was in touch with all classes. I think this was possible only in Russia.

I remember myself at a very early age. I have several quite clear mental pictures of events which happened before I was two years old. From the age of three I remember myself quite clearly. I remember Moscow River about thirty miles west of Moscow. I remember the river there, boats with a smell of tar, hills covered with forests, the old monastery, etc. I remember the exhibition of 1882 in Moscow and the coronation of Alexander III in 1883, chiefly the illuminations.

About that time I began to read. When I was about six I read two books which produced an enormous impression on me.

They were Lermontoff's *A Hero of Our Time* and Turgenleff's *A Sportsman's Sketches*. Soon after that I became very interested in poetry and painting, I mean reading poetry and looking at pictures. Poetry and painting became <u>the arts</u> for me. I was also very fond of all kinds of engravings and prints of which there was a large collection in the house; I could also sketch at that time. About eight I began to feel a great interest in natural science; everything about plants and animals had an enormous fascination for me at that time.

Work at school was dull; I was lazy; I hated Greek and school routine in general. Happily the boys at school were left very much to themselves, and although I lived in school I managed to read a great deal. About thirteen I became interested in dreams and consequently in psychology. At sixteen I first found Nietzsche. In 1896, when I was eighteen, I began my first independent travels, and at the same time I began to write. I was very anarchistically inclined at that time. I particularly distrusted all forms of academic science and took a firm decision never to pass any examinations and never to take any degrees. At the same time I worked very intensely on biology, mathematics and psychology. I was enormously excited by the idea of the fourth dimension and subsequently, terribly disappointed by the usual 'scientific' treatment of it.

I mistrusted and disliked all kinds of socialism even more than industrialism and militarism, and did not believe in any kind of secret revolutionary parties, with which all Russian 'Intelligentsia' sympathized. But when I became interested in journalism I could only work on 'left' papers because 'right' papers did not smell well. It was one of the complexities of Russian life.

I became dissatisfied with science. I felt that there was a dead wall everywhere, even in mathematics, and I used to say at that time that professors were killing science in the same way as priests were killing religion. For several years I was in journalistic work; I travelled—in Russia, in the East, in Europe. In 1905, during the months of strikes and disorders which ended in the armed insurrection in Moscow, I wrote a novel based on the idea of eternal recurrence. It was published only ten years later.

In 1907 I found theosophical literature, which was prohibited in Russia—Blavatsky, Olcott, Annie Besant, Sinnett, etc. It produced a very strong impression on me although I at once saw its weak side. The weak side was that, such as it was, it had no continuation. But it opened doors for me into a new and bigger world. I discovered the idea of esotericism, found a possible angle for the study of religion and mysticism, and received a new impulse for the study of 'higher dimensions'. In 1908 I was in Constantinople, Smyrna, Greece and Egypt. Early in 1909 I finally left Moscow and after that lived in St. Petersburg. I studied occult literature; made all kinds of psychological experiments by the Yogi and magical methods: published several books, 'Tertium Organum' among them, and gave public lectures on the Tarot, on Superman, on Yogis, etc.

In 1913 and 1914 I was in Egypt, Ceylon and India, and returned to Russia soon after the beginning of the war. In the beginning of 1915 I gave, first in St. Petersburg and later in Moscow, several public lectures on my travels and on my search for the miraculous.

In the spring of 1915 I met in Moscow a strange man who had a kind of philosophical school. This was G.I. Gurdjieff. He and his ideas produced a very great impression on me. Very soon I realized that he had found many things for which I had been looking in India. I realized that I had met with a completely new system of thought surpassing all I knew before. This system threw quite a new light on psychology and explained what I could not understand before in esoteric ideas and 'school principles'. I spent a week with G. in Moscow and returned to St. Petersburg with very great expectations. In the autumn of 1915 G. came to St. Petersburg and after that began to come regularly, giving lectures to small groups which I arranged for him.

At the end of 1916 I found myself in the Guards Sappers. It was a strange but not unpleasant experience. Four months afterwards I was given my discharge on account of bad sight. This was two weeks before the revolution. I had no illusions about the revolution and I realized that the days of Russia were numbered. I decided to go abroad, wait for the end of the war in one of the neutral countries, and afterwards continue my work in London where, on my way back from India, I had made some preparations for publishing my books.

My departure from Russia was delayed because of my connection with G. G. went to the Caucasus just before the revolution, and for some time I had no news of him. I heard from him only in June, and immediately went to his native place in Transcaucasia. Next month G. invited members of the Moscow and

Petersburg groups to the Caucasus. We spent the end of the summer of 1917 at Essentuki, a place with mineral waters in North Caucasus, and in September we came to Touapse, on the Black Sea. I went to St. Petersburg for the last time in the autumn of 1917 and I left it a week before the overthrow of the provisional government by the bolsheviks. I came back to the Caucasus and after that stayed there a little more than two years, first on the Black Sea shore and later, again at Essentuki.

During the first year I was with G., but in the summer of 1918 I began to feel that I had ceased to understand him, or his views had changed, and I found it necessary to separate G. and the system, of which I had no doubts. But it did not help very much, so in the end I broke with G. and soon afterwards he left Essentuki and went to Tiflis. I spent a very difficult winter in Essentuki. It was in the hands of the bolsheviks at that time, and there was civil war round about us. In January 1919 we were liberated by the whites. But it was clear that it was only temporary liberation. If I wanted to continue my work it was necessary to go abroad, according to my original plan.

I passed the summer and autumn of 1919 between Ekaterinodar, Rostov and Novorossisk, and in January 1920 I left Russia for Constantinople and stayed there about a year and a half. Constantinople then was full of Russians. I began lectures there on psychology, on my travels, etc., and in the summer of 1920 I met G. who had come there from Tiflis. I tried to work with him again but soon found it impossible for the same reasons as before.

In August 1921 I left Constantinople for London. I started my lectures in London and met many people interested in the same kind of ideas. In February 1922 G. visited London; he then lived in Germany. I was still very interested in his work, but this time I very firmly decided to stand apart. G. went to France. I helped him in many ways to organize his work there, and in 1922 and in 1923 went many times to Paris and to Fontainbleau. At the end of 1923 I found that I could not remain connected with G. because I ceased to understand him completely, and I broke with him finally in January 1924.

After that I continued my work in London. In 1931 I published 'A New Model of the Universe' in English. It was a very long work. The correction of the translation took about two years. After 1931 my work was chiefly connected with the development of a psychological system based on the study of 'self-consciousness' and 'objective consciousness'. These terms need explanations. I am preparing a book on this system and it may be published in a year or two.

London 1935

Index